The Civil Junglees Collective is a group of Indian and British wildlife and literature enthusiasts who meet occasionally to go on jungle treks, birdwatching expeditions and tours of museums and libraries. The youngest and most excitable of the group is 83, the oldest and wisest is 29. The former, a founding member of the group, was born in Assam and grew up in Sri Lanka, where her parents ran an animal shelter. She settled in Nepal with her partner in the 1970s. The other two founding members, English doctors who met and married and spent most of their lives in Bombay, are both deceased. The wise 29-year-old, a nurse by profession and tour guide by hobby, is their grandson.

BIG CAT TALES

VINTAGE ENCOUNTERS AND STORIES

Jim Corbett, J.H. Patterson, Mrs W.W. Baillie, Saki and Others

Compiled and edited by The Civil Junglees Collective

Illustrations by Devashish Verma

SPEAKING TIGER

SPEAKING TIGER BOOKS LLP
4381/4, Ansari Road, Daryaganj
New Delhi 110002, India

First published by Speaking Tiger Books 2020

ISBN: 978-93-89958-49-2
eISBN: 978-93-89958-50-8

10 9 8 7 6 5 4 3 2 1

Typeset in Adobe Garamond Pro by Jojy Philip, New Delhi
Printed at Shree Maitrey Printech Pvt. Ltd., Noida

CONTENTS

INTRODUCTION

These pages throb and thrum with adventure, drama and narrative tension. Men, and some women, often alone, stalking big cats in the wild—or being stalked themselves—make for thrilling, memorable reading. Especially when the danger to both hunter and hunted is immense and equal.

Many of these pages are also soaked in blood. There's no getting away from that. You will be entertained and enthralled by the records and stories of shikar in this anthology, several of them timeless, but you will also find there is violence—sadly inevitable, given the subject.

Our attempt in the collection has been to find humanity in a context where its absence was not only justified, but even celebrated. As in war, in hunting, too, our humanity is redeemed and affirmed by unexpected compassion, regret or, at the very least, honesty and self-awareness. We were surprised by how many examples of this we found when we began to look.

The history of human-big cat interaction has been for the most part one of conflict, and modern civilization is most to blame. It is a romantic notion that no animal will harm you. There is no evidence yet that lions, tigers and leopards are naturally forgiving of innocent trespass, or that they understand a fisherman's need to make a living in the Sunderbans or a Tanzanian farmer's need to harvest the crop in her little field at the edge of a wilderness. But they have never come into our streets and homes armed with guns in order to test or prove their virility, or simply for diversion. And they don't plunder our villages and cities for uranium or bulldoze our ancient homesteads to build massive highways.

As the noted wildlife conservationist Theodore Bhaskaran writes, 'When humans hunted for food, there was no problem. A human being was a predator, like any cat. The trouble began when humans began to kill for sport and commerce.' (See his review of Donald Anderson's memoir, *The Last White Hunter*, in *The Wire*.) He then reminds us that hunting as a mad and bloody sport, and as a display of imperial power, came to South Asia (and much of Africa) when the British colonized it and began to use guns indiscriminately. 'Coming from a land with practically no wildlife or forests, the British saw Indian forests, with their bewildering variety of wildlife, as unguarded bounty. They went berserk. Tiger hunting became a ritual, even a rite of passage. And they began writing of their "adventures" in journals, such as the *Blackwood's Magazine*, for the benefit of readers back home. The articles proved hugely popular, and hunter literature began to take shape as a dimension of life in colonial India.'

We must make a brief digression at this point: It is worth remembering that the Mughals in India had already made big-game shikar a grand, awe-inspiring spectacle and had started using guns as well. The British would only outdo them. We are reminded of this by many Indian scholars and commentators, but few of them go back further in history to tell us that kings, princes and their nobles had been hunting animals, including tigers, for centuries in India before the Mughals came on the scene. There is evidence of this everywhere in the epics, and in sculpture, art and scripture. (In religious iconography, too: the depiction of gods and sages sitting on tiger skins says something about a society's extreme comfort with hunting.) Bow-and-arrow and spears would have been the favoured weapons back then, but had guns been invented these would certainly have been used, and there would probably have been slaughter.

But returning to recent centuries, it is undeniable that the worst excesses began with the British, and shikar was closely linked to the imperial project. It was a display of power, a means of claiming vast tracts of land, and a way of legitimizing the White man's rule—and, in Africa, also legitimizing poaching for massive profits. White men, young and old, many of them delinquent or damaged in different ways, went out routinely to 'bag big game'. It was their favourite pastime. They 'bagged' thousands of lions, tigers, leopards and cheetahs, among other wild animals. The maharajas of India and Nepal went several steps further.

With shikar came shikar literature—journal after journal, book after book, many of them bragging accounts full of blood and gore and an obsession with masculinity, vigour, honour and other such things. Protecting the cowering 'natives' from marauding beasts was, of course, part of the narrative, but 99 of 100 such claims were mere mythmaking. The habitual 'sportsman' only had contempt for the 'natives', who were used mainly to beat the forests and drive wild animals into the open for the sahibs to shoot.

All of this is true and awful. And if this was all there was to shikar literature, it would be best forgotten. But there is also this:

> With rifle to shoulder and elbows on knees I now waited for the tiger to project his head a second time, and this I felt sure he would presently do. Minutes passed, and then I heard the tiger. He had skirted round the bushes and, approaching from behind, started to claw my tree where the thick growth of small branches on the trunk made it impossible for me to see him. Purring with pleasure the tiger once and again clawed the tree with vigour, while I sat on my branch and rocked with silent laughter.
>
> I know that crows and monkeys have a sense of humour, but until that day I did not know that tigers also possessed this sense. Nor did I know that an animal could have the luck, and the impudence, that particular tiger had. In five days he had killed five cows, four of them in broad daylight. In those five days I had seen him eight times and on four occasions I had pressed a trigger on him. And now, after staring at me for half an hour and eating while doing so, he was clawing the tree on which I was sitting and purring to show his contempt of me…
>
> I visited Dabidhura several times in subsequent years while hunting man-eaters, and I never heard of anyone having killed [that] tiger. So I hope that in the fullness of time this old warrior, like an old soldier, just faded away.

This is the legendary Jim Corbett. A shikari and storyteller whose defining trait was empathy—for his fellow human beings and for the animals he hunted at great risk, most of them man-eaters who had terrorized entire villages. He did, on a few occasions, kill when he did not need to, and though the gentlest of men who had bonds of deep friendship with his fellow-villagers, he was a half-sahib all his life. But a finer sensibility and a more compassionate voice will be difficult to find in the pages of a book.

Corbett, in fact, was one of many hunters who chose to live outside the toxic code of traditional shikar. Like David Wilson, a forest officer and occasional hunter posted in Burma at the turn of the twentieth century:

> In a private letter to me Mr Allan wrote, 'Had I missed the second shot [the tigress] would have had us…She was very angry. She was hungry and meant business. On opening her we found that she had evidently not had a meal for some days.'
>
> This illustrates a truth which is often forgotten by us. The big beasts live from hand to mouth, like improvident working men. A dog may bury a bone, a tiger return to a kill, and a leopard has been known to put half a corpse or an unfinished bit of venison up a tree for security. But beyond the next meal they never look…Think of her empty stomach, and perhaps hungry cubs in her lair; and then this big, strong Englishman, with his diabolical machinery in his hand, molesting her as she was stalking the wild cattle. 'She meant business,' said he. Of course she did. Did anyone think she was hunting for amusement?
>
> No matter now! Her body lies inert enough, a subject for their inquisitive knives[.]

Or A.I.R. Glasfurd, a captain in the British Indian army who was, by his own admission, an enthusiastic hunter. In 'The Biography of a Tiger', he writes:

> It would not be difficult to paint in the life story of our tiger, becoming an adult, in ultra-lurid tints and make him into a dreaded man-eater, a monster, the terror of a

> countryside—for such things are too literally true. But they are the exception…[In] the ordinary everyday habits and incidental life of the jungle-king, usually one of retirement and inoffensive monotony, such things have no place… The life of the jungle and its denizens runs its course full of incident and colour, tragedy and romance, with the ever-recurring refrain of unalterable savage Nature. And that of the tiger is no exception. He follows the seasons—hot, cold and wet—wandering on lengthy rounds or tied to a locality. He goes hungry or luxuriates in easy circumstance at the nod of Fate.

Even a racist with little sympathy for native customs and creatures, in this case a lady called Mrs Handley, who glories in her husband's endless hunting exploits, surprises us with something like tenderness:

> Turning only my eyes, I saw the beautiful, sleek body lying almost flat as he drank. Meanwhile he had caught sight of my reflection, and lifted his head, the water dripping from his jaws, and gazed full at me. Then he backed, absolutely without a sound or the faintest rustle of the fallen leaves, just like a scared cat (which indeed he was), creeping away into safety for itself. That was all he cared about; that is all they ever do care about, these wild things, no matter what stories sensation-writers may invent.
>
> But the beauty of him! His coat was of gleaming tawny satin, with jetty rosettes, and his eyes of aquamarine, as I could see while they were glaring into mine. I felt quite sorry he had let himself be interrupted before finishing his drink comfortably…

In compiling this anthology, we have been partial—more than partial—to sentiments such as these. But it would be wrong to blot out the larger, ugly truth about shikar, so there are three excerpts from books of the kind that Glasfurd once described as 'little more than a butcher's bill'.

Finally, it is great storytelling that we looked for—thrilling narratives of adventure, yes, but also prose that would communicate the magic of the jungle. Here's a sample of what we found:

> As the piercing rays of the blistering sun decline towards late afternoon, and are intercepted by the taller trees, the jungle begins to awake from the diurnal siesta to the anticipated delight of another tropical night. Cooler airs begin to move with light stirrings to and fro…The painted sandgrouse come chuckling and whirling in twos and threes along the winding riverbed, drop suddenly on the damp sand, and run to become brown stones at the water's shining edge. The monkeys whoop and swing; the red spur-fowls cackle in the rustling leaves; the kakar barks hoarsely to his mate on the hillside... Under the bamboo clumps, a frog croaks sleepily in the riverbed; from the forest beyond it a nightjar utters his first low 'Chuckoo-chuckoo'; something heavy is heard in the distance, stealthily crackling in the leaves uphill; a tiny fluffy owlet emerges, round and wonder-eyed, from a hole in a great dead tree, and chatters volubly of the coming night.
>
> Then, somehow or other, it is full yellow moonlight; a light scarcely less bright than the evening glow so lately departed, but such a wondrous welcome change from its heat, turning greens to blue, blues to grey, casting a silvern fairy charm over the calm scene with its soothing, cool, deliciously peaceful effulgence.
>
> The greater fauna of the jungle are now issuing forth to seek food and water; to roam, prowl, browse, slay, or be seized in turn, until the breaking of the distant dawn. Above them all, it is the tiger's hour.

> Away in the distance, faint but clear, rises the unaccustomed sound of a cart bumping over the rough boulders of the dry Sipna river, and the staccato cry of a jungle-man, no doubt anxiously urging on his belated bullocks as they return to their forest village…

Reading this, one of us sighed, transported back half a century to a jungle night in the Terai. She was still young, her marriage had ended and she had come to the forest to deal with the mess. She wasn't looking for tigers. She had just closed the book she was reading and put out the lamp when something drew her to the window—'I don't know what it was, because there had been no sound,' she said, 'maybe it was a shift in the scale of the silence, or the crickets had stopped singing.' And there, metres ahead, in the open patch in front of the lodge, three grey-blue liquid shadows stood listening under the moon. A tigress and her cubs, proud and perfectly still. They owned the night.

H.S. Bedi
(for the CJ Collective)
September 2020

ENCOUNTERS

THE PIPAL PANI TIGER

JIM CORBETT

The finest and perhaps most widely read 'shikar' writer of all time, Jim Corbett (1875–1955) was born in the Nainital district of Kumaon, now in the Indian state of Uttarakhand. He spent much of his childhood and teens roaming the surrounding hills and forests, and his deep connection with the people and wildlife of the area shaped his life: he became a legendary hunter of man-eating tigers and leopards; a keen naturalist and one of India's earliest conservationists; and the author of books based on his jungle encounters that are today considered classics. While it is a misconception that Corbett never killed a big cat unless he was convinced that it was a man-eater, his respect for these and other wild animals and his love for the villagers at whose request he hunted man-eaters are apparent in the kind of life he chose to live, and they shine through in all his writing. Author and journalist Mrinal Pande, who also grew up in Uttarakhand, has written that people in Kumaon and Garhwal remember Corbett 'not so much as an iconic hunter of tigers and leopards, but as a compassionate naturalist and conservationist'.

The following story about a tiger Corbett first noticed as a solitary cub and tracked for fifteen years is one of the most poignant in shikar literature.

BEYOND the fact that he was born in a ravine running deep into the foothills and was one of a family of three, I know nothing of his early history.

He was about a year old when, attracted by the calling of a chital hind early one November morning, I found his pug-marks in the sandy bed of a little stream known locally as Pipal Pani. I thought at first that he had strayed from his mother's care, but, as week succeeded week and his single tracks showed on the game paths of the forest, I came to the conclusion that the near approach of the breeding season was sufficient reason for his being alone. Jealously guarded one day—protected at the cost of the parent life if necessary—and set adrift the next, is the lot of all jungle folk; nature's method of preventing inbreeding.

That winter he lived on peafowl, kakar, small pig and an occasional chital hind, making his home in a prostrate giant of the forest felled for no apparent reason, and hollowed out by time and porcupines. Here he brought most of his kills, basking, when the days were cold, on the smooth bole of the tree, where many a leopard had basked before him.

It was not until January was well advanced that I saw the cub at close quarters. I was out one evening without any definite object in view, when I saw a crow rise from the ground and wipe its beak as it sat on the branch of a tree. Crows, vultures and magpies always interest me in the jungle, and many are the kills I have found both in India and in Africa with the help of these birds. On the present occasion the crow led me to the scene of an overnight tragedy. A chital had been killed and partly eaten and, attracted to the spot probably as I had been, a party of men passing along the road had cut up and removed the remains. All that was left of the chital were a few splinters of bone and a little congealed blood off which the crow had lately made his meal. The absence of thick cover and the proximity of the road convinced me that the animal responsible for the kill had not witnessed the removal and that it would return in due course; so I decided to sit up, and made myself as comfortable in a plum tree as the thorns permitted.

I make no apology to you, my reader, if you differ with me on the ethics of the much-debated subject of sitting up over kills. Some of my most pleasant shikar memories centre round the hour or two before sunset that I have spent in a tree over a natural kill, ranging from the time when, armed with a muzzleloader whipped round with brass wire to prevent the cracked barrel from bursting, I sat over a langur killed by a leopard, to a few days ago, when with the most modern rifle across my knees, I watched a tigress and her two full-grown cubs eat up the sambar stag they had killed, and counted myself no poorer for not having secured a trophy.

True, on the present occasion there is no kill below me, but, for the reasons given, that will not affect any chance of a shot; scent to interest the jungle folk there is in plenty in the blood-soaked ground, as witness the old grey-whiskered boar who has been quietly rooting along for the past ten minutes, and who suddenly stiffens to attention as he comes into the line of the blood-tainted wind. His snout held high, and worked as only a pig can work that member, tells him more than I was able to glean from the ground which showed no tracks; his method of approach, a short excursion to the right and back into the wind, and then a short excursion to the left and again back into the wind, each manoeuvre bringing him a few yards nearer, indicates the chital was killed by a tiger. Making sure once and again that nothing worth eating has been left, the boar finally trots off and disappears from view.

Two chital, both with horns in velvet, now appear and from the fact that they are coming down-wind, and making straight for the blood-soaked spot, it is evident they were witnesses to the overnight tragedy. Alternately snuffing the ground, or standing rigid with every muscle tensed for instant flight, they satisfy their curiosity and return the way they came.

Curiosity is not a human monopoly; many an animal's life is cut short by indulging in it. A dog leaves the veranda to bark at a shadow, a deer leaves the herd to investigate a tuft of grass that no wind agitated, and the waiting leopard is provided with a meal.

The sun is nearing the winter line when a movement to the right attracts attention. An animal has crossed an opening between two bushes at the far end of a wedge of scrub that terminates thirty yards from my tree. Presently the bushes at my end part, and out into the open, with never a look to right or left, steps the cub. Straight up to the spot where his kill had been he goes, his look of expectancy giving place to one of disappointment as he realizes that his chital, killed possibly after hours of patient stalking, is gone. The splinters of bone and congealed blood are rejected, and his interest centres on a tree stump lately used as a butcher's block, to which some shreds of flesh are adhering. I was not the only one who carried fire-arms in these jungles and, if the cub was to grow into a tiger, it was necessary he should be taught the danger of carelessly approaching kills in daylight. A scatter-gun and dust-shot would have served my purpose better, but the rifle will have to do this time; and, as he raises his head to smell the stump, my bullet crashes into the hard wood an inch from his nose. Only once in the years that followed did the cub forget that lesson.

The following winter I saw him several times. His ears did not look so big now and he had changed his baby hair for a coat of rich tawny red with well-defined stripes. The hollow tree had been given up to its rightful owners, a pair of leopards, new quarters found in a thick belt of scrub skirting the foothills, and young sambar added to his menu.

On my annual descent from the hills next winter, the familiar pug-marks no longer showed on the game paths and at the drinking places, and for several weeks I thought the cub had abandoned his old haunts and gone further afield. Then one morning his absence was explained for, side by side with his tracks, were the smaller and more elongated tracks of the mate he had gone to find. I only once saw the tigers, for the cub was a tiger now, together. I had been out before dawn to try to bag a serow that lived on the foothills, and returning along a fire track my attention was arrested by a vulture, perched on the dead limb of a sal tree.

The bird had his back towards me and was facing a short stretch of scrub with dense jungle beyond. Dew was still heavy on the ground, and without a sound I reached the tree and peered round. One antler of a dead sambar, for no living deer would lie in that position, projected above the low bushes. A convenient moss-covered rock afforded my rubber-shod feet silent and safe hold, and as I drew myself erect, the sambar came into full view. The hind quarters had been eaten away and, lying on either side of the kill, were the pair, the tiger being on the far side with only his hind legs showing. Both tigers were asleep. Ten feet straight in front, to avoid a dead branch, and thirty feet to the left would give me a shot at the tiger's neck, but in planning the stalk I had forgotten the silent spectator. Where I stood I was invisible to the vulture, but before the ten feet had been covered I came into view and, alarmed at my near proximity, he flapped off his perch, omitting as he did so to notice a thin creeper dependent from a branch above him against which he collided, and came ignominiously to ground. The tigress was up and away in an instant, clearing at a bound the kill and her mate, the tiger not being slow to follow—a possible shot, but too risky with thick jungle ahead where a wounded animal would have all the advantages. To those who have never tried it, I can recommend the stalking of leopards and tigers on their kills as a most pleasant form of sport. Great care should however be taken over the shot, for if the animal is not killed outright, or anchored, trouble is bound to follow.

A week later the tiger resumed his bachelor existence. A change had now come over his nature. Hitherto he had not objected to my visiting his kills but, after his mate left, at the first drag I followed up I was given very clearly to understand that no liberties would in future be permitted. The angry growl of a tiger at close quarters, than which there is no more terrifying sound in the jungles, has to be heard to be appreciated.

Early in March the tiger killed his first full-grown buffalo. I was near the foothills one evening when the agonized bellowing of a buffalo, mingled with the angry roar of a

tiger, rang through the forest. I located the sound as coming from a ravine about six hundred yards away. The going was bad, mostly over loose rocks and through thorn bushes, and when I crawled up a steep bluff commanding a view of the ravine the buffalo's struggles were over, and the tiger nowhere to be seen. For an hour I lay with finger on trigger without seeing anything of the tiger. At dawn next morning I again crawled up the bluff, to find the buffalo lying just as I had left her. The soft ground, torn up by hoof and claw, testified to the desperate nature of the struggle and it was not until the buffalo had been hamstrung that the tiger had finally succeeded in pulling her down, in a fight which had lasted from ten to fifteen minutes. The tiger's tracks led across the ravine and, on following them up, I found a long smear of blood on a rock, and, a hundred yards further on, another smear on a fallen tree. The wound inflicted by the buffalo's horns was in the tiger's head and sufficiently severe to make the tiger lose all interest in the kill, for he never returned to it.

Three years later the tiger, disregarding the lesson received when a cub (his excuse may have been that it was the close season for tigers), incautiously returned to a kill, over which a zamindar and some of his tenants were sitting at night, and received a bullet in the shoulder which fractured the bone. No attempt was made to follow him up, and thirty-six hours later, his shoulder covered with a swarm of flies, he limped through the compound of the Inspection Bungalow, crossed a bridge flanked on the far side by a double row of tenanted houses, the occupants of which stood at their doors to watch him pass, entered the gate of a walled-in compound and took possession of a vacant godown. Twenty-four hours later, possibly alarmed by the number of people who had collected from neighbouring villages to see him, he left the compound the way he had entered it, passed our gate, and made his way to the lower end of our village. A bullock belonging to one of our tenants had died the previous night and had been dragged into some bushes at the edge of the village; this the tiger found, and here he remained a few days, quenching his thirst at an irrigation furrow.

When we came down from the hills two months later the tiger was living on small animals (calves, sheep, goats, etc.) that he was able to catch on the outskirts of the village. By March his wound had healed, leaving his right foot turned inwards. Returning to the forest where he had been wounded, he levied heavy toll on the village cattle, taking, for safety's sake, but one meal off each and in this way killing five times as many as he would ordinarily have done. The zamindar who had wounded him and who had a herd of some four hundred head of cows and buffaloes was the chief sufferer.

In the succeeding years he gained as much in size as in reputation, and many were the attempts made by sportsmen, and others, to bag him.

One November evening, a villager, armed with a single-barrel muzzle-loading gun, set out to try to bag a pig, selecting for his ground machan an isolated bush growing in a twenty-yard-wide rowkah (dry watercourse) running down the centre of some broken ground. This ground was rectangular, flanked on the long sides by cultivated land and on the short sides by a road, and by a ten-foot canal that formed the boundary between our cultivation and the forest. In front of the man was a four-foot-high bank with a cattle track running along the upper edge; behind him a patch of dense scrub. At 8 p.m. an animal appeared on the track and, taking what aim he could, he fired. On receiving the shot the animal fell off the bank, and passed within a few feet of the man, grunting as it entered the scrub behind. Casting aside his blanket, the man ran to his hut two hundred yards away. Neighbours soon collected and, on hearing the man's account, came to the conclusion that a pig had been hard hit. It would be a pity, they said, to leave the pig for hyenas and jackals to eat, so a lantern was lit and as a party of six bold spirits set out to retrieve the bag, one of my tenants (who declined to join the expedition, and who confessed to me later that he had no stomach for looking for wounded pig in dense scrub in the dark) suggested that the gun should be loaded and taken.

His suggestion was accepted and, as a liberal charge of powder was being rammed home, the wooden ramrod jammed and broke inside the barrel. A trivial accident which undoubtedly saved the lives of six men. The broken rod was eventually and after great trouble extracted, the gun loaded, and the party set off.

Arrived at the spot where the animal had entered the bushes, a careful search was made and, on blood being found, every effort to find the 'pig' was made; it was not until the whole area had been combed out that the quest for that night was finally abandoned. Early next morning the search was resumed, with the addition of my informant of weak stomach, who was a better woodsman than his companions and who, examining the ground under a bush where there was a lot of blood, collected and brought some blood-stained hairs to me which I recognized as tiger's hairs.

A brother sportsman was with me for the day and together we went to have a look at the ground.

The reconstruction of jungle events from signs on the ground has always held great interest for me. True, one's deductions are sometimes wrong, but they are also sometimes right. In the present instance I was right in placing the wound in the inner forearm of the right foreleg, but was wrong in assuming the leg had been broken and that the tiger was a young animal and a stranger to the locality.

There was no blood beyond the point where the hairs had been found and, as tracking on the hard ground was impossible, I crossed the canal to where the cattle track ran through a bed of sand. Here from the pug-marks I found that the wounded animal was not a young tiger as I had assumed, but my old friend the Pipal Pani tiger who, when taking a shortcut through the village, had in the dark been mistaken for a pig.

Once before when badly wounded he had passed through the settlement without harming man or beast, but he was older now, and if driven by pain and hunger might do considerable damage. A disconcerting prospect, for the locality was thickly populated, and I was due to leave within the week, to keep an engagement that could not be put off.

For three days I searched every bit of the jungle between the canal and the foothills, an area of about four square miles, without finding any trace of the tiger. On the fourth afternoon, as I was setting out to continue the search, I met an old woman and her son hurriedly leaving the jungle. From them I learnt that the tiger was calling near the foothills and that all the cattle in the jungle had stampeded. When out with a rifle I invariably go alone; it is safer in a mix-up, and one can get through the jungle more silently. However, I stretched a point on this occasion, and let the boy accompany me since he was very keen on showing me where he had heard the tiger.

Arrived at the foothills, the boy pointed to a dense bit of cover, bounded on the far side by the fire-track to which I have already referred, and on the near side by the Pipal Pani stream. Running parallel to and about a hundred yards from the stream was a shallow depression some twenty feet wide, more or less open on my side and fringed with bushes on the side nearer the stream. A well-used path crossed the depression at right angles. Twenty yards from the path, and on the open side of the depression, was a small tree. If the tiger came down the path he would in all likelihood stand for a shot on clearing the bushes. Here I decided to take my stand and, putting the boy into the tree with his feet on a level with my head and instructing him to signal with his toes if from his raised position he saw the tiger before I did, I put my back to the tree and called.

You, who have spent as many years in the jungle as I have, need no description of the call of a tigress in search of a mate, and to you less fortunate ones I can only say that the call, to acquire which necessitates close observation and the liberal use of throat salve, cannot be described in words.

To my great relief, for I had crawled through the jungle for three days with finger on trigger, I was immediately answered from a distance of about five hundred yards, and for half an hour thereafter it may have been less and certainly appeared more the call was tossed back and forth. On the one side the urgent summons of the king, and on the other, the subdued and coaxing answer of his handmaiden. Twice the boy signalled, but I had as yet seen nothing of the tiger, and it was not until the setting sun was flooding the forest with golden light that he suddenly appeared, coming down the path at a fast walk with never a pause as he cleared the bushes. When halfway across the depression, and just as I was raising the rifle, he turned to the right and came straight towards me.

This manoeuvre, unforeseen when selecting my stand, brought him nearer than I had intended he should come and, moreover, presented me with a head shot which at that short range I was not prepared to take. Resorting to an old device, learned long years ago and successfully used on similar occasions, the tiger was brought to a stand without being alarmed. With one paw poised, he slowly raised his head, exposing as he did so his chest and throat. After the impact of the heavy bullet, he struggled to his feet and tore blindly through the forest, coming down with a crash within a few yards of where, attracted by the calling of a chital hind one November morning, I had first seen his pug-marks.

It was only then that I found he had been shot under a misapprehension, for the wound which I feared might make him dangerous proved on examination to be almost healed and caused by a pellet of lead having severed a small vein in his right forearm.

Pleasure at having secured a magnificent trophy—he measured 10’ 3” over curves and his winter coat was in perfect condition—was not unmixed with regret, for never again would the jungle folk and I listen with held breath to his deep-throated call resounding through the foothills, and never again would his familiar pug-marks show on the game paths that he and I had trodden for fifteen years.

FIRST ENCOUNTERS IN TSAVO

J.H. PATTERSON

*John Henry Patterson (1867-1947) was a British soldier who became better known as a hunter after his time in Africa, where he shot man-eating lions, encounters that he later recounted in the book that made him famous—*The Man-Eaters of Tsavo *(1907). Patterson first went to Africa in early 1898, commissioned to supervise the construction of a railway bridge over the Tsavo river in present-day Kenya. Lion attacks began almost as soon as construction started; workers, most of them African and Indian, were dragged out of their tents at night by the lions and eaten. Patterson, who had experience of hunting tigers in India, planned a mission to eliminate the two rogue lions who were confirmed to be the killers. It was seven months before he succeeded, shooting the first lion on 9th December 1898 and the second one twenty days later. The following excerpt from* The Man-Eaters of Tsavo *describes his first few encounters with the lions.*

IT was towards noon on March 1st, 1898, that I first found myself entering the narrow and somewhat dangerous harbour of Mombasa on the east coast of Africa. The town lies on an island of the same name, separated from the mainland only by a very narrow channel, which forms the harbour; and as our vessel steamed slowly in, under the quaint old Portuguese fortress built over three hundred years ago, I was much struck with the strange beauty of the view which gradually opened out before me. Contrary to my anticipation, everything looked fresh and green, and an oriental glamour of enchantment seemed to hang over the island. The old town was bathed in brilliant sunshine and reflected itself lazily on the motionless sea; its flat roofs and dazzlingly white walls peeped out dreamily between waving palms and lofty cocoanuts, huge baobabs and spreading mango trees [...]

My object in coming out to East Africa at this time was to take up a position to which I had been appointed by the Foreign Office on the construction staff of the Uganda Railway. As soon as I landed, therefore, I enquired from one of the Customs officials where the headquarters of the railway were to be found, and was told that they were at a place called Kilindini, some three miles away, on the other side of the island. The best way to get there, I was further informed, was by gharri, which I found to be a small trolley, having two seats placed back to back under a little canopy and running on narrow rails which are laid through the principal street of the town. Accordingly, I secured one of these vehicles, pushed by two strapping Swahili boys, and was soon flying down the track...On arrival at Kilindini, I made my way to the Railway Offices and was informed that I should be stationed inland and should receive further instructions in the course of a day or two. [...]

I had spent nearly a week in Mombasa, and was becoming very anxious to get my marching orders, when one morning I was delighted to receive an official letter instructing me to proceed to Tsavo, about one hundred and thirty-two miles from the coast, and to take charge of the construction of the section of the line at that place, which had just then been reached by railhead. I accordingly started at daylight next morning in a special train with Mr Anderson, the Superintendent of Works, and Dr McCulloch, the principal Medical Officer.

Our journey was slow, as every now and again we stopped to inspect the permanent works in progress; but eventually, towards dusk, we arrived at our destination, Tsavo. I slept that night in a little palm hut which had been built by some previous traveller, and which was fortunately unoccupied for the time being. It was rather broken-down and dilapidated, not even possessing a door, and as I lay on my narrow camp-bed I could see the stars twinkling through the roof. I little knew then what adventures awaited me in this neighbourhood; and if I had realized that at that very time two savage brutes were prowling around, seeking whom they might devour, I hardly think I should have slept so peacefully in my rickety shelter.

Next morning I was up betimes, eager to make acquaintance with my new surroundings. My first impression on coming out of my hut was that I was hemmed in on all sides by a dense growth of impenetrable jungle; and on scrambling to the top of a little hill close at hand, I found that the whole country as far as I could see was covered with low, stunted trees, thick undergrowth and 'wait-a-bit' thorns. The only clearing, indeed, appeared to be where the narrow track for the railway had been cut. This interminable nyika, or wilderness, of whitish and leafless dwarf trees presented a ghastly and sun-stricken appearance; and here and there a ridge of dark-red heat-blistered rock jutted out above the jungle and added by its rugged barrenness to the dreariness of the picture. Away to the north-east stretched the unbroken line of the N'dungu Escarpment, while far off to the south I could just catch a glimpse of the snow-capped top of towering Kilimanjaro.

The one redeeming feature of the neighbourhood was the river from which Tsavo takes its name. This is a swiftly flowing stream, always cool and always running, the latter being an exceptional attribute in this part of East Africa; and the fringe of lofty green trees along its banks formed a welcome relief to the general monotony of the landscape.

When I had thus obtained a rough idea of the neighbourhood, I returned to my hut, and began in earnest to make preparations for my stay in this out-of-the-way place. The stores were unpacked, and my 'boys' pitched my tent in a little clearing close to where I had slept the night before and not far from the main camp of the workmen. Railhead had at this time just reached the western side of the river, and some thousands of Indian coolies and other workmen were encamped there. As the line had to be pushed on with all speed, a diversion had been made and the river crossed by means of a temporary bridge. My principal work was to erect the permanent structure, and to complete all the other works for a distance of thirty miles on each side of the Tsavo [river]. I accordingly made a survey of what had to be done, and sent my requisition for labour, tools and material to the headquarters at Kilindini. In a short time workmen and supplies came pouring in, and the noise of hammers and sledges, drilling and blasting, echoed merrily through the district.

The First Appearance of the Man-Eaters

Unfortunately, this happy state of affairs did not continue for long, and our work was soon interrupted in a rude and startling manner. Two most voracious and insatiable man-eating lions appeared upon the scene, and for over nine months waged an intermittent warfare against the railway and all those connected with it in the vicinity of Tsavo. This culminated in a perfect reign of terror in December 1898, when they actually succeeded in bringing the railway works to a complete standstill for about three weeks. At first they were not always successful in their efforts to carry off a victim, but as time went on they stopped at nothing and indeed braved any danger in order to obtain their favourite food. Their methods then became so uncanny, and their man-stalking so well-timed and so certain of success, that the workmen firmly believed that they were not real animals at all, but devils in lions' shape. Many a time the coolies solemnly assured me that it was absolutely useless to attempt to shoot them. They were quite convinced that the angry spirits of two departed native chiefs had taken this form in order to protest against a railway being made through their country, and by stopping its progress to avenge the insult thus shown to them.

I had only been a few days at Tsavo when I first heard that these brutes had been seen in the neighbourhood. Shortly afterwards one or two coolies mysteriously disappeared, and I was told that they had been carried off by night from their tents and devoured by lions. At the time I did not credit this story, and was more inclined to believe that the unfortunate men had been the victims of foul play at the hands of some of their comrades. They were, as it happened, very good workmen, and had each saved a fair number of rupees, so I thought it quite likely that some scoundrels from the gangs had murdered them for the sake of their money. This suspicion, however, was very soon dispelled. About three weeks after my arrival, I was roused one morning about daybreak and told that one of my jemadars, a fine powerful Sikh named Ungan Singh, had been seized in his tent during the night, and dragged off and eaten.

Naturally I lost no time in making an examination of the place, and was soon convinced that the man had indeed been carried off by a lion, as its 'pug' marks were plainly visible in the sand, while the furrows made by the heels of the victim showed the direction in which he had been dragged away. Moreover, the jemadar shared his tent with half a dozen other workmen, and one of his bedfellows had actually witnessed the occurrence. He graphically described how, at about midnight, the lion suddenly put its head in at the open tent door and seized Ungan Singh who happened to be nearest the opening by the throat. The unfortunate fellow cried out '*Chor oe*!' ('Let go!'), and threw his arms up round the lion's neck. The next moment he was gone, and his panic-stricken companions lay helpless, forced to listen to the terrible struggle which took place outside. Poor Ungan Singh must have died hard; but what chance had he? As a coolie gravely remarked, 'Was he not fighting with a lion?'

On hearing this dreadful story I at once set out to try to track the animal, and was accompanied by Captain Haslem, who happened to be staying at Tsavo at the time, and who, poor fellow, himself met with a tragic fate very shortly afterwards. We found it an easy matter to follow the route taken by the lion, as he appeared to have stopped several times before beginning his meal. Pools of blood marked these halting-places, where he doubtless indulged in the man-eaters' habit of licking the skin off so as to get at the fresh blood. (I have been led to believe that this is their custom from the appearance of two half-eaten bodies which I subsequently rescued: the skin was gone in places, and the flesh looked dry, as if it had been sucked.) On reaching the spot where the body had been devoured, a dreadful spectacle presented itself. The ground all round was covered with blood and morsels of flesh and bones, but the unfortunate jemadar's head had been left intact, save for the holes made by the lion's tusks on seizing him, and lay a short distance away from the other remains, the eyes staring wide open with a startled, horrified look in them. The place was considerably cut up, and on closer examination we found that two lions had been there and had probably struggled for possession of the body. It was the most gruesome sight I had ever seen. We collected the remains as well as we could and heaped stones on them, the head with its fixed, terrified stare seeming to watch us all the time, for it we did not bury, but took back to camp for identification before the Medical Officer.

Thus occurred my first experience of man-eating lions, and I vowed there and then that I would spare no pains to rid the neighbourhood of the brutes. I little knew the trouble that was in store for me, or how narrow were to be my own escapes from sharing poor Ungan Singh's fate.

That same night I sat up in a tree close to the late jemadar's tent, hoping that the lions would return to it for another victim. I was followed to my perch by a few of the more terrified coolies, who begged to be allowed to sit up in the tree with me; all the other workmen remained in their tents, but no more doors were left open. I had with me my 303 and a 12-bore shot gun, one barrel loaded with ball and the other with slug. Shortly after settling down to my vigil, my hopes of bagging one of the brutes were raised by the sound of their ominous roaring coming closer and closer. Presently this ceased, and quiet reigned for an hour or two; as lions always stalk their prey in complete silence. All at once, however, we heard a great uproar and frenzied cries coming from another camp about half a mile away; we knew then that the lions had seized a victim there, and that we should see or hear nothing further of them that night.

Next morning I found that one of the brutes had broken into a tent at Railhead Camp whence we had heard the commotion during the night and had made off with a poor wretch who was lying there asleep. After a night's rest, therefore, I took up my position in a suitable tree near this tent. I did not at all like the idea of walking the half-mile to the place after dark, but all the same I felt fairly safe, as one of my men carried a bright lamp close behind me. He in his turn was followed by another leading a goat, which I tied under my tree in the hope that the lion might be tempted to seize it instead of a coolie. A steady drizzle commenced shortly after I had settled down to my night of watching, and I was soon thoroughly chilled and wet. I stuck to my uncomfortable post, however, hoping to get a shot, but I well remember the feeling of impotent disappointment I experienced when about midnight I heard screams and cries and a heartrending shriek, which told me that the man-eaters had again eluded me and had claimed another victim elsewhere.

At this time the various camps for the workmen were very scattered, so that the lions had a range of some eight miles on either side of Tsavo to work upon; and as their tactics seemed to be to break into a different camp each night, it was most difficult to forestall them. They almost appeared, too, to have an extraordinary and uncanny faculty of finding out our plans beforehand, so that no matter in how likely or how tempting a spot we lay in wait for them, they invariably avoided that particular place and seized their victim for the night from some other camp. Hunting them by day, moreover, in such a dense wilderness as surrounded us, was an exceedingly tiring and really foolhardy undertaking. In a thick jungle of the kind round Tsavo the hunted animal has every chance against the hunter, as however careful the latter may be, a dead twig or something of the sort is sure to crackle just at the critical moment and so give the alarm. Still I never gave up hope of some day finding their lair, and accordingly continued to devote all my spare time to crawling about through the undergrowth. Many a time when attempting to force my way through this bewildering tangle I had to be released by my gun bearer from the fast clutches of the 'wait-a-bit' [bushes]; and often with immense pains I succeeded in tracing the lions to the river after they had seized a victim, only to lose the trail from there onwards, owing to the rocky nature of the ground which they seemed to be careful to choose in retreating to their den.

At this early stage of the struggle, I am glad to say, the lions were not always successful in their efforts to capture a human being for their nightly meal, and one or two amusing incidents occurred to relieve the tension from which our nerves were beginning to suffer. On one occasion an enterprising bania (Indian trader) was riding along on his donkey late one night, when suddenly a lion sprang out on him, knocking over both man and beast. The donkey was badly wounded, and the lion was just about to seize the trader, when in some way or other his claws became entangled in a rope by which two empty oil tins were strung across the donkey's neck. The rattle and clatter made by these as he dragged them after him gave him such a fright that he turned tail and bolted off into the jungle, to the intense relief of the terrified bania, who quickly made his way up the nearest tree and remained there, shivering with fear, for the rest of the night.

Shortly after this episode, a Greek contractor named Themistocles Pappadimitrini had an equally marvellous escape. He was sleeping peacefully in his tent one night, when a lion broke in, and seized and made off with the mattress on which he was lying. Though rudely awakened, the Greek was quite unhurt and suffered from nothing worse than a bad fright. This same man, however, met with a melancholy fate not long afterwards. He had been to the Kilimanjaro district to buy cattle, and on the return journey attempted to take a shortcut across country to the railway, but perished miserably of thirst on the way.

On another occasion fourteen coolies who slept together in a large tent were one night awakened by a lion suddenly jumping on to the tent and breaking through it. The brute landed with one claw on a coolie's shoulder, which was badly torn; but instead of seizing the man himself, in his hurry he grabbed a large bag of rice which happened to be lying in the tent, and made off with it, dropping it in disgust some little distance away when he realized his mistake.

These, however, were only the earlier efforts of the man-eaters. Later on, as will be seen, nothing flurried or frightened them in the least, and except as food they showed a complete contempt for human beings. Having once marked down a victim, they would allow nothing to deter them from securing him, whether he were protected by a thick fence, or inside a closed tent, or sitting round a brightly burning fire. Shots, shouting and firebrands they alike held in derision.

The Attack on the Goods Wagon

All this time my own tent was pitched in an open clearing, unprotected by a fence of any kind round it. One night when the medical officer, Dr Rose, was staying with me, we were awakened about midnight by hearing something tumbling about among the tent ropes, but on going out with a lantern we could discover nothing. Daylight, however, plainly revealed the 'pug' marks of a lion, so that on that occasion I fancy one or other of us had a narrow escape. Warned by this experience, I at once arranged to move my quarters, and went to join forces with Dr Brock, who had just arrived at Tsavo to take medical charge of the district. We shared a hut of palm leaves and boughs, which we had constructed on the eastern side of the river, close to the old caravan route leading to Uganda; and we had it surrounded by a circular boma, or thorn fence, about seventy yards in diameter, well made and thick and high. Our personal servants also lived within the enclosure, and a bright fire was always kept up throughout the night. For the sake of coolness, Brock and I used to sit out under the veranda of this hut in the evenings; but it was rather trying to our nerves to attempt to read or write there, as we never knew when a lion might spring over the boma, and be on us before we were aware. We therefore kept our rifles within easy reach, and cast many an anxious glance out into the inky darkness beyond the circle of the firelight. On one or two occasions, we found in the morning that the lions had come quite close to the fence; but fortunately they never succeeded in getting through.

By this time, too, the camps of the workmen had also been surrounded by thorn fences; nevertheless the lions managed to jump over or to break through some one or other of these, and regularly every few nights a man was carried off, the reports of the disappearance of this or that workman coming in to me with painful frequency. So long, however, as Railhead Camp with its two or three thousand men scattered over a wide area remained at Tsavo, the coolies appeared not to take much notice of the dreadful deaths of their comrades. Each man felt, I suppose, that as the man-eaters had such a large number of victims to choose from, the chances of their selecting him in particular were very small. But when the large camp moved ahead with the railway, matters altered considerably. I was then left with only some few hundred men to complete the permanent works; and as all the remaining workmen were naturally camped together, the attentions of the lions became more apparent and made a deeper impression. A regular panic consequently ensued, and it required all my powers of persuasion to induce the men to stay on. In fact, I succeeded in doing so only by allowing them to knock off all regular work until they had built exceptionally thick and high bomas round each camp.

Within these enclosures fires were kept burning all night, and it was also the duty of the night-watchman to keep clattering half a dozen empty oil tins suspended from a convenient tree. These he manipulated by means of a long rope, while sitting in safety within his tent; and the frightful noise thus produced was kept up at frequent intervals during the night in the hopes of terrifying away the man-eaters. In spite of all these precautions, however, the lions would not be denied, and men continued to disappear.

When the railhead workmen moved on, their hospital camp was left behind. It stood rather apart from the other camps, in a clearing about three-quarters of a mile from my hut, but was protected by a good thick fence and to all appearance was quite secure. It seemed, however, as if barriers were of no avail against the 'demons', for before very long one of them found a weak spot in the boma and broke through. On this occasion the Hospital Assistant had a marvellous escape. Hearing a noise outside, he opened the door of his tent and was horrified to see a great lion standing a few yards away looking at him. The beast made a spring towards him, which gave the Assistant such a fright that he jumped backwards, and in doing so luckily upset a box containing medical stores. This crashed down with such a loud clatter of breaking glass that the lion was startled for the moment and made off to another part of the enclosure. Here, unfortunately, he was more successful, as he jumped on to and broke through a tent in which eight patients were lying. Two of them were badly wounded by his spring, while a third poor wretch was seized and dragged off bodily through the thorn fence. The two wounded coolies were left where they lay, a piece of torn tent having fallen over them;

and in this position the doctor and I found them on our arrival soon after dawn next morning. We at once decided to move the hospital closer to the main camp; a fresh site was prepared, a stout hedge built round the enclosure, and all the patients were moved in before nightfall.

As I had heard that lions generally visit recently deserted camps, I decided to sit up all night in the vacated boma in the hope of getting an opportunity of bagging one of them; but in the middle of my lonely vigil I had the mortification of hearing shrieks and cries coming from the direction of the new hospital, telling me only too plainly that our dreaded foes had once more eluded me. Hurrying to the place at daylight I found that one of the lions had jumped over the newly erected fence and had carried off the hospital bhisti (water-carrier), and that several other coolies had been unwilling witnesses of the terrible scene which took place within the circle of light given by the big campfire. The bhisti, it appears, had been lying on the floor, with his head towards the centre of the tent and his feet nearly touching the side. The lion managed to get its head in below the canvas, seized him by the foot and pulled him out. In desperation the unfortunate water-carrier clutched hold of a heavy box in a vain attempt to prevent himself being carried off, and dragged it with him until he was forced to let go by its being stopped by the side of the tent. He then caught hold of a tent rope, and clung tightly to it until it broke. As soon as the lion managed to get him clear of the tent, he sprang at his throat and after a few vicious shakes the poor bhisti's agonizing cries were silenced for ever. The brute then seized him in his mouth, like a huge cat with a mouse, and ran up and down the boma looking for a weak spot to break through. This he presently found and plunged into, dragging his victim with him and leaving shreds of torn cloth and flesh as ghastly evidences of his passage through the thorns. Dr Brock and I were easily able to follow his track, and soon found the remains about four hundred yards away in the bush. There was the usual horrible sight. Very little was left of the unfortunate bhisti, only the skull, the jaws, a few of the larger bones and a portion of the palm with one or two fingers attached. On one of these was a silver ring, and this, with the teeth (a relic much prized by certain castes), was sent to the man's widow in India.

Again it was decided to move the hospital; and again, before nightfall, the work was completed, including a still stronger and thicker boma. When the patients had been moved, I had a covered goods-wagon placed in a favourable position on a siding which ran close to the site which had just been abandoned, and in this Brock and I arranged to sit up that night. We left a couple of tents still standing within the enclosure, and also tied up a few cattle in it as bait for the lions, who had been seen in no less than three different places in the neighbourhood during the afternoon (April 23). Four miles from Tsavo they had attempted to seize a coolie who was walking along the line. Fortunately, however, he had just time to escape up a tree, where he remained, more dead than alive, until he was rescued by the Traffic Manager, who caught sight of him from a passing train. They next appeared close to Tsavo Station, and a couple of hours later some workmen saw one of the lions stalking Dr Brock as he was returning about dusk from the hospital.

In accordance with our plan, the doctor and I set out after dinner for the goods-wagon, which was about a mile away from our hut. In the light of subsequent events, we did a very foolish thing in taking up our position so late; nevertheless, we reached our destination in safety, and settled down to our watch about ten o'clock. We had the lower half of the door of the wagon closed, while the upper half was left wide open for observation: and we faced, of course, in the direction of the abandoned boma, which, however, we were unable to see in the inky darkness. For an hour or two everything was quiet, and the deadly silence was becoming very monotonous and oppressive, when suddenly, to our right, a dry twig snapped, and we knew that an animal of some sort was about. Soon afterwards we heard a dull thud, as if some heavy body had jumped over the boma. The cattle, too, became very uneasy, and we could hear them moving about restlessly. Then again came dead silence.

At this juncture I proposed to my companion that I should get out of the wagon and lie on the ground close to it, as I could see better in that position should the lion come in our direction with his prey. Brock, however, persuaded me to remain where I was; and a few seconds afterwards I was heartily glad that I had taken his advice, for at that very moment one of the man-eaters, although we did not know it, was quietly stalking us, and was even then almost within springing distance. Orders had been given for the entrance to the boma to be blocked up, and accordingly we were listening in the expectation of hearing the lion force his way out through the bushes with his prey. As a matter of fact, however, the doorway had not been properly closed, and while we were wondering what the lion could be doing inside the boma for so long, he was outside all the time, silently reconnoitring our position.

Presently I fancied I saw something coming very stealthily towards us. I feared, however, to trust to my eyes, which by that time were strained by prolonged staring through the darkness, so under my breath I asked Brock whether he saw anything, at the same time covering the dark object as well as I could with my rifle. Brock did not answer; he told me afterwards that he, too, thought he had seen something move, but was afraid to say so lest I should fire and it turn out to be nothing after all. After this there was intense silence again for a second or two, then with a sudden bound a huge body sprang at us. 'The lion!' I shouted, and we both fired almost simultaneously—not a moment too soon, for in another second the brute would assuredly have landed inside the wagon. As it was, he must have swerved off in his spring, probably blinded by the flash and frightened by the noise of the double report which was increased a hundredfold by the reverberation of the hollow iron roof of the truck. Had we not been very much on the alert, he would undoubtedly have got one of us, and we realized that we had had a very lucky and very narrow escape. The next morning we found Brock's bullet embedded in the sand close to a footprint; it could not have missed the lion by more than an inch or two. Mine was nowhere to be found.

Thus ended my first direct encounter with one of the man-eaters [of Tsavo].

EIGHT ANNAS A TAIL

HUGH ALLEN

Hugh Allen came to India in 1942, after a head wound during World War II put him out of service. At a time when the British were leaving the country, he bought a farm at the edge of a forest in Madhya Pradesh and settled there. As is evident in 'Eight Annas a Tail', Allen was a reluctant hunter, who took up his rifle only when left with no other option. The title of this story refers to the reward the government gave at the time for killing a monkey, in order to deal with the 'menace' of monkeys raiding crops. Allen opposed the policy and made constant efforts to drive away poachers from his land. It was during one such instance, when he was chasing poachers, that his dog Jumbo was killed and eaten by a leopard. A distraught Allen then took up his rifle and set out to kill the leopard.

IT was six o'clock of a May morning and already unpleasantly warm. As Babs and I sipped our early tea under the shade of the trees near the house we told each other quite unnecessarily that it was going to be another scorching day. Speaking for myself I did not really mind: the hot month of May is a slack one and I was going to spend the morning on a cool veranda with a new book; after lunch I might raise the energy to answer some letters.

Jumbo, one of the dogs, was feeling lazy too and lay stretched at my feet, a shaggy and rather oversized cocker spaniel. He had always hated the heat, and unless I took him down to the river to bathe he would not stir out until the cool of evening for he was a wise old man of twelve summers.

Those were our plans at six in the morning and for a hot day they were sound. Unfortunately they did not last very long; for even as we made them fate and the jungle were decreeing that our day should be very different indeed. For me it was to be a day that is still branded across my memory; for poor old Jumbo it was to mark the end of the road...

Bandar wallahs! Bandar wallahs! It was Kalu racing up through the orchards and shouting as he came. I knew at once what he was coming to tell me, another raid by the 'monkey-men' who had already visited us twice before. As soon as Kalu had caught up with his breath I asked him where he had seen them. When he had told me I gulped down my tea and then went in to dress.

This time I was really going to catch them and discourage further visits; for these are cruel devils that come armed with nets, clumsy traps and old muzzle-loading guns. The live monkeys—and they prefer them to be very young—are for export and vivisection; the ones they cannot catch in their traps are shot down for the new government reward of eight annas a tail.

Now you might well imagine that as a farmer with large orchards I should be only too happy to let these men go over the estate as often as they pleased. That, however, would be a wrong idea because by now I have the monkey situation pretty much under control whenever any fruits are on the trees. The monkeys of course always do some damage, but this is more than offset by the help these little animals give you about the jungles. Indeed, they might even save your life for they will often tell where a tiger or a leopard is hiding after a badly placed bullet.

Besides, the business of protecting orchards developed long ago into an exciting game which I believe is enjoyed by the monkeys just as much as by us. I play it often for it takes me back to those early days when I was a senior member of the Black Hand and known over a widish area as 'that bloody little horror with the catapult'. Now, alas, most of that puerile cunning with this weapon has gone, but some of the old magic of those times still returns when I pull back an elastic. But my own accuracy is no longer important as it is more than made up for by a little band of dusky 'sure-shots'—eager volunteers from the kids on the estate.

These young rustics know nothing of space-suits and ray-guns, and even cowboys and Indians are as yet unknown. They are thoroughly old-fashioned kids and so content with a simple 'catty' and a pocketful of smooth pebbles—and the red bottoms of the monkeys in the tree-tops...

That morning, as soon as I was dressed, I set off after the monkey-men with Jumbo at my heels. We walked fast for I was hoping to find them before they could do much damage. I was carrying a rifle while Jumbo had his old red and blue ball bulging from his mouth. Somewhere, he hoped, we should stop by water and play his favourite game.

I was making for a deep and shady nullah which runs diagonally through the estate and divides it into two almost equal halves. The banks of this are lined with magnificent trees, most of them tall stately kohas, which are loved by the monkeys for the cool shade of their topmost branches. So it was somewhere along here that I expected to find the monkey-men at work because this nullah is more than three miles long and the trees above it 'home' for at least six troops of monkeys.

The estate is roughly square, so I started the search at the far north-eastern corner and intended to stalk along the nullah until I found the raiders. By now the morning was really hot. There was little breeze and even under the shade of the trees the fierce heat from the sun was unpleasant. During the rains this nullah is a raging torrent, but now the flow of water had dried up leaving along the winding bed a series of crystal-clear pools with little fish darting above the pepper-and-salt of their sandy bottoms. By the side of most of these pools, at the foot of the high bank, are small ledges a foot or two wide and a few inches above the surface of the water. These are paths that have been beaten out by game and are much used at night by all kinds of animals. As the days grow warmer and the smaller pools elsewhere dry up, tigers and leopards begin to haunt the banks of this nullah.

For the first mile I found no sign of the raiders. Then I picked up what were almost certainly their tracks: five pairs of human feet, the prints fresh and over the marks of the hooves and pads left by last night's visitors. At one spot these men had stopped to rest. The ground here was littered with bidis, the Indian leaf cigarette; and in one place against the bank some heavy bundles had been thrown down, one of them leaving on the sand a criss-crossed pattern like a net.

If those signs had not been enough to tell me that the monkey-men were not far ahead, the next pool two hundred yards down the nullah left no doubt of it. The grey bodies of two langur monkeys lay just by the water's edge. One was dead and nearly cold, the other still lived though its life was flowing rapidly away into a pool of blot seeping into the sand. Both bodies were peppered with red-brown spots where the shot that had brought them tumbling from the trees had slammed in. Neither of the monkeys had a tail.

I had known the troop from which these monkeys came for many years and had always regarded its little members as some of my best jungle friends. In many ways this was the most useful troop of all along the whole stretch of the nullah. The ground here is tricky; beyond the banks it is covered with heavy forest and to the north rises steeply to several hundred feet. Towards the summit of this high ground are patches of open rocky scrub. These places are difficult to reach: the way up to them is over large boulders which have between them a mass of 'wait-a-bit' thorns and other rampageous weeds; these hide deep crevices so completely that a false step can mean a heavy fall; end up at the bottom of one of these with a broken limb and you might never be found.

All these high places are loved by leopards. They come up in the early morning to take the sun and stretch out on the flat-topped rocks. As the day gets warmer they move to some shady spot to doze away the drowsy hours until night; but although they appear to sleep one eye is always cocked towards the nullah below. Long stretches of it are laid bare from these high places and anything moving on the sandy bed can be seen plainly. It is seldom that there is not a leopard somewhere about here, and whenever one of these sneaking brutes becomes a nuisance, this is the spot I come to first. Then it was that the monkeys used to help, for if a leopard was indeed about they would tell me—sooner or later—where it was.

As I looked up from the bodies of the two monkeys a cold anger took hold of me. The whole troop seemed to have been wiped out for there was no sign of the others anywhere. No swaying branches up in the trees as they swung from bough to bough, and in the air were none of their usual cries as they quarrelled and played above the pool. For the next fifteen minutes my anger mounted and there was but one thought in my mind: to catch these men, free whatever captives they had, and—but that could wait until I caught them.

That morning, however, I was not to catch them. Indeed, that satisfaction only came many years later when I surprised a big camp of them one morning just before dawn. But on that occasion I got them all: men, women and children, all their monkeys and all their goods and chattels. The chattels included the skins of buck, chital and barking deer, as well as an enormous bundle of peacock feathers. The skins and the feathers were a lucky find; for although those rascals had no licence to trap I could not have touched them for the monkeys alone.

All that, however, was still in the future and not known to me that morning when I set off after finding the dead monkeys to track their killers. In the sand I could see that two men had stayed in the nullah while the other three had probably worked the banks. At two places they had stopped to smoke again; then, at a spot where a game-path crosses the nullah, the footsteps of all five led away to the left and were lost on the harder surface of the track up on the bank.

Now, I suspected, they were making for the river half-a-mile away where they would find a lot more monkeys.

I was about to go after them when I noticed that Jumbo was no longer at my heels. I whistled softly to bring him up from the pool in the nullah below. He was probably there wallowing like a buffalo with his beloved ball near his nose waiting for me to come and play. But there was no time for that now, so I sent down another and more urgent whistle when he did not come up to the first one.

I felt the first tinge of anxiety when a third call failed to bring him up. In a flash every other thought was swept from my mind and I raced back to the pool. Jumbo was not in sight, and when I started back the way I had come I saw none of his pug-marks following mine. Now I was really worried. He was an obedient dog who without word to break would not have gone far on his own affairs.

From the pool I had just left to the one where we had found the two monkeys was just over a quarter of a mile with the nullah between them shaped like the letter S. Slowly I worked back scanning the sand for sign of Jumbo. But there was none, the soft surface showed only my own boots, the feet of the monkey-men and the tracks of wild animals.

There was still no trace of him when at last I was standing by the pool on the far side of which were the two monkeys. Across that placid surface was the last spot where I positively remembered Jumbo at my heels. So, from somewhere between where I stood now and the other end of the water—a distance of only eighty yards—that faithful old dog had vanished into thin air.

My eyes went to the little ledge running along by the water at the foot of the bank. A feeling of sick apprehension was churning inside me and every instinct was warning of what I should find when I went along that ledge.

For five minutes more I stood still and listened to the jungle. Nothing was excited; all the birds were going about their business in a calm way, and from nowhere around me came the slightest sign that anything was wrong. What I needed to tell me the truth was monkeys, but when I scanned the trees again there was still not one in sight. Slowly I started towards the ledge by the side of the pool.

Halfway along it I stopped. In the firm clay at my feet was the whole story and it told me that Jumbo was dead.

Almost at the water's edge was the single imprint of a leopard's paw. The pad had rammed hard into the clay with the toes wide-cleft and the claws straining out. A little to the left of the pug a small patch on the ledge had been swept clean of the debris and dead leaves fallen from the trees above. The leopard had sprung down from the bank, seized Jumbo by the neck, and then shaken him so violently that his body had swept that patch. And about a yard from the ledge, motionless and just showing above the surface of the pool, a spot of faded red and blue that was Jumbo's old ball.

Of the attack I had heard nothing, and why Jumbo had stayed so far behind me I shall never know. I can only think that he must have lingered about the bodies of the two monkeys and then, when he set out to follow me, he had picked up the leopard's scent. That would have stopped him, for he was well aware of the danger from these sneaking cats. By then I must have been round the first bend of the S in the nullah.

From the swept patch the leopard had gone on along the ledge carrying Jumbo with his legs trailing through the dead leaves by the water's edge. Then, a few yards beyond the pool, Jumbo—still alive—had broken the leopard's grip and shaken free. For a few glorious seconds, for he was a fighting man, he had kept the leopard off. The sand here had been wildly churned by both the leopard's pugs and Jumbo's in what had been a short but furious melee. Then sheer brute force had driven Jumbo back against the bank where he had been seized again. From here the leopard had gone on down the nullah and then had bounded up the bank towards that rocky and difficult ground.

I followed slowly, the trail made easy by frequent spots of blood. After climbing steeply for about fifteen minutes I stopped. From a dense patch of scrub farther up the slope I had suddenly heard the leopard.

I am not going to try to describe my feelings. All I can say, passing over the agony, is that a burning fury was urging me on to rush forward and stop those dreadful sounds by any means. But I fought the urge back. To rush forward now would probably send the leopard flying from the back of the scrub and leave him free to operate another day. It might have been very unwise, too, and no help to Jumbo now, to rush straight at an unsuspecting leopard on a fresh kill. Patience was the only thing. If I held my hand and waited I might get the revenge I wanted.

But not from here. When I had looked around me again I soon saw that I could get no nearer to the leopard without giving myself away. The ground was too difficult: the fifty or so yards I still had to climb before I stood the slightest chance were strewn with rocks and crackling leaves. The leopard had picked his spot with instinctive cunning and from no side could he be surprised; the only thing was to leave him where he was and then set a trap on ground of my own choosing.

The morning by now was so hot that there was one place the leopard was sure to come to when he had finished. That place was the pool immediately below me. When he came down to drink, as he must, I could kill him from the other side of the nullah.

With the greatest care I crept away from those heart-rending sounds, back down the rocks, then across the nullah and up the opposite bank where I found some cover to hide me.

The leopard took his time. It was over half-an-hour before I heard him moving on the hill—an animal unsuspicious of any danger. About halfway down he started to roll in the dead leaves; then he spent some time cleaning his claws, tearing them through the bark of a tree with sharp, plucking little jerks. All at once I saw him weaving through the trees at the foot of the high ground across the nullah—a comparatively small animal as his pugs had shown. When he reached the bank above the pool he paused and looked to his right and left. A moment later he came down the bank in a gracefully controlled slide to stand on the ledge beside the water.

He gave me a beautiful broadside shot as he bent to drink with the points of his elbows sharp above his back. But I was a little too eager to see him dead and raised the rifle a shade too quickly. The leopard saw the movement from the corner of his eye. In a flash his head was up and looking straight towards me. As he braced for the spring that would take him away to safety I snatched at the trigger.

I heard the bullet strike and saw the leopard leap into the air. At the top of his jump he twisted and clawed for the bank. For one uncertain moment he hung there fighting for a hold with a blur of scrabbling paws. As I ripped back the bolt I thought he was going to drop; but with a sudden effort he was up and racing away through the trees. The bullet I sent after him hit a rock well behind his tail.

Although the first shot had been poorly placed he was nevertheless a badly wounded animal and that mad rush would not take him far. Or so I thought, but when I went to look for him I sought in vain for over an hour. There was no sign of him anywhere about the spot where I thought he should have fallen; nor on the high ground was there any trace of his passing; and nowhere was there a single drop of blood. At last I came to the conclusion that I must have left him somewhere behind me and so decided to go back to the beginning—the claw marks at the top of the nullah bank.

From here, as I had seen before, his first wild rush had taken him about a hundred yards. Then all trace of him was lost as the ground began to rise and became rocky. I started to search around the end of this trail again, and I had only been going for about a minute when I suddenly found a clue. Across the side of a rock was a heavy smear of blood. As I bent down to examine it I was wondering how I could have missed it the first time.

But had I missed It? The rock had been catching the full rays of the sun for some time and was burning hot when I touched it. Now my follow-up had started more than an hour before, yet this blood was still wet and just beginning to trickle down the rock. *I've walked right into it!* As the thought hit me I froze beside the rock: the leopard had been here within the last few minutes and now was probably watching me from somewhere close by.

Any sudden movement now might bring the enraged beast on top of me. He might come even if I did not move, but it was safer to stay crouched by the rock and let my eyes search as far as they could from under the brim of my hat. There was no sign of him in front of me, so fervently hoping that he was not somewhere close behind I started slowly to my feet. A few breathless moments later, after I had looked all round, the tension slackened. The sudden rush would have come before now if the leopard had been really near.

It had been a nasty scare and I now started off much more cautiously. Not far from the blood-smeared rock a game-path led towards the nullah. That was the way I thought the leopard would have gone. The heat now was like a furnace and a burning thirst had probably driven him back to the pool. I was, however, taking no more chances; for it was just as possible that he had moved on from the rock because he had heard me coming and might now be waiting in ambush somewhere ahead.

As I moved slowly towards the pool I found more blood on the path. This certainly was the way he had gone and I doubled my precautions. Every bit of cover likely to conceal a leopard was now suspect indeed and had to be scrutinized carefully before going on. After I had stalked forward for another hundred yards the ground in front of me rose in a gentle fold before it rolled down to the nullah on the other side. If the leopard was planning mischief, just over the crest of that was a likely place for him to spring it.

A little before the fold started to rise I left the game-path and went thirty yards to the right of it. From this new position I began to creep up the slope as carefully as I could. At the top of it I paused with my finger on the trigger and my eyes everywhere at once. Suddenly I knew that the leopard was not here. Of that I was perfectly sure, for on one of the topmost branches of a koha tree almost above my head was a monkey.

From where it sat it could take in a sizable piece of the surrounding jungle. Yet it was calm and quiet, and from the ground appeared to be dozing. That told me that no leopard was or recently had been anywhere near here; for if that monkey had caught even a glimpse of its spotted hide it would now be racing round the tree and screaming in high alarm.

With the tension suddenly slackened and the leopard heaven knew where, I fished out a pipe. Why, I wondered as I filled it, had the leopard so abruptly changed his mind and avoided the nullah? The most probable answer was that he had either seen or heard me close behind him and had realized the danger of going down to the pool. If that was true, then he had for a certainty doubled back to the high ground. One thing, however, was sure: the leopard knew where I was and so it would be unwise to go back from my present position. The safest thing was to let him think I had lost his trail by going on to the nullah. Then, once I was by the pool and out of sight, I could fool him by working round to the high ground from behind.

As I started towards the path leading down to the pool I was thinking again of Jumbo. Once more I was living through the agony of hearing the leopard at his meal. So it happened that as I reached the path the memory of that ordeal was undoubtedly dulling my mind and in some odd way splitting it into two differently thinking parts. I was halfway down the path when I came abruptly into the deep shadow cast by the trees along the bank. Just beyond this and straight ahead of me was a patch of blinding sunlight and the dazzling reflection from the pool. The two together were so bright that for a moment I closed my eyes.

When I opened them again it seemed that one part of my mind showed me the spotted back of a leopard crouched half behind the root of a tree and a small bush on the path six feet ahead. At the same time the other part of my mind was assuring me that no leopard could be there while a monkey sat silent overhead. A little confused but nevertheless sure that this could not be a leopard I walked on expecting to see that spotted back resolve into the litter of dead leaves it had to be.

It was only one pace short of the bush that my confusion vanished when the full length of the leopard leapt into view. For a second that seemed eternity I looked down at him. Neither of us moved and for one brief moment I thought he was dead. But he was alive, and an instant later, with a snarl of rage, he reared up in a blur of flailing paws. I tried to leap clear and went crashing into the bank. As I fought to keep my balance sharp claws raked down my left leg. I raised my foot to kick them off and the leopard's jaws snapped shut round the heel of my boot. I slammed it down with his head still clamped to it. But with my foot caught tight I lost the last of my balance and fell heavily to the path.

Now he had me. A quick spring and the game was his. But he did not move. He might have been dead except for his furious eyes screaming hate into mine. I knew then that he was at his last gasp, but even though his strength was failing fast I could feel his jaws straining tighter round my boot. By now I had found and grabbed up the rifle.

The next second I jammed the muzzle into his mouth and pulled the trigger.

He died at once. But although I had felt the blast through my boot it was some little time before I had prised his fangs from the rubber heel. Reaction hit me as soon as my foot was free. I was trembling with shock and my heart was pounding at top speed while the deep claw marks down my leg were streaming blood. I should have liked to lie down beside the dead leopard, but before I could move a wild scream of terror ripped through the air. It came so abruptly and held such a chilling note that I was on my feet in a flash and grabbing for the rifle expecting I knew not what.

All at once I remembered the monkey. It had to be that for the scream had come from high above me. From where I was I could not see it through the leaves of the trees, but the scream had startled me so much that I began to run towards the top of the bank. Just as I reached it and was looking up the scream came again and stopped me in utter amazement.

What sort of monkey was this? It didn't call at leopards and seemed so bad at climbing trees that it was about to fall off the one it was on; for it was hanging from a branch with its arms at full stretch and kicking its legs feebly in the air. Without warning the scream rent the air again. Then before my startled eyes the monkey let go its hold. It dropped like a stone, a sudden twisting flash of grey that hurtled down thumping from branch to branch until it hit the ground with a sickening thud sixty feet below.

I was still surprised, but as I made my way down to it an idea was forming in my mind. The monkey had fallen by the water's edge with its face upwards and one quick look was enough to tell me why it had not called at the leopard and why it had fallen off the tree. It was a young male monkey and it had been dying for hours. Its body was peppered with the shot from a muzzle-loading gun and it had been blinded in both eyes. It would have fallen from the tree in any case, but I believe that the sudden report of my shot at the leopard had so terrified it anew that it slipped from its perch; then, weak from loss of blood and hanging over a sixty-foot drop in a strange and frightening world of blackness and pain—well, who wouldn't scream?

At last I slung the rifle and started to limp up the slope towards home. As I stepped out a whistle instinctively formed on my lips to call up Jumbo before I remembered. At the top of the slope I paused and looked down at the dead monkey. Its little face seemed slightly ashamed and saying, 'I couldn't really help it, you know.'

THE MUKTESAR MAN-EATER

JIM CORBETT

Corbett's deep bond with the people he lived among is nowhere more apparent than in this story. It is also one where, as in the best of his stories, the hunted animal becomes the main protagonist, the epic and tragic figure that is the defining spirit of the story.

EIGHTEEN miles to the north–north-east of Naini Tal is a hill eight thousand feet high and twelve to fifteen miles long, running east and west. The western end of the hill rises steeply and near this end is the Muktesar Veterinary Research Institute, where lymph and vaccines are produced to fight India's cattle diseases. The laboratory and staff quarters are situated on the northern face of the hill and command one of the best views to be had anywhere of the Himalayan snowy range. This range, and all the hills that lie between it and the plains of India, run east and west, and from a commanding point on any of the hills an uninterrupted view can be obtained not only of the snows to the north but also of the hills and valleys to the east and to the west as far as the eye can see. People who have lived at Muktesar claim that it is the most beautiful spot in Kumaon, and that its climate has no equal.

A tiger that thought as highly of the amenities of Muktesar as human beings did, took up her residence in the extensive forests adjoining the small settlement. Here she lived very happily on sambar, kakar, and wild pig, until she had the misfortune to have an encounter with a porcupine. In this encounter she lost an eye and got some fifty quills, varying in length from one to nine inches, embedded in the arm and under the pad of her right foreleg. Several of these quills after striking a bone had doubled back in the form of a U, the point and the broken-off end being close together. Suppurating sores formed where she endeavoured to extract the quills with her teeth, and while she was lying up in a thick patch of grass, starving and licking her wounds, a woman selected this particular patch of grass to cut as fodder for her cattle. At first the tigress took no notice, but when the woman had cut the grass right up to where she was lying, the tigress struck once, the blow crushing the woman's skull. Death was instantaneous, for, when found the following day, she was grasping her sickle with one hand and holding a tuft of grass, which she was about to cut when struck, with the other. Leaving the woman lying where she had fallen, the tigress limped off for a distance of over a mile and took refuge in a little hollow under a fallen tree. Two days later a man came to chip firewood off this fallen tree, and the tigress who was lying on the far side killed him also. The man fell across the tree, and as he had removed his coat and shirt and the tigress had clawed his back while killing him, it is possible that the sight of blood trickling down his body as he hung across the bole of the tree first gave her the idea that he was something that she could satisfy her hunger with. However that may be, before leaving him she ate a small portion from his back. A day later she killed her third victim deliberately, and without having received any provocation. Thereafter she became an established man-eater.

I heard of the tigress shortly after she started killing human beings, and as there were a number of sportsmen at Muktesar, all of whom were keen on bagging the tigress—who was operating right on their doorsteps—I did not consider it would be sporting of an outsider to meddle in the matter. When the toll of human beings killed by the tigress had risen to twenty-four, however, and the lives of all the people living in the settlement and neighbouring villages were endangered and work at the Institute slowed down, the veterinary officer in charge of the Institute requested the Government to solicit my help.

My task, as I saw it, was not going to be an easy one, for, apart from the fact that my experience of man-eaters was very limited, the extensive ground over which the tigress was operating was not known to me and I therefore had no idea where to look for her.

Accompanied by a servant and two men carrying a roll of bedding and a suitcase, I left Naini Tal at midday and walked ten miles to the Ramgarh Dak Bungalow, where I spent the night. The Dak Bungalow khansama (cook, bottle-washer, and general factotum) was a friend of mine, and when he learnt that I was on my way to Muktesar to try to shoot the man-eater, he warned me to be very careful while negotiating the last two miles into Muktesar for, he said, several people had recently been killed on that stretch of road.

Leaving my men to pack up and follow me I armed myself with a double-barrelled .500 express rifle using modified cordite, and making a very early start next morning arrived at the junction of the Naini Tal/Almora road with the Muktesar road just as it was getting light. From this point it was necessary to walk warily for I was now in the man-eater's country. Before zigzagging up the face of a very steep hill the road runs for some distance over flat ground on which grows the orange-coloured lily, the round hard seeds of which can be used as shot in a muzzle-loading gun. This was the first time I had ever climbed that hill and I was very interested to see the caves, hollowed out by wind, in the sandstone cliffs overhanging the road. In a gale I imagine these caves must produce some very weird sounds, for they are of different sizes and, while some are shallow, others appear to penetrate deep into the sandstone.

Where the road comes out on a saddle of the hill there is a small area of flat ground flanked on the far side by the Muktesar Post Office, and a small bazaar. The post office was not open at that early hour, but one of the shops was and the shopkeeper very kindly gave me directions to the Dak Bungalow which, he said, was half a mile away on the northern face of the hill. There are two Dak Bungalows at Muktesar, one reserved for government officials and the other for the general public. I did not know this and my shopkeeper friend, mistaking me for a government official, possibly because of the size of my hat, directed me to the wrong one and the khansama in charge of the bungalow, and I, incurred the displeasure of the red tape brigade, the khansama by providing me with breakfast, and I by partaking of it. However, of this I was at the time happily ignorant, and later I made it my business to see that the khansama did not suffer in any way for my mistake.

While I was admiring the superb view of the snowy range, and waiting for breakfast, a party of twelve Europeans passed me carrying service rifles, followed a few minutes later by a sergeant and two men carrying targets and flags. The sergeant, a friendly soul, informed me that the party that had just passed was on its way to the rifle range, and that it was keeping together because of the man-eater. I learnt from the sergeant that the officer in charge of the Institute had received a telegram from the Government the previous day informing him that I was on my way to Muktesar. The sergeant expressed the hope that I would succeed in shooting the man-eater for, he said, conditions in the settlement had become very difficult. No one even in daylight, dared to move about alone, and after dusk everyone had to remain behind locked doors. Many attempts had been made to shoot the man-eater but it had never returned to any of the kills that had been sat over.

After a very good breakfast I instructed the khansama to tell my men when they arrived that I had gone out to try get news of the man-eater, and that I did not know when I would return. Then, picking up my rifle, I went up to the post office to send a telegram to my mother to let her know I had arrived safely.

From the flat ground in front of the post office and the bazaar the southern face of the Muktesar hill falls steeply away, and is cut up by ridges and ravines overgrown with dense brushwood, with a few trees scattered here and there. I was standing on the edge of the hill, looking down into the valley and the well-wooded Ramgarh hills beyond, when I was joined by the Postmaster and several shopkeepers. The Postmaster had dealt with the Government telegram of the previous day, and on seeing my signature on the form I had just handed in, he concluded I was the person referred to in the telegram and his friends and he had now come to offer me their help. I was very glad of the offer for they were in the best position to see and converse with everyone coming to Muktesar, and as the man-eater was sure to be the main topic of conversation where two or more were gathered together, they would be able to collect information that would be of great value to me. In rural India, the post office and the bania's shop are to village folk what taverns and clubs are to people of other lands, and if information on any particular subject is sought, the post office and the bania's shop are the best places to seek it.

In a fold of the hill to our left front, and about two miles away and a thousand feet below us, was a patch of cultivation. This I was informed was Badri Sah's apple orchard. Badri, son of an old friend of mine, had visited me in Naini Tal some months previously and had offered to put me up in his guest house and to assist me in every way he could to shoot the man-eater. This offer, for the reason already given, I had not accepted. Now, however, as I had come to Muktesar at the request of the Government I decided I would call on Badri and accept his offer to help me, especially as I had just been informed by my companions that the last human kill had taken place in the valley below his orchard.

Thanking all the men who were standing round me, and telling them I would rely on them for further information, I set off down the Dhari road. The day was still young and before calling on Badri there was time to visit some of the villages farther along the hill to the east. There were no milestones along the road, and after I had covered what I considered was about six miles and visited two villages, I turned back. I had retraced my steps for about three miles when I overtook a small girl having difficulties with a bullock. The girl, who was about eight years old, wanted the bullock to go in the direction of Muktesar, while the bullock wanted to go in the opposite direction, and when I arrived on the scene the stage had been reached when neither would do what the other wanted. The bullock was a quiet old beast, and with the girl walking in front holding the rope that was tied round his neck and I walking behind to keep him on the move he gave no further trouble. After we had proceeded a short distance I said:

'We are not stealing Kalwa, are we?' I heard her addressing the black bullock by that name.

'N—o,' she answered indignantly, turning her big brown eyes full on me.

'To whom does he belong?' I next asked.

'To my father,' she said.

'And where are we taking him?'

'To my uncle.'

'And why does uncle want Kalwa?'

'To plough his field.'

'But Kalwa can't plough uncle's field by himself

'Of course not,' she said. I was being stupid, but then you could not expect a sahib to know anything about bullocks and ploughing.

'Has uncle only got one bullock?' I next asked.

'Yes,' she said; 'he has only got one bullock now, but he did have two.'

'Where is the other one?' I asked, thinking that it had probably been sold to satisfy a debt.

'The tiger killed it yesterday,' I was told. Here was news indeed, and while I was digesting it we walked on in silence, the girl every now and then looking back at me until she plucked up courage to ask:

'Have you come to shoot the tiger?'

'Yes,' I said, 'I have come to try to shoot the tiger.'

'Then why are you going away from the kill?'

'Because we are taking Kalwa to uncle.' My answer appeared to satisfy the girl, and we plodded on. I had got some very useful information, but I wanted more and presently I said:

'Don't you know that the tiger is a man-eater?'

'Oh, yes,' she said, 'it ate Kunthi's father and Bonshi Singh's mother, and lots of other people.'

'Then why did your father send you with Kalwa? Why did he not come himself?'

'Because he has bhabari bokhar (malaria).'

'Have you no brothers?'

'No. I had a brother but he died long ago.'

'A mother?'

'Yes, I have a mother; she is cooking the food.'

'A sister?'

'No, I have no sister.' So on this small girl had devolved the dangerous task of taking her father's bullock to her uncle, along a road on which men were afraid to walk except when in large parties, and on which in four hours I had not seen another human being.

We had now come to a path up which the girl went, the bullock following, and I bringing up the rear. Presently we came to a field on the far side of which was a small house. As we approached the house the girl called out and told her uncle that she had brought Kalwa.

'All right,' a man's voice answered from the house, 'tie him to the post, Putli, and go home. I am having my food.' So we tied Kalwa to the post and went back to the road. Without the connecting link of Kalwa between us, Putli (dolly) was now shy, and as she would not walk by my side I walked ahead, suiting my pace to hers. We walked in silence for some time and then I said:

'I want to shoot the tiger that killed uncle's bullock but I don't know where the kill is. Will you show me?'

'Oh, yes,' she said eagerly, 'I will show you.'

'Have you seen the kill?' I asked.

'No,' she said, 'I have not seen it, but I heard uncle telling my father where it was.'

'Is it close to the road?'

'I don't know.'

'Was the bullock alone when it was killed?'

'No, it was with the village cattle.'

'Was it killed in the morning or the evening?'

'It was killed in the morning when it was going out to graze with the cows.'

While talking to the girl I was keeping a sharp lookout all round, for the road was bordered on the left by heavy tree jungle, and on the right by dense scrub. We had proceeded for about a mile when we came to a well-used cattle track leading off into the jungle on the left. Here the girl stopped and said it was on this track that her uncle had told her father the bullock had been killed. I had now got all the particulars I needed to enable me to find the kill, and after seeing the girl safely to her home I returned to the cattle track. This track ran across a valley and I had gone along it for about a quarter of a mile when I came upon a spot where cattle had stampeded. Leaving the track, I now went through the jungle, parallel to and about fifty yards below the track. I had only gone a short distance when I came on a drag-mark. This drag-mark went straight down into the valley, and after I had followed it for a few hundred yards I found the bullock, from which only a small portion of the hindquarters had been eaten. It was lying at the foot of a bank about twenty feet high, and some forty feet from the head of a deep ravine. Between the ravine and the kill was a stunted tree, smothered over by a wild rose. This was the only tree within a reasonable distance of the kill on which I could sit with any hope of bagging the tiger, for there was no moon, and if the tiger came after dark—as I felt sure it would—the nearer I was to the kill the better would be my chance of killing the tiger.

It was now 2 p.m. and there was just time for me to call on Badri and ask him for a cup of tea, of which I was in need for I had done a lot of walking since leaving Ramgarh at four o'clock that morning. The road to Badri's orchard takes off close to where the cattle track joins the road, and runs down a steep hill for a mile through dense brushwood. Badri was near his guest house, attending to a damaged apple tree when I arrived, and on hearing the reason for my visit he took me up the guest house which was on a little knoll overlooking the orchard. While we sat on the veranda waiting for the tea and something to eat that Badri had ordered his servant to prepare for me, I told him why I had come to Muktesar, and about the kill the young girl had enabled me to find. When I asked Badri why this kill had not been reported to the sportsmen at Muktesar, he said that owing to the repeated failures of the sportsmen to bag the tiger the village folk had lost confidence in them, and for this reason kills were no longer being reported to them. Badri attributed the failures to the elaborate preparations that had been made to sit over kills. These preparations consisted of clearing the ground near the kills of all abstractions in the way of bushes and small trees, the building of big machans, and the occupation of the machans by several men. Reasons enough for the reputation the tiger had earned of never returning to a kill. Badri was convinced that there was only one tiger in Muktesar district and that it was slightly lame in its right foreleg, but he did not know what had caused the lameness, nor did he know whether the animal was male or female.

Sitting on the veranda with us was a big Airedale terrier. Presently the dog started growling, and looking in the direction in which the dog was facing, we saw a big langur sitting on the ground and holding down the branch of an apple tree, and eating the unripe fruit. Picking up a shotgun that was leaning against the railing of the veranda, Badri loaded it with No. 4 shot and fired. The range was too great for the pellets, assuming any hit it, to do the langur any harm, but the shot had the effect of making it canter up the hill with the dog in hot pursuit. Frightened that the dog might come to grief, I asked Badri to call it back, but he said it would be all right for the dog was always chasing this particular animal, which he said had done a lot of damage to his young trees. The dog was now gaining on the langur, and when it got to within a few yards the langur whipped round, got the dog by the ears, and bit a lump off the side of its head. The wound was a very severe one, and by the time we had finished attending to it my tea and a plate of hot puris (unleavened bread fried in butter) was ready for me.

I had told Badri about the tree I intended sitting on, and when I returned to the kill he insisted on going with me accompanied by two men carrying materials for making a small machan. Badri and the two men had lived under the shadow of the man-eater for over a year and had no illusions about it, and when they saw that there were no trees near the kill—with the exception of the one I had selected—in which a machan could be built, they urged me not to sit up that night, on the assumption that the tiger would remove the kill and provide me with a more suitable place to sit up the following night. This was what I myself would have done if the tiger had not been a man-eater, but as it was I was disinclined to miss a chance which might not recur on the morrow, even if it entailed a little risk. There were bears in this forest and if one of them smelt the kill, any hope I had of getting a shot at the tiger would vanish, for Himalayan bears are no respecters of tigers and do not hesitate to appropriate their kills. Climbing into the tree, smothered as it was by the rose bush, was a difficult feat, and after I had made myself as comfortable as the thorn permitted and my rifle had been handed up to me Badri and his men left, promising to return early next morning.

I was facing the hill, with the ravine behind me. I was in clear view of any animal coming down from above, but if the tiger came from below, as I expected, it would not see me until it got to the kill. The bullock, which was white, was lying on its right side with its legs towards me, and at a distance of about fifteen feet. I had taken my seat at 4 p.m. and an hour later a kakar started barking on the side of the ravine two hundred yards below me. The tiger was on the move, and having seen it the kakar was standing still and barking. For a long time it barked and then it started to move away, the bark growing fainter and fainter until the sound died away round the shoulder of the hill. This indicated that after coming within sight of the kill, the tiger had lain down. I had expected this to happen after having been told by Badri the reasons for the failures to shoot the tiger over a kill. I knew the tiger would now be lying somewhere nearby with his eyes and ears open, to make quite sure there were no human beings near the kill, before he approached it. Minute succeeded long minute; dusk came; objects on the hill in front of me became indistinct and then faded out. I could still see the kill as a white blur when a stick snapped at the head of the ravine and stealthy steps came towards me, and then stopped immediately below. For a minute or two there was dead silence, and then the tiger lay down on the dry leaves at the foot at the tree.

Heavy clouds had rolled up near sunset and there was now a black canopy overhead blotting out the stars. When the tiger eventually got up and went to the kill, the night could best be described as pitch black. Strain my eyes as I would, I could see nothing of the white bullock, and still less of the tiger. On reaching the kill the tiger started blowing on it. In the Himalayas, and especially in the summer, kills attract hornets, most of which leave as the light fades but those that are too torpid to fly remain, and a tiger—possibly after bitter experience—blows off the hornets adhering to the exposed portion of the flesh before starting to feed. There was no need for me to hurry over my shot for, close though it was, the tiger would not see me unless I attracted its attention by some movement or sound. I can see reasonably well on a dark night by the light of the stars, but there were no stars visible that night nor was there a flicker of lightning in the heavy clouds. The tiger had not moved the kill before starting to eat, so I knew he was lying broadside on to me, on the right-hand side of the kill.

Owing to the attempts that had been made to shoot the tiger I had suspicion that it would not come before dark, and it had been my intention to take what aim I could—by the light of the stars—and then move the muzzle of my rifle sufficiently for my bullet to go a foot or two to the right of the kill. But now that the clouds had rendered my eyes useless, I would have to depend on my ears (my hearing at that time was perfect). Raising the rifle and resting my elbows on my knees, I took careful aim at the sound the tiger was making, and while holding the rifle steady, turned my right ear to the sound, and then back again. My aim was a little too high, so, lowering the muzzle a fraction of an inch, I again turned my head and listened. After I had done this a few times and satisfied myself that I was pointing at the sound, I moved the muzzle a little to the right and pressed the trigger. In two bounds the tiger was up the twenty-foot bank. At the top there was a small bit of flat ground, beyond which the hill went up steeply. I heard the tiger on the dry leaves as far as the flat ground, and then there was silence. This silence could be interpreted to mean either that the tiger had died on reaching the flat ground or that it was unwounded. Keeping the rifle to my shoulder I listened intently for three or four minutes, and as there was no further sound I lowered the rifle. This movement was greeted by a deep growl from the top of the bank. So the tiger was unwounded, and had seen me. My seat on the tree had originally been about ten feet up but, as I had nothing solid to sit on, the rose bush had sagged under my weight and I was now possibly no more than eight feet above ground, with my dangling feet considerably lower. And a little above and some twenty feet from me a tiger that I had every reason to believe was a man-eater was growling deep down in his throat.

The near proximity of a tiger in daylight, even when it has not seen you, causes a disturbance in the blood stream. When the tiger is not an ordinary one, however, but a man-eater and the time is ten o'clock on a dark night, and you know the man-eater is watching you, the disturbance in the blood stream becomes a storm. I maintain that a tiger does not kill beyond its requirements, except under provocation. The tiger that was growling at me already, had a kill that would last it for two or three days, and there was no necessity for it to kill me. Even so, I had an uneasy feeling that on this occasion this particular tiger might prove an exception to the rule. Tigers will at times return to a kill after being fired at, but I knew this one would not do so. I also knew that in spite of my uneasy feeling I was perfectly safe so long as I did not lose my balance—I had nothing to hold on to—or go to sleep and fall off the tree. There was no longer any reason for me to deny myself a smoke, so I took out my cigarette case and as I lit a match I heard the tiger move away from the edge of the bank. Presently it came back and again growled. I had smoked three cigarettes, and the tiger was still with me, when it came on to rain. A few big drops at first and then a heavy downpour. I had put on light clothes when I started from Ramgarh that morning and in a few minutes I was wet to the skin, for there was not a leaf above me to diffuse the raindrops. The tiger, I knew, would have hurried off to shelter under a tree or on the lee of a rock the moment the rain started. The rain came on at 11 p.m.; at 4 a.m. it stopped and the sky cleared. A wind now started to blow, to add to my discomfort, and where I had been cold before I was now frozen. When I get a twinge of rheumatism I remember that night and others like it, and am thankful that it is no more than a twinge.

Badri, good friend that he was, arrived with a man carrying a kettle of hot tea just as the sun was rising. Relieving me of my rifle the two men caught me as I slid off the tree, for my legs were too cramped to function. Then as I lay on the ground and drank the tea they massaged my legs and restored circulation. When I was able to stand, Badri sent his man off to light a fire in the guest house. I had never previously used my ears to direct a bullet and was interested to find that I had missed the tiger's head by only a few inches. The elevation had been all right but I had not moved the muzzle of the rifle far enough to the right, with the result that my bullet had struck the bullock six inches from where the tiger was eating.

The tea and the half-mile walk up to the road took all the creases out of me, and when we started down the mile-long track to Badri's orchard, wet clothes and an empty stomach were my only discomfort. The track ran over red clay which the rain had made very slippery. In this clay were three tracks: Badri's and his man's tracks going up, and the man's tracks going down. For fifty yards there were only these three tracks in the wet clay, and then, where there was a bend in the track, a tigress had jumped down from the bank on the right and gone down the track on the heels of Badri's man. The footprints of the man and the pug-marks of the tigress showed that both had been travelling at a fast pace. There was nothing that Badri and I could do, for the man had a twenty-minute start from us, and if he had not reached the safety of the orchard he would long have been beyond any help we could give him. With uneasy thoughts assailing us, we made what speed we could on the slippery ground and were very relieved to find, on coming to a footpath from where the orchard and a number of men working in it were visible, that the tigress had gone down the path while the man had carried on to the orchard. Questioned later, the man said he did not know that he had been followed by the tigress.

While drying my clothes in front of a roaring wood-fire in the guest house, I questioned Badri about the jungle into which the tigress had gone. The path which the tigress had taken, Badri told me, ran down into a deep and densely wooded ravine which extended down the face of a very steep hill, for a mile or more, to where it was met by another ravine coming down from the right. At the junction of the two ravines there was a stream and here there was an open patch of ground which, Badri said, commanded the exit of both ravines. Badri was of the opinion that the tigress would lie up for the day in the ravine into which we had every reason to believe she had gone, and as this appeared to be an ideal place for a beat, we decided to try this method of getting a shot at the tigress, provided we could muster sufficient men to carry out the beat. Govind Singh, Badri's head gardener, was summoned and our plan explained to him. Given until midday, Govind Singh said he could muster a gang of thirty men to do the beat, and in addition carry out his master's orders to gather five mounds (four hundred and ten pounds) of peas. Badri had an extensive vegetable garden in addition to his apple orchard and the previous evening he had received a telegram informing him that the price of marrowfat peas on the Naini Tal market had jumped to four annas (four pence) a pound. Badri was anxious to take advantage of this good price and his men were gathering the peas to be dispatched by pack pony that night, to arrive in Naini Tal for the early morning market.

After cleaning my rifle and walking round the orchard, I joined Badri at his morning meal—which had been put forward an hour to suit me—and at midday Govind produced his gang of thirty men. It was essential for someone to supervise the pea-pickers, so Badri decided to remain and send Govind to carry out the beat. Govind and the thirty men were local residents and knew the danger to be apprehended from the man-eater. However, after I had told them what I wanted them to do, they expressed their willingness to carry out my instructions. Badri was to give me an hour's start to enable me to search the ravine for the tigress and, if I failed to get a shot, to take up my position on the open ground near the stream. Govind was to divide his men into two parties, take charge of one party himself, and put a reliable man in charge of the other. At the end of the hour Badri was to fire a shot and the two parties were to set off, one on either side of the ravine, rolling rocks down, and shouting and clapping their hands. It all sounded as simple as that, but I had my doubts, for I have seen many beats go wrong.

Going up the track down which I had come that morning, I followed the path that the tigress had taken, only to find after I had gone a short distance that it petered out in a vast expanse of dense brushwood. Forcing my way through for several hundred yards I found that the hillside was cut up by a series of deep ravines and ridges. Going down a ridge which I thought was the right-hand boundary of the ravine to be beaten, I came to a big drop at the bottom of which the ravine on my left met a ravine coming down from the right, and at the junction of the two ravines there was stream. While I was looking down and wondering where the open ground was on which I was to take my stand, I heard flies buzzing near me and on following the sound found the remains of a cow that had been killed about a week before. The marks on the animal's throat showed that it had been killed by a tiger. The tiger had eaten all of the cow, except a portion of the shoulders, and the neck and head. Without having any particular reason for doing so, I dragged the carcass to the edge and sent it crashing down the steep hill. After rolling for about a hundred yards the carcass fetched up in a little hollow a short distance from the stream. Working round to the left I found an open patch of ground on a ridge about three hundred yards from the hollow into which I had rolled the remains of the cow. The ground down here was very different from what I had pictured it to be. There was no place where I could stand to overlook the hillside that was to be beaten, and the tigress might break out anywhere without my seeing her. However, it was then too late to do anything, for Badri had fired the shot that was to let me know the beat had started. Presently, away in the distance, I heard men shouting. For a time I thought the beat was coming my way and then the sounds grew fainter and fainter until they eventually died away. An hour later I again heard the beaters. They were coming down the hill to my right, and when they were on a level with me I shouted to them to stop the beat and join me on the ridge. It was no one's fault that the beat had miscarried, for without knowing the ground and without previous preparation we had tried to beat with a handful of untrained men a vast area of dense brushwood that hundreds of trained men would have found difficult to cope with.

The beaters had had a very strenuous time forcing their way through the brushwood, and while they sat in a bunch removing thorns from their hands and feet and smoking my cigarettes, Govind and I stood facing each other, discussing his suggestion of carrying out a beat on the morrow in which every available man in Muktesar and the surrounding villages would take part. Suddenly, in the middle of a sentence, Govind stopped talking. I could see that something unusual had attracted his attention behind me, for his eyes narrowed and a look of incredulity came over his face. Swinging round I looked in the direction in which he was facing, and there, quietly walking along a field that had gone out of cultivation, was the tigress. She was about four hundred yards away on the hill on the far side of the stream, and was coming towards us.

When a tiger is approaching you in the forest—even when you are far from human habitations—thoughts course through your mind of the many things that can go wrong to spoil your chance of getting the shot, or the photograph, you are hoping for. On one occasion I was sitting on a hillside overlooking a game track, waiting for a tiger. The track led to a very sacred jungle shrine known as Baram ka Than. Baram is a jungle God who protects human beings and does not permit the shooting of animals in the area he watches over. The forest in the heart of which this shrine is situated is well stocked with game and is a favourite hunting ground of poachers for miles around, and of sportsmen from all parts of India. Yet, in a lifetime's acquaintance with that forest, I do not know of a single instance of an animal having been shot in the vicinity of the shrine. When therefore I set out that day to shoot a tiger that had been taking toll of our village buffaloes, I selected a spot a mile from Baram's shrine. I was in position, behind a bush, at 4 p.m. and an hour later a sambar belled in the direction from which I was expecting the tiger. A little later and a little nearer to me a kakar started barking; the tiger was coming along the track near which I was sitting. The jungle was fairly open and consisted mostly of young jamun trees, two to three feet in girth. I caught sight of the tiger—a big male—when he was two hundred yards away. He was coming slowly and had reduced the distance between us to a hundred yards when I heard the swish of leaves, and on looking up saw that one of the jamun trees whose branches were interlaced with another was beginning to lean over. Very slowly the tree heeled over until it came in contact with another tree of the same species and of about the same size. For a few moments the second tree supported the weight of the first and then it, too, started to keel over. When the two trees were at an angle of about thirty degrees from the perpendicular, they fetched up against a third and smaller tree. For a moment or two there was a pause, and then all three trees crashed to the ground. While watching the trees, which were only a few yards from me, I had kept an eye on the tiger. At the first sound of the leaves he had come to a halt and when the trees crashed to the ground he turned and, without showing any sign of alarm, went back in the direction from which he had come. What made the occurrence I had witnessed so unusual was that the trees were young and vigorous; that no rain had fallen recently to loosen their roots; that not a breath of air was stirring in the forest; and, finally, that the trees had fallen across the track leading to the shrine when the tiger had only another seventy yards to cover to give me the shot I was waiting for.

The chances of a shot being spoilt are greatly increased when the quarry is in an inhabited area in which parties of men may be travelling from one village to another or going to or from markets, or where shots may be fired to scare away langurs from apple orchards. The tigress still had three hundred yards to go to reach the stream, and two hundred yards of that was over open ground on which there was not a single tree or bush. The tigress was coming towards us at a slight angle and would see any movement we made, so there was nothing I could do but watch her, and no tigress had ever moved more slowly. She was known to the people of Muktesar as the lame tiger, but I could see no sign of her being lame. The plan that was forming in my head as I watched her was to wait until she entered the scrub jungle, and then run forward and try to get a shot at her either before or after she crossed the stream. Had there been sufficient cover between me and the point the tigress was making for, I would have gone forward as soon as I saw her and tried either to get a shot at her on the open ground or, failing that, to intercept her at the stream. But unfortunately there was not sufficient cover to mask my movements, so I had to wait until the tigress entered the bushes between the open ground and the stream. Telling the men not to move or make a sound until I returned, I set off at a run as the tigress disappeared from view. The hill was steep and as I ran along the contour I came to a wild rose bush which extended up and down the hill for many yards. Through the middle of the bush there was a low tunnel, and as I bent down to run through it my hat was knocked off, and raising my head too soon at the end of the tunnel I was nearly dragged off my feet by the thorns that entered my head. The thorns of these wild roses are curved and very strong and as I was not able to stop myself some embedded themselves and broke off in my head—where my sister Maggie had difficulty in removing them when I got home—while others tore through the flesh. With little trickles of blood running down my face I continued to run until I approached the hollow into which I had rolled the partly eaten kill from the hill above. This hollow was about forty yards long and thirty yards wide. The upper end of it where the kill was lying, the hill above the kill, and the further bank, were overgrown with dense brushwood. The lower half of the hollow and the bank on my side were free of bushes. As I reached the edge of the hollow and peered over, I heard a bone crack. The tigress had reached the hollow before me and, on finding the old kill, was trying to make up for the meal she had been deprived of the previous night.

If after leaving the kill, on which there was very little flesh, the tigress came out on to the open ground I would get a shot at her, but if she went up the hill or up the far bank I would not see her. From the dense brushwood in which I could hear the tigress, a narrow path ran up the bank on my side and passed within a yard to my left; a yard beyond the path, there was a sheer drop of fifty feet into the stream below. I was considering the possibility of driving the tigress out of the brushwood on to the open ground by throwing a stone on to the hill above her, when I heard a sound behind me. On looking round I saw Govind standing behind me with my hat in his hand. At that time no European in India went about without a hat, and having seen mine knocked off by the rose bush Govind had retrieved it and brought it to me. Near us there was a hole in the hill. Putting my finger to my lips I got Govind by the arm and pressed him into the hole. Sitting on his hunkers with his chin resting on his drawn-up knees, hugging my hat, he just fitted into the hole and looked a very miserable object, for he could hear the tigress crunching bones a few yards away. As I straightened up and resumed my position on the edge of the bank, the tigress stopped eating. She had either seen me or, what was more probable, she had not found the old kill to her liking. For a long minute there was no movement or sound, and then I caught sight of her. She had climbed up the opposite bank, and was now going along the top of it towards the hill. At this point there were a number of six-inch-thick poplar saplings, and I could only see the outline of the tigress as she went through them. With the forlorn hope that my bullet would miss the saplings and find the tigress I threw up my rifle and took a hurried shot. At my shot the tigress whipped round, came down the bank, across the hollow, and up the path on my side, as hard as she could go. I did not know, at the time, that my bullet had struck a sapling near her head, and that she was blind of one eye. So what looked like a very determined charge might only have been a frightened animal running away from danger, for in that restricted space she would not have known from which direction the report of my rifle had come. Be that as it may, what I took to be a wounded and a very angry tigress was coming straight at me; so, waiting until she was two yards away, I leaned forward and with great good luck managed to put the remaining bullet in the rifle into the hollow where her neck joined her shoulder. The impact of the heavy .500 bullet deflected her just sufficiently for her to miss my left shoulder, and her impetus carried her over the fifty-foot drop into the stream below, where she landed with a great splash. Taking a step forward I looked over the edge and saw the tigress lying submerged in a pool with her feet in the air, while the water in the pool reddened with her blood.

Govind was still sitting in the hole, and at a sign he joined me. On seeing the tigress he turned and shouted to the men on the ridge, 'The tiger is dead. The tiger is dead.' The thirty men on the ridge now started shouting, and Badri on hearing them got hold of his shot gun and fired off ten rounds. These shots were heard at Muktesar and in the surrounding villages, and presently men from all sides were converging on the stream. Willing hands drew the tigress from the pool, lashed her to a sapling, and carried her in triumph to Badri's orchard. Here she was put down on a bed of straw for all to see, while I went to the guest house for a cup of tea. An hour later by the light of hand lanterns, and with a great crowd of men standing round, among whom were several sportsmen from Muktesar, I skinned the tigress.

It was then that I found she was blind of one eye and that she had some fifty porcupine quills, varying in length from one to nine inches, embedded in the arm and under the pad of her right foreleg. By ten o'clock my job was finished, and declining Badri's very kind invitation to spend the night with him I climbed the hill in company with the people who had come down from Muktesar, among whom were my two men carrying the skin. On the open ground in front of the post office the skin was spread out for the Postmaster and his friends to see. At midnight I lay down in the Dak Bungalow reserved for the public, for a few hours' sleep. Four hours later I was on the move again and at midday I was back in my home at Naini Tal after an absence of seventy-two hours.

The shooting of a man-eater gives one a feeling of satisfaction. Satisfaction at having done a job that badly needed doing. Satisfaction at having outmanoeuvred, on his own ground, a very worthy antagonist. And, the greatest satisfaction of all, at having made a small portion of the earth safe for a brave little girl to walk on.

THE MYSTERIOUS YELLOW MAN-EATER OF PACHWARA

MRS E. MINSHULL

This story first appeared in The Illustrated Weekly of India *and was later included in a collection of shikar stories—*Big Game Encounters*—edited by Stanley Jepson, then editor of the* Weekly, *and published in 1936. There is no information about the author, except that she was a resident of Mussoorie, the hill station that almost rivalled Shimla in popularity and importance during the Raj. She would have been English, of course, and probably the spouse of someone senior in the police or the army to have a 'daffadar'—a local Indian employee of the British Indian police or army—to send off on errands.*

WE hastily gave orders for fires to be kept burning all night round the camp. Rifles were left ready loaded beside our beds in case of any *khubber* [early news] being brought, but nothing happened and we marched on to meet the D.S.P., who was also out to bag the creature. Then began nights of sitting up over *puddahs* [buffaloes tied up as bait] and days of chasing off in all directions after the latest news. But still the creature killed and killed, and gave no sign by which it could be identified...

The memory of that chase will live with me for ever—stalking a ferocious and unidentified man-eater of the jungle.

It happened some years ago—actually it was in the cold weather of 1928—but the incidents were so thrilling that it seems as if they happened only yesterday. I remember that we were on our usual cold weather tour, and eventually came to Bansi, a small village in the Jhansi district, lying at the foot of a low range of hills covered with scrub jungle. The camp, as usual, had marched the night before, but when we arrived in the morning our surprise and indignation can be better imagined than described when we discovered that no tents had been pitched, and pandemonium reigned everywhere.

We were not left long in doubt as to the cause of this apparent neglect of duty on the part of our staff, as our car was soon surrounded by the servants, headed by our venerable *khitmatgar*. Throwing himself almost under the car wheels in his agitation he moaned pitifully, beating his breast and crying: 'Huzoor, let us be gone from this accursed place as soon as possible. A fearful demon haunts it and has killed hundreds of villagers. Yet no one has seen it, and down in the village they tell us that it is the spirit of a dhobi, who lived on the banks of the river.'

'An evil spirit entered into him,' continued the cowering *khitmatgar*, 'and he slew his wife and devoured her. Now he wanders through the jungle with matted hair and nails like claws, going on all fours and destroying all he meets.'

He told us more in this strain with frightful embellishments, but sifting his story, we realised that something unusual was happening. So we sent off the *duffadar* to Bansi village for more information. He more or less confirmed our *khitmatgar*'s story on his return, and was quite definite that an animal of a ferocious nature had been haunting the range of hills that ran up to Pachwara. It had killed twenty people in Bansi alone.

One of its favourite methods was to steal up behind a cart travelling through the jungle paths, and snatch the poor unsuspecting occupants. Then again it made a speciality of carrying off the lonely watchers from the machans in the fields. The night before our arrival, we were told this fearsome prowler had entered a village, where all the terrified inhabitants were safely behind barricaded doors, with the exception of the village chowkidar. The latter—sad to relate—provided the evening meal for that day. His headless body was found near his charpoy.

Then it was that we decided on immediate action, as the beginning of this story tells. But all to no purpose. We were very disappointed at not finding any trace of this weird creature, and almost gave up in despair, but our hopes of a kill were revived when an old man appeared at the camp. He came from a village twenty miles away, running practically all the way. After he had calmed down he told us that the previous evening he was sitting by the fire in his hut, with his grandson lying on the charpoy behind him. The door was open as it was still only six o'clock. 'Suddenly,' he went on, 'an enormous yellow monster with a great ruff of yellow hair round his neck crept through the door, sprang upon the charpoy and seized the child.'

This brave old warrior was too bashful to tell us the sequel, but by judicious questioning we learnt that with flashing presence of mind, he seized a burning faggot from the fire and dashed it in the creature's face. With a roar of fear and pain it dropped the child and fled. We found out afterwards that no permanent harm was done to the child, except that it suffered a good deal from shock—in fact, it nearly died from fright.

This incident, therefore, only served to intensify our longing to get at this monster, but we were impotent. Every day brought fresh news of a kill generally forty to fifty miles away from the last, but none of the khubber was of any use to us in identifying the beast. Then we heard that it had killed a woman in the fields. So we went there and found the marks of its pads. The creature was obviously lame in the off foreleg but the marks were not those of either a leopard or a tiger!

Excitement now ran high among the seasoned shikaris, and many were the arguments as to what it really was. After many consultations, we decided that the beast must have been a lion.

Now that part of the mystery was fairly easy compared to the subsequent question. How did it get there? A possible explanation was offered by one of the party who said that some years before the incident of which I am writing took place, Gwalior State, hoping to raise a fresh stock of lions in their jungles, had let loose four of the animals imported from Kathiawar. They were not seen again until one was shot in 1928. The one that was giving us all this excitement was probably another.

Be that as it may, one and all were determined to seek out this beast of the jungle. Government offered a reward of five hundred rupees, but our quarry scented like a sambar, and even when one was lucky enough to happen on a kill within an hour or two, he was away. Finally it was decided, at a round-the-camp-fire conference, to make an attack in force on his favourite haunt, Pachwara. Officials collected in large numbers, and tents, ringed with camp fires, were pitched in the valley. Our baby and I were parked in solitary state in the bungalow on the ridge, this being deemed the safest place. Night after night we dined at five p.m. and the men were in their machans by six o'clock sitting over the juiciest puddahs that could be found. But never another sight nor sound of our jungle friend did anyone get.

He had disappeared into the blue, and to this day has not been heard of since.

When he included this story in Big Game Encounters, *Stanley Jepson added an update, which he called 'The Mystery of the Lion Man-eaters Solved':*

> *The Administrative Officer, Forest Department of Gwalior State, writes in reply to an inquiry that 'His Late Highness the Maharajah, for the sake of experiment, had imported four pairs of lions direct from Africa, and not from Kathiawar. These lions were let loose in the State jungles of Sheopur District, so that they might get used to our jungles and breed there. But as time went on, it was found that for various reasons these African lions and their progeny did not like the environment; and later on, most of them turned into man-eaters. They have now all been accounted for, except for a lioness which is still at large. Out of these lions, a few strayed away into our other neighbouring districts, and out of these, one must have gone over to Datia State border, and from there found its way into Jhansi District. But I cannot say with certainty that the lion that was killed in Jhansi District was a man-eater or not.'*

A MAN-EATER IN A RAILWAY CARRIAGE

J.H. PATTERSON

Long after he had shot the two man-eating lions that had terrorised workers building a railway bridge under his supervision (see 'First Encounters in Tsavo'), Patterson had dinner with a police officer in a railway carriage. In one of the concluding chapters of The Man-Eaters of Tsavo, *he describes what happened to his host just a few months later.*

TOWARDS the end of my stay in British East Africa, I dined one evening with Mr Ryall, the Superintendent of the Police, in his inspection carriage on the railway. Poor Ryall! I little thought then what a terrible fate was to overtake him only a few months later in that very carriage in which we dined.

A man-eating lion had taken up his quarters at a little roadside station called Kimaa, and had developed an extraordinary taste for the members of the railway staff. He was a most daring brute, quite indifferent as to whether he carried off the stationmaster, the signalman, or the pointsman; and one night, in his efforts to obtain a meal, he actually climbed up on to the roof of the station buildings and tried to tear off the corrugated-iron sheets. At this the terrified baboo in charge of the telegraph instrument below sent the following laconic message to the Traffic Manager: 'Lion fighting with station. Send urgent succour.' Fortunately, [the lion] was not victorious in his 'fight with the station'; but he tried so hard to get in that he cut his feet badly on the iron sheeting, leaving large bloodstains on the roof. Another night, however, he succeeded in carrying off the native driver of the pumping-engine, and soon afterwards added several other victims to his list. On one occasion an engine-driver arranged to sit up all night in a large iron water-tank in the hope of getting a shot at him, and had a loop-hole cut in the side of the tank from which to fire. But as so often happens, the hunter became the hunted; the lion turned up in the middle of the night, overthrew the tank and actually tried to drag the driver out through the narrow circular hole in the top through which he had squeezed in. Fortunately the tank was just too deep for the brute to be able to reach the man at the bottom; but the latter was naturally half paralyzed with fear and had to crouch so low down as to be unable to take anything like proper aim. He fired, however, and succeeded in frightening the lion away for the time being.

It was in a vain attempt to destroy this pest that poor Ryall met his tragic and untimely end. On June 6, 1900, he was travelling up in his inspection carriage from Makindu station to Nairobi, accompanied by two friends, Mr Huebner and Mr Parenti. When they reached Kimaa, which is about two hundred and fifty miles from Mombasa, they were told that the man-eater had been seen close to the station only a short time before their train arrived, so they at once made up their minds to remain there for the night and endeavour to shoot him. Ryall's carriage was accordingly detached from the train and shunted into a siding close to the station, where, owing to the unfinished state of the railway line, it did not stand perfectly level, but had a pronounced list to one side. In the afternoon the three friends went out to look for the lion, but finding no traces of him whatever, they returned to the carriage for dinner. Afterwards, they all sat up on guard for some time; but the only noticeable thing they saw was what they took to be two very bright and steady glow-worms. After events proved that these could have been nothing else than the eyes of the man-eater steadily watching them all the time and studying their every movement.

The hour now growing late, and there being apparently no sign of the lion, Ryall persuaded his two friends to lie down, while he kept the first watch. Huebner occupied the high berth over the table on one side of the carriage, the only other berth being on the opposite side of the compartment and lower down. This Ryall offered to Parenti, who declined it, saying that he would be quite comfortable on the floor, and he accordingly lay down to sleep, with his feet towards the sliding door which gave admission to the carriage.

It is supposed that Ryall, after watching for some considerable time, must have come to the conclusion that the lion was not going to make its appearance that night, for he lay down on the lower berth and dozed off. No sooner had he done so, doubtless, than the cunning man-eater began cautiously to stalk the three sleepers. In order to reach the little platform at the end of the carriage, he had

to mount two very high steps from the railway line, but these he managed to negotiate successfully and in silence. The door from this platform into the carriage was a sliding one on wheels, which ran very easily on a brass runner; and as it was probably not quite shut, or at any rate not secured in any way, it was an easy matter for the lion to thrust in a paw and shove it open. But owing to the tilt of the carriage and to his great extra weight on the one side, the door slid to and snapped into the lock the moment he got his body right in, thus leaving him shut up with the three sleeping men in the compartment.

He sprang at once at Ryall, but in order to reach him had actually to plant his feet on Parenti, who, it will be remembered, was sleeping on the floor. At this moment Huebner was suddenly awakened by a loud cry, and on looking down from his berth was horrified to see an enormous lion standing with his hind feet on Parenti's body, while his forepaws rested on poor Ryall. Small wonder that he was panic-stricken at the sight. There was only one possible way of escape, and that was through the second sliding door communicating with the servants' quarters, which was opposite to that by which the lion had entered. But in order to reach this door Huebner had literally to jump on to the man-eater's back, for its great bulk filled up all the space beneath his berth. It sounds scarcely credible, but it appears that in the excitement and horror of the moment he actually did this, and fortunately the lion was too busily engaged with his victim to pay any attention to him. So he managed to reach the door in safety; but there, to his dismay, he found that it was held fast on the other side by the terrified coolies, who had been aroused by the disturbance caused by the lion's entrance. In utter desperation he made frantic efforts to open it, and exerting all his strength at last managed to pull it back sufficiently far to allow him to squeeze through, when the trembling coolies instantly tied it up again with their turbans.

A moment afterwards a great crash was heard, and the whole carriage lurched violently to one side; the lion had broken through one of the windows, carrying off poor Ryall with him. Being now released, Parenti lost no time in jumping through the window on the opposite side of the carriage, and fled for refuge to one of the station buildings; his escape was little short of miraculous, as the lion had been actually standing on him as he lay on the floor. The carriage itself was badly shattered, and the woodwork of the window had been broken to pieces by the passage of the lion as he sprang through with his victim in his mouth. All that can be hoped is that poor Ryall's death was instantaneous.

His remains were found next morning about a quarter of a mile away in the bush, and were taken to Nairobi for burial. I am glad to be able to add that very shortly afterwards, the terrible brute who was responsible for this awful tragedy was caught in an ingenious trap constructed by one of the railway staff. He was kept on view for several days, and then shot.

SURPRISED BY PANTHERS

MRS M.A. HANDLEY

A forest officer's wife, Mrs Handley writes with astonishing sensitivity in her book Roughing It in Southern India *(1911) about her encounters with leopards. Astonishing because in the same book she also writes with pride, delight and obvious exaggeration about her husband (to whom she dedicates the book) routinely destroying tigers, leopards and other wildlife. And her sensitivity to India's leopards does not extend to India's people; but in that she ranks with Kipling, after all. Here are the surprising bits from her book, lightly edited for continuity and coherence:*

WE were in the cardamom forests [of the Malabar region], where much of my husband's work lay, and near our camp was a small mountain pool by which I loved to sit. One day, for a wonder, the dogs were not with me; they had started, but something attracted them back, and I went on alone—very fortunately, as it chanced; for as I sat by the pool, looking into the still, darkening water and at the pretty shifting light falling between the boughs overhead, I descried the reflection of a panther's face, much too near me, the animal being on my bank of the pool.

At such times one's instinct is to keep quiet, holding one's breath, unless one be of the screaming order. Turning only my eyes, I saw the beautiful, sleek body lying almost flat as he drank. Meanwhile he had caught sight of my reflection, and lifted his head, the water dripping from his jaws, and gazed full at me. Then he backed, absolutely without a sound or the faintest rustle of the fallen leaves,

just like a scared cat (which indeed he was), creeping away into safety for itself. That was all he cared about; that is all they ever do care about, these wild things, no matter what stories sensation-writers may invent.

But the beauty of him! His coat was of gleaming tawny satin, with jetty rosettes, and his eyes of aquamarine, as I could see while they were glaring into mine. I felt quite sorry he had let himself be interrupted before finishing his drink comfortably; for I may truly say that all fear on my side vanished on seeing how he behaved, keeping his eyes on me furtively—for fear of my flying at him, I suppose!—whilst in reality he could have made such very short work of me had he but known it.

On the second and similar occasion I almost stumbled over a panther, again close to the tents. We came face to face as I was turning the angle of a rock, under the shelving base of which he had been enjoying his noon-day siesta. He was in the act of stretching himself preparatory to strolling off, and so near were we that he could have laid his paw upon me had he not been as frightened as I was. Far from wanting to do anything of the sort, he shrank back, flattened himself, and then turned on his stomach as on a pivot, and so crawled for a little way, till he could pluck up heart to gather his limbs together for a bound into cover.

These encounters did not last long, not so much as a minute perhaps, but on each occasion my eyes met those of the panther, and we looked full at each other. What they saw in mine I cannot imagine, but I saw in theirs abject terror, and the question as to how to save themselves without my stopping them. I suppose my appearance filled them with such fright as something they did not understand. The unknown is always terrifying to the wild nature, whether of a tiny field-mouse that scurries back to its nest in the hedge, scared to death at a footstep, or of the princely tiger himself, who slinks away into the familiar, friendly depths of his jungles at the scent or sight of man.

Yet it is certain that as we moved about in those forests, we were observed by many a creature that we never saw. Of all animals commend me to a panther for inquisitiveness; he will follow, nay downright stalk, you from no other motive than just to stalk—himself, I need hardly say, well hidden all the while... [As my husband] F. discovered one day when he suspected the presence of some creature watching him. He was after bison, and would not let any other quest turn him aside, only seeing that the dogs kept to heel. The next day, on searching about, he found plain proofs that a panther had followed him. Through the long day this espionage had been kept up!

I may mention here a strange error I have often noticed in drawings and paintings of lions, tigers, and other animals of the same family. All the felines, small and great alike, walk with the legs of the same side moving together in a step, while other animals move theirs, as it were, cornerwise. This distinction is commonly ignored, though the tabby proof of it may lie no farther off than on the hearthrug.

With regard to the panther incidents related above, F. was rather envious of my 'unheard of luck'—so thrown away upon me—for though he went about in search of such meetings they never fell to his lot accidentally. I do not wish to represent myself as wonderfully courageous. In neither of those two instances was there any leading up on my part; indeed, had I known of a panther being anywhere near the pool or the rock most surely I would not have stirred out of camp. To walk open-eyed up to danger when necessary, that is where the courage comes in.

--

Rain, as known in the tropics, cannot be rightly imagined by those who have not seen it. It is a very wall or sheet of water, lowered and lowered, hour after hour, day after day, sometimes week after week. For six weeks in succession have I known rain of that tropical sort to fall continuously; if it stopped at all during that time it was at night, for it certainly did not do so by day for so much as half an hour. One night it surpassed itself; without storm or sound it steadily descended, and in the morning the rain-gauges were found to register twenty-four inches for the twelve hours! That was phenomenal, and happened at Tellicherry, on the west coast (only to be beaten at Cherapoonji, in northern India, which has the greatest rainfall in India, if not in the world).

The year of that night of rain was a disastrous one, and was long remembered for its consequences—devastation by floods, the bursting of dams, the annihilation of villages, the destruction of the people's very livelihood by the drowning of their animals. Of these, many were also to be seen lying dead from exposure on the roadside or in the grazing pastures. The very crows fell off the trees, so drenched with the rain and cramped with cold were they.

The place—Manantavadi, in the Wynad—where we were then living was some two thousand five hundred feet or more above sea-level, and to make it comfortable for people who were better used to a temperature of ninety degrees in the shade, fires had to be kept up for quite six months every year, let alone this exceptional one. One morning, not far from the bungalow, F. came upon a panther, on his very path, all but dead from starvation, and killed it in sheer pity for its wasted condition. Our people brought in two, and a fourth they found more dead than alive, famished and spiritless with misery; all four in the space of a week!

There was much unreclaimed forest and scrub in the neighbourhood, and the wild things that inhabited it suffered frightfully from the continuous cold and wet, which seemed to alter all the accustomed conditions of their lives, and it was at this time that we got up one morning to find that we had unawares entertained as a guest during the night a panther, who had adventured his precious but most miserable self under our roof—anything for shelter—curling himself up on a sofa in the veranda! This veranda was a closed-in one, with windows round three sides, and a very rough door, never shutting properly, which, being made of unseasoned planks, shrank in the dry and swelled in the wet weather, in this matching the rest of this special habitation, so that we looked for nothing better, nor sought to remedy it. Hence the distressed creature, finding no hindrance, crept in, enticed by the warmth, and perhaps the chance of a bite of food—emboldened or, it may be, tamed by stress of misery.

When the dogs were let out they tore about the place like mad things, baying and whining in deafening chorus, and would have dragged and torn the sofa to pieces, only we shut them out of the veranda as we wanted to look round first.

The dried muddy pugs were quite distinctly recognizable for those of a full-grown panther; the sofa rug and a flannel coat of F.'s were damp where they had been lain on, and were covered, too, with a quantity of jet-black hairs, proving that this special panther was one of the rarest and most beautiful of the species; and very strange it was that just then a large reward was being offered by the Government for a specimen, dead or alive, of a black panther.

The animal had doubtless taken himself off at the first streak of dawn, very much the better for his good square meal and warm night's rest. Perhaps, with an eye to repeating the experiment, he had not gone very far either; but most surely no harm should have befallen him under our roof, he having 'eaten our salt' in the form of dog biscuits, which we felt quite glad should have been left in his way overnight, and of which just a remnant remained to prove that he could eat no more.

A panther coming to the bungalow thus for food and shelter was a very unusual and incautious act on the part of one of the wariest of animals, only showing him to have been at his wits' end for a living. He would be used to a certain amount of wet and cold, the monsoon being heavy here as compared with some places, but this was an exceptional season—not a dry inch anywhere—and all the denizens of the forest were suffering.

For six weeks we tasted no bread, except what was homemade, as the road was impassable for the coolies upon whom we depended for some of our supplies. They had thirty miles to travel to the nearest stores, and the few Europeans in the place joined in a sort of club to send for things in this way every fortnight. Neither could we have potatoes; as a substitute we ate, and thankfully, the boiled seeds of the jackfruit, which are not unlike chestnuts in taste.

This district was at all times and in all parts what we called a 'panthery' region. The native town of Manantavadi, which was the seat of Government locally, lay in the low flat land between surrounding and isolated low hills, and consisted of one irregular street with countless alleys. All around was the ubiquitous lantana, forming by its thick growth a very nursery for young panthers. There were four European bungalows besides the hospital: one for the doctor and his household; one for the Superintendent of Police; one for the District Magistrate; and one for the Forest Officer. Each bungalow was perched on the summit of its own hill, and set apart from the gardens; very little more of the jungle was cleared round it than enough to make it approachable by a carriage drive, or maybe by only a bridle path. The 'carriage drives' were as far removed as possible from the idea that word usually conveys. They were steep, stony, narrow, winding; nothing to mind, however, when [one was] used to them.

I had been 'tiffing' with the doctor's wife, and was riding leisurely home one evening after dark, the syce walking ahead with a lantern, when I fancied I smelt a panther. I was not sure, however, and my pony Charlie's quicker senses were beforehand with me. Without the least warning he simply laid legs to the ground, took a bee-line for his stable, and tore home, the syce being nowhere. That pony knew all the shortcuts, and took them. Though not anything of a rider, I had learnt the knack of sticking on, but the difficulty now was not so much that, but keeping myself from being dragged off by the strong overhanging boughs, some of which were thorny and clinging. The monsoon being high, all vegetation was at its thickest growth; indeed, only by going in this headlong fashion could I have got through it at all. The ground was full of holes and puddles, but little cared my pony of such trifles; on he flew—while the panther, doubtless, was going just as fast in an opposite direction, but I had not had enough experience to be sure of it in those days, and I had no mind to be left behind!

At length the home lights appeared, and all danger from the panther was at an end, but with Charlie heading straight for his stable there was another danger and all I could do to avoid being brained in passing through the wickedly low doorway was to bury my face in his mane. We were both scratched and bleeding, and it took some time, and a good deal of bread and sugar, before the terrified little animal was soothed and quieted.

The panthers, however, though not usually aggressive, were sometimes pretty bold, and would even snatch a dog from off the very doorstep if not prevented. This happened once to my knowledge, and the dog's rescue was miraculous. It was near the dinner hour—eight o'clock—at the bungalow of a coffee planter and his wife, Mr and Mrs N., friends of ours, who lived about twelve miles from where we were. He and she, as very usual at that hour, were bathing and dressing. The servants were laying the table in the dining-room, which opened on a wide veranda, having a deep flight of ten or more steps leading into the garden. Crotons and various other large shrubs grew round about, but nothing to be considered as cover. Lights there were in plenty on all sides. Several dogs lay taking their ease in the veranda, and one had stretched herself on a step, not far down, and quite within the light. Her a lurking panther dared to seize, and was making off with, without a sound from either, under the very eyes of the servants, one of whom, however, saw what was happening, and raised the outcry which brought master and mistress upon the scene. That something had happened to Dido they could just about make out amid the din of cries...Before this time Mr N. would simply have stared at the idea of leaving his room apparelled in a bath-sheet, but such was the preoccupation of every mind at the moment that, as we were told afterwards, he actually did so on this occasion, armed with a rifle, when, lo and behold!—a few yards from the bottom step lay the gasping, half-choked, but unhurt Dido, her collar beside her!

It was evident that the panther must have caught Dido up by that collar, and, what with the weight, and the leather being probably worn thin, it gave way at the buckle, so setting the dog free, for she had not so much as a tooth-mark on her! The only pity was that the scene could not be snapshotted.

It was no rare occurrence, however, for dogs to be carried off, without hope of a miracle, if loose after four o'clock, or farther away than beside one's chair. Invasion of the kennel was even attempted, and after one such fright, when it had a reasonably strong thatched roof, we had this replaced by tiles, and we, and the dogs too, slept in peace; till one night when a very bold, hungry panther clambered on to the tile-roof and began clawing his way inside. Needless to say, the inmates raised such a bedlam as woke every one about the place, and the panther was glad to take himself off as quickly as possible, leaving a claw or two behind. Lucky for him that F. was away that night!

It was at Manantavadi, too, that we once had a whole afternoon's amusement and interest watching the gambols of a couple of panther cubs, sitting the while in our veranda and looking across to the opposite hillside, no great distance away. The hills being scarcely more than eminences, only a few hundred yards lay between their playground and our bungalow. These little creatures played with each other's tails, and rolled over and over, exactly like kittens, without a touch of malice or savagery—all was pure mischief and fun. Very young, they were just fat round things, with fuzzy, yellowish-grey coats; not sleek as yet, nor had the tawny colour and distinct black rosettes even begun to appear. There was nothing as yet of the lithe, cruel grace of the panther-form—only rounded baby limbs. Their mother could not have been far off, but we neither saw nor heard anything of her till quite late, when the two babies had romped and tumbled themselves tired, and were lying on their sides, paws in air, after the manner of kittens. Then a deep sharp note or call from somewhere we did hear, very different from the harsh roar we knew so well when it echoed through the jungle. The cubs were keen to hear it too; they scrambled to their feet and scampered off, tails on end.

THE FIRST PANTHER

MRS W.W. BAILLIE

Mrs Baillie arrived in India with her husband, a British army clergyman who also appears to have been a busy hunter. His wife would not be denied the outdoor life either, and became an enthusiastic hunter herself—even a horrific bear attack wouldn't stop her; she was out hunting again before her wounds had fully healed. In her sixties she began to put together her hunting notes and journals and published them in a book, Days and Nights of Shikar *(1921), of which the historian Jane Robinson writes: 'This book is less bloodthirsty than many; the worst moments in it are not concerned with the poor animals' appointment with death, but with the author's own.' Mrs Baillie's humour and self-deprecation and, for the most part, the easy, no-humbug camaraderie she shared with local Indians wherever she went are great antidotes to the self-importance, grandstanding and bigotry of a lot of shikar literature.*

For the first few years that my husband and I were in India I had most extraordinary bad luck in every way in shooting. I sat up night after night over kills to try and get a leopard. I never saw or heard one. I went out with parties tiger-beating, under really favourable circumstances, the beat sometimes arranged by an Indian prince, sometimes by a sahib, and I was generally given the most likely place. But though I heard an occasional bang to right or left, nothing ever came my way. I was beginning to grow rather despondent about it.

There were several thieving panthers at Mount Abu. At that time we were taking care of a little brown spaniel, Flirt, for a friend. One night when we were at dinner she ran round to the back of our quarters and stood in the veranda where the light from the cookhouse fell on her. Servants were going backwards and forwards with dinner and the butler was bringing something from the cookhouse when he saw a panther spring into the veranda, snap up poor little Flirt and go off with her. I tied up a goat outside and sat hidden in the veranda night after night, as long as the moon endured; but the panther was too wary for me.

Some weeks afterwards, when we were packing up to leave the hill, a friend put us up for the night. My husband and I chained up our dog Banjo, a fat, smiling thing who thought himself a terrier, to the heavy zinc tub in the bathroom and closed the outside door. In the morning he was gone. We found the chain broken and the door ajar. The panther must have pushed his way in. As we were leaving for Deesa that day, we could not try for our revenge. But a friend next door tied up a goat that evening and went out to dine. When he returned late at night, the goat had just been killed, and he saw the panther glide away. He sat up for a few minutes watching, from his window, when back came the animal for his feed, and we were delighted to hear afterwards that he was slain.

I wasted many more good nights, that I might have spent better in sleep, in vain attempts. I did manage to shoot one tiger in a beat. He came slowly, creeping on, dragging himself along the ground and trying to look as if he were not there. I was up in a machan and, as I put up my rifle and shifted my position, a branch of the tree caught my big pith helmet and knocked it off my head. It went rattling down with a clatter among the dry leaves. The tiger stopped and looked and then glanced up and saw me. His stopping gave me a good chance of a shot. He rolled over, got up, and only went a few yards further, when he died. I was with my brother, Herbert, and he had very nobly, I think, given me the shot.

This was very nice, but I did not feel the joy of triumph that the first panther gave me when I began to go out altogether on my own account. And another thing was, I dare say, that he took so much getting.

We were stationed in a much cultivated part of the Deccan, with no jungle anywhere round worth speaking of. A poor place for big or small game.

A village man, who called himself a shikari, came in one day in May with the news that a panther had been doing much damage among the villagers' flocks, and would I go out and shoot him. There had been a goat killed that morning, and I must go out at once. I asked him where the place was and how far away.

'Near,' he said.

'Three miles, six miles?'

It was farther than that. I brought the map and looked it up, and suggested thirty miles. (It was nearer forty, I found afterwards.) He thought it might be, but it was still 'near'.

'You must have done very quick time to come in thirty miles by midday, after finding the dead goat.'

He had to admit the goat was killed the day before, but was very insistent about the necessity of coming out soon; so I settled to go, told him to go back again and make arrangements, ordered a cart to send out the small tent and a servant, and went out myself in a hired tonga with two little ponies.

It was in the middle of the hot weather and we did not travel very fast. After about thirty miles the tonga man said that he had orders to turn off the road at that point. So we drove on some distance over bare fields. Then he pulled up and said, as well as I could understand, that he had lost his way and could go no farther. He talked Marathi, and I knew only a word or two of that language, but I made him understand that he was to go to the shikari's village.

There was no village to be seen and he did not know even in which direction it was: besides, the ponies had done enough.

By this time the sun had set, out got the driver, unharnessed his ponies and said he was going to find them water. Of course they must have a drink after that long hot march, so I told him to go, thinking he and his ponies would be back soon. But he never did come back, that is, not until the next morning.

I sat and waited for some time, then darkness came on, and beautiful stars shone out, but there was no moon.

I ate some sandwiches and drank some claret, which was very soothing! And when that was over, I thought it seemed a pity my night's rest should be spoiled by any tongawala, so took the cushions out of the cart, put my guns under my head so that they should not be stolen, and soon was fast asleep.

In the middle of the night I was awakened by a bright light shining in my eyes, and three men were standing round me with a lantern. It was the patel of the village for which I was bound, and his servants. He said he had heard that I was there and came to see that I was all right, as there was a party of dacoits on the other side of some small hills nearby, and I had much better come back with him to the village, where I could have a charpoy to sleep on.

I thanked him for coming, and said I was very comfortable where I was, and would come in the morning.

He squatted down on his heels and began to talk:

'I have not seen many white sahibs, but I knew one very well, sahib.' (As a rule, I found the Indians in the country parts do not call a woman 'memsahib', as our servants always do.) 'He was a missionary and was a very good man. He used to give us medicine, or dress our wounds at any time, day or night. Whenever anyone went to him for help he was always ready and kind and in a good temper. And we talked among ourselves and said, "If this is the Christian religion, then it is a good and great religion, better than ours." And we thought and wondered about it, whether we should join him. Then he had to go away and another sahib came. He was a very different. He often lost his temper and got very angry. He was a big gussawala. Then we said, "No, this is no religion for us, no better than ours."'

It was very amusing to hear his ideas on the subject. He went on and told me a good deal about his religion which was very interesting. They had a holy man of their own a long time ago. He was so good that when he died both Mussulmans and Hindus built a temple to him on a hill, and both worshipped there, and did so still.

I got rather sleepy at last, and said we would finish our talk next day, so he went away leaving two of his men to keep watch over me. Next morning the patel, pony-man and shikari came early and I drove to the village, where my servant had already arrived.

The shikari was disappointed that I had been too late to sit up over the goat and so missed a good chance. However, I sat and watched until dark that evening. Nothing happened and I began to think there was no panther there and that I had been 'had', just to bring a little baksheesh to the village. I drove home, but, before starting, the shikari said he should not give up the hope of killing the panther and would come and tell me when he saw his tracks again.

About a week after this he came. Another goat had been killed. Would I come out? I thought not. He begged me to come as the panther was causing them so much loss among their flocks.

I thought I had been rather a fool to go on the previous occasion, as I was told in the Station by those who knew that it was most unlikely I should find any panther in this district. I was lazy, and it was grilling out in camp. So I hedged, and said, 'Go to every sahib in the Regiment and Indian Regiment, and if no one will go, I will.' Two days afterwards he came back. 'Some sahibs won't go; some sahibs can't get leave; and memsahib said she would go if no sahib would come.'

I did not start in quite such a hurry this time, but sent the servants and kit and a horse on overnight. Then I drove out in the early morning, found the horse waiting halfway and cantered on. The tent was pitched in a grove of mango trees; it was a beautiful camp with lovely shade not far from the village.

Bumps and Bristler, the spaniel and terrier, had been brought with the cart, and after the sun had risen had been allowed to run alongside. I was playing with them and was rubbing Bumps down the back, when he wrenched himself free and screamed with pain. I looked, and could see nothing to account for it, so asked the boy what was the matter. He said that when the spaniel was running with the cart, the sun was very hot and that the dog dropped down unconscious as if he had had a fit. He was put back in the cart and gradually recovered. Afterwards, a long deep blister appeared down the length of his back, and all the hair came off, leaving a scar for life. The veterinary surgeon told me it was a case of sunstroke and he thought that the dog would certainly have died, had it not been for the healing relief of the blister.

At night both dogs seemed uneasy. The horse was stamping, and I woke up hearing the servants talking. They said there were some terrible animals crawling all over their legs and biting them, and that no one could sleep. I, being off the ground, in my camp-bed, was free. There was no help for it until morning, except that the dogs were called on to the tent carpet, where they seemed fairly content; but the servants and horse suffered badly.

When dawn came, we searched about to find out what these insects were. We had not far to look. The ground was simply alive with them—things that looked like wood-lice, almost covering the ground under the mango trees. Beyond in the open there were none. I have never seen or heard of the ground wood-lice anywhere else.

The friendly patel was called and I told him it was impossible to stay in this spot; we must have shade, and the only shade to be had was in this mango tope. The servants could not bear themselves; the horse was stamp-stamping all night long, and sleep was impossible.

He thought for a time, and then said:

'Will the sahib come and live in the temple?'

'*May* I live in the temple?'

He thought I might, but the several heads of the Hindus and Mohammedans would have to be consulted; he was one among them and would give his sanction. There was a hasty conclave and there were one or two small points to which I was asked to agree, and then, in a few minutes, the whole camp was shifting up to the temple.

The temple was a big building with enormously thick walls, standing on a hill with a long flight of steps to climb up to it—easy steps, but many of them. Shelters were made for the horse and servants below, close to the village. My bedroom had open archways and carved ornamental window frames; and the dining-room was anywhere in the spacious, open centre court where the shade happened to fall.

And so it was that ground wood-lice obtained lodgings for me, and the dogs too, in a combined Hindu-Mussulman temple!

When all things were settled, we turned our attention to the panther and I sat up till dark over a goat. He came after I had left, and killed. We had a beat next day and he was seen for a second in some prickly pear and then disappeared into a cave.

The same thing happened again on the following day. The beaters were very bad, they huddled all together in a pack so that the panther could go where he liked. I called them up and gave them a short harangue.

'Those who are afraid can go, and need not come again as long as I stay here. Those who want to stay must obey orders and beat as I tell them. They will receive baksheesh if they beat the panther to me.'

All the Marathi people melted away, and there was only one family left, a big one, of people belonging to the Bhil tribe, whom I had noticed before as being very staunch. There was a very old man who looked the great-grandfather of the family, very thin, almost a skeleton, aged, I should think, about eighty; some men, women and children of all ages, and one woman with a small baby carried on her hip. They were ready for anything, and determined at once to try and drive the panther out of his cave. It took a long time to make a start and I found it fearfully hot standing out on burning rocks with absolutely no shade. I tried sitting down, but jumped up again very quickly, the ground being like hot bricks. The shikari tied an old bit of cloth he was wearing on to a cactus bush to give me shelter from the sun, and I squatted down under it and poured water from my drinking bottle over my head and down my back; but it was grilling all the same.

The Bhils started off from different points towards the cave, creeping through cactus and prickly pear scrub where they could. The panther was lying outside the cave and, from my point of vantage on the opposite side of a wide deep ravine, I saw him for the first time, creeping along, but only for a second, and then he disappeared under bushes, making for his cave. A Bhil woman went up a tangled narrow path, the only one that led to the mouth of the cave. She took with her a bundle of dry grass which she placed inside the mouth of the cave and then set fire to it in order to smoke the panther out. I did not at first realize what she was doing, but when I understood, I shouted to her to come back from her dangerous position; she would not stir, however, until she had got the grass well alight. She was enveloped in smoke which blew the wrong way, towards us, so did not do much good, but not till then did she come away.

The panther may have had another outlet, or he may not have liked the smoke, for next morning the Bhils discovered, by some tracks, that he had gone off to another nullah in the bare hill where there was no place for him to hide. They said that this time we should surely get him. I was posted on a small stone a foot or two high (for safety!) on the side of the hill. The Bhil family climbed to the top, and then beat the nullah down towards me. The panther was at home. He tried to climb the hill, so they told me afterwards, and get away over the top, but was driven back by shouts and showers of stones.

When I first saw him, he was some distance below me, galloping round a slope, off towards his cave again. I waited for a space clear from undulating ground and rocks and took my shot. He spoke, but galloped on, untouched, as I thought. I was on the point of turning round on the shikari and telling him that his bandobast was rotten, for how could I hit a thing travelling at that pace so far away? Then it struck me that I was still more rotten not to fire again. During this small space of time the panther had done another twenty yards or so. I raised my rifle, but before I could fire again, over he went, head over heels, rolling down the hill, stone dead.

I was never, I think, so pleased at anything before. And what a fluke! We measured and found that he was over 120 yards away, and I might have shot another forty times and never have hit him once.

The shikari and Bhils salaamed to the ground and laid their heads on my feet. Then, as I tried to walk down, they lifted and moved my feet for me, which made progression rather difficult. Several of them ran on ahead up to the panther, not staying to throw stones at him from a distance to make sure that he was really dead. I told them how well they had beaten—so they had—and what a good bandobast it was to have managed to beat an animal over that difficult lie of country anywhere near me. We measured him—7 ft 2 in.—and they carried him back to the village to be skinned.

That evening we had a village concert in the courtyard of the temple. The schoolmaster asked if the villagers might come up to hear my music! I had a banjo which always comes out camping with me, as often after dinner the flies and insects are so troublesome, swarming round a light, that one has perforce to sit in darkness. Then I strum on in the dark till bedtime.

Of course I said that the schoolmaster and the villagers could come up, and quite a little gathering of men and children assembled; the children stood in the archway. The men did not think much of my performances, however, and soon suggested that they should give me some of their own music. The schoolmaster said he would sing an English song. I believe he did not know any English at all excepting the words of his song, which were as follows:

'God made the sun that shines so bright;
God made the moon that shines at night;
God made the stars to give us light—'

I forget the last line: but he sang sufficiently in tune for me to gather that he started on the top key-note and descended the scale to the octave below, which was repeated for each line. He burst into loud fits of laughing at the end of each line, and I joined in. I encored him and we had it several times over. He was the *primo donno*, as it were, the other performers not doing great things.

He asked as a favour if I would spare him a bottle of soda-water, so some was ordered and was brought in a glass. 'No, not like that,' he said. 'I want to take it home.' So it was poured into a black bottle, and next day he told me that he had drunk ten drops and had given two to his small daughter and that they both felt much better. He said that he intended to continue this treatment daily!

THE ONE-EYED MAN-EATER

A. MERVYN SMITH

Mervyn Smith's accounts of his own shikar adventures and those of several others appeared regularly in newspapers like the Statesman, published from Calcutta, at the turn of the twentieth century. These were later collected in a book entitled Sport and Adventure in the Indian Jungle *(1904). Reading many of the pieces in that book, especially the one that follows, we wish he had written more.*

SOME years ago, I was engaged in prospecting for gold on the north-west-frontier of Mysore, between the districts of Chittaldroog and Shimoga. The forest tracts of Ubrani and Gangur, where my work lay, are made up of stunted growths of bamboo, babul and date-palm—a very desolate country, the villages being few and far between and the cultivation limited to the margins of the few streams that drain this hilly region. This portion of the country had a very evil reputation, for it was said to be infested with tigers, which found ready shelter in the low thorny jungle seen all over these hills. At the time of my visit, a notorious man-eater was ravaging the country around Gangur, and it was reported that twenty-six human victims had fallen prey to the savage monster in the past six months.

A large reward had been offered for his slaughter by the Mysore Government, and some of the most noted native shikaris had been after him but had failed to bag the cunning brute. Several parties of British officers from the military stations of Bangalore and Belgaum had also been after him, and although a number of other tigers had been shot, the famous man-eater was still at large. There could be no mistaking him. He was said to have but one eye, the other having been knocked out by a native when out duck-shooting on the Sulikeray tank (a large artificial lake in this neighbourhood). The man's story was that he was perched in the fork of a large tree on the margin of the lake, waiting for daylight in order to shoot the wild geese which frequent this tank. At daybreak he noticed an enormous tiger go down to the lake to drink. It then came and stretched itself under the very tree on which he was perched. After a time, it appeared to go to sleep, with its head between its paws. He had only small shot in his single-barrel fowling-piece, but he thought at this short range he might be able to kill the brute, and the Government reward appeared to be within his grasp. He took careful aim at its eye and fired, dropping his gun at the same time in his agitation. With a fearful roar the tiger rushed away, tearing the bark from the trees with his teeth in his savage fury. After the lapse of some considerable time, and when the sun was well up in the heavens, the man got off his perch and made his way as quickly as he could to his village. The next day a careful search was made for the tiger, but nothing was seen of him. A few weeks later a man was carried off from the path between Ubrani and Gangur and partially eaten by the tiger. This happened again, and then it became a common occurrence, not a week passing but a

human being was carried off. The brute seemed to frequent the high road between the district stations of Chittaldroog and Shimoga, and so daring had he become that all traffic between these two towns was at a standstill for the time.

He had been seen several times by villagers and goat-herds, and the loss of one of his eyes was noted. Probably it was this very loss of an eye that led him to take to man-eating, as when wounded he would have been unable to roam far in search of his natural prey, and driven by hunger to attack man, he found him so easy a victim that thenceforth he hunted man instead of beast. He had been known to carry off a cartman and leave the bullocks from an ox-waggon conveying goods along the road. Latterly he had taken to killing the dak-men, or native runners who carry the post from station to station in outlying parts of the country. These dak-runners carry the letter-bags slung on a stick thrown over the shoulder. At the further end of the stick is a bunch of small bells which make a kind of rhythmic jangle as the men trot along. The sound of these bells can be heard a considerable way off, and evidently this tiger had learned to associate their tinkle-tinkle with approaching prey. He would lie in wait in some unfrequented corner and then pounce on the unfortunate dak-runner as he passed with the mails. Four poor wretches had fallen in succession to the maw of the fearful creature, and none would now venture to carry the mails.

I had with me at the time as my assistant a young Cornish man named Provis, out from England for the first time. We had pitched our camp at a wayside overseer's bungalow, about ten miles from the village of Gangur and on the Chittaldroog side. The country was open for several miles on all sides of the bungalow, the forest beginning some four miles west, where the road descended a kind of ghat (hill-side) into the valley leading to the Badra river. It was this spot that the man-eater was said chiefly to frequent, although his range extended to villages many miles away. Owing to four dak-men having been carried off by the tiger we could not get our letters from the nearest postal station, but had to ride in ourselves once a week to Shimoga, forty miles off. None of our servants nor the villagers dared to go alone any distance from the bungalow. Provis had heard and read so much of tiger-shooting that he was eager to have a shot at the tiger, all the more so from the fact of its being a man-eater, for great would be the kudos should he bag him.

We scoured the country for miles, doing our gold prospecting at the same time, but never got sight of the tiger. We sat out night after night in a machan in all the most likely places, with a fine buffalo as a bait; yet no tiger came. When we were at Gangur we heard of him at Ubrani; when we got there, he had 'killed' at some village ten miles off. We should have grown sceptical as to the existence of the tiger if it were not for the gruesome sight of the partially eaten body of a young woman taken from the fields in broad daylight at a village seven miles from our camp. If we could have induced the poor weeping relatives to leave the body where it was found, we might probably have got a shot at the monster on his return to complete his meal. But we had not the heart to urge it on them, when they wished to remove what was left of their kinswoman for burial. We gave them sufficient money to bury their dead and drown their sorrow in arrack, and turned away heart-sick at the ghastly spectacle we had just witnessed, vowing that we would not relax our efforts to rid the place of the brute.

Talking over the events of the day at the bungalow, Provis suggested that if one of us disguised himself as a dak-man and carried the bells over his shoulder and trudged the bit of ghat road where the tiger had carried off the four dak-men, while the other perched himself in a machan just near the spot where the tiger had made his previous attacks, we might probably get a shot at him. He thought that even if nothing came of it, the attempt would still serve to hearten the natives and show them that dak-running was not so dangerous after all. This last argument, the inconvenience we had ourselves suffered from the stoppage of the post together with the need of a little excitement in our hum-drum life, induced me to consent to his proposal. No thought of danger ever entered my mind for the moment. The toss of a rupee soon decided that I was to enact the dak-man and Provis do the shooting from the machan. We sat up long, talking over the details of our mad-cap scheme, and probably dreamt of it that night. Next morning we got together a number of villagers, and set off for the scene of the night's operations.

The news of our plot to circumvent Master Stripes soon got wind, and the whole male population of the village assembled to help to erect the machan. Halfway down the declivity was a large tree which overhung the road at the angle of a zig-zag. In order to cut off this corner the natives took a shortcut across the zig-zag. This path was worn into deep ruts, and it was along these ruts that the tiger concealed himself when lying in wait for the dak-men. From the machan in the tree the roadway on both sides, as well as the shortcut, could be plainly seen. Provis was to ride over at four o'clock in the afternoon and conceal himself in the machan. I was to ride over at about six, dismount some distance away from the edge of the jungle, send the pony back and then begin my experience as a dak-man. Nothing would induce our syces to remain with the ponies anywhere near the ghat, so we arranged to walk back to the bungalow after our adventure. Prompt to the hour Provis set out and ensconced himself in the machan, taking with him our whole battery of two double-barrel smooth-bores and a Snider carbine. Meanwhile I got myself up in a dark serge suit, shikar shoes, a white cummerbund and turban, and, provided with a stout staff and bells to complete my personation of a native post-runner, I set off amid the plaudits of the natives, who assembled in crowds to witness this escapade of the pitheya dorays (mad gentlemen).

It was just dusk when I got to within a mile of the head of the ghat. A bright moon was soon shining, so objects were clear enough. I dismounted and sent back my pony and began my tramp towards the jungle, shaking my bells as I went. I had two miles in all to go before reaching the machan. The first mile was in comparatively open ground; after that the forest deepened and but little of the roadway could be seen. I had started my tramp in a careless mood, thinking more of my ludicrous disguise than of any danger to myself. As I descended the declivity I began to realize my position. Supposing the tiger actually attacked me, what was I to do? I was wholly unarmed with the exception of the wooden staff, but what was that when matched against a tiger! I felt more than half-inclined to turn back and concoct some tale as to my return. But what of Provis? Could I shout to him from where I was? Might not this very shouting attract the tiger? To turn back then was perhaps as dangerous as to go forward, for the tiger might already be behind me. A glance backward sent a cold shiver all over me, and I set off at a sharp trot to join Provis. The jingling of the bells seemed to reassure me, and I went along for a few hundred yards. Suddenly I came to a stop, my heart beating furiously. There was a dark object standing by the road. The tiger! Should I run from it? My sudden stopping evidently alarmed the beast and it scampered off into the jungle, with the unmistakable lope of a jackal. I cannot recollect what happened in the next few minutes, but I found myself under the machan and Provis shouting, 'What on earth has scared you, old man? Did you see the tiger?' A strong nip from Provis's flask and I was able to give some garbled account of having been out of wind with the trot. Shouldering our guns we walked down the ghat and then back to camp, but saw no signs of the tiger. Several times that night I got up with a feeling of the 'creeps' and imagined I was being stalked by the man-eater.

Next morning Provis insisted that we must make another attempt, this time changing places. No argument of mine would alter his determination. 'If you don't come, old man, I go alone and do the dak-man. I won't have the natives say that the chick doray (little gentleman) is afraid.' I tried to persuade him to take one of the double guns with him; but no, he would go just as I went. Well, I got into the machan at 5 o'clock and made a nice little opening on three sides, so as to rest my gun and command the road on both sides, as well as the shortcut. After that I sat down to wait quietly but found it a most difficult matter, as at dusk the mosquitoes got scent of me and kept me on the move trying to beat them away from my ears. At last I heard the bells in the distance, when it occurred to me that should anything happen to Provis, I would be seriously to blame. I ought at any cost to have dissuaded him from his rash attempt. Every tinkle of the bells, I feared, would be the last, and it was with the utmost relief that at length I saw his figure looming in the distance. Now he has left the main road and got into the shortcut. He is still about two hundred yards off, when Merciful Heaven! What is that I see stealing along some thirty yards behind him? The ruts hide it from view for a moment, but there it is again. There is no mistaking that huge head. It is the tiger! The bright moonlight shows up his yellow body between the little ridges in the road, as crouching low he stealthily follows my friend, actually stalking him. I was in an agony of nervous tremor. Should I shout to warn Provis? But that would probably cause him to stop, and the tiger would be on to him. Every moment seemed an age, yet there was my friend in the jaws of death and yet wholly unconscious of his extreme danger. Could I but stay the shaking of my hands there was a chance yet, as I could depend on my Snider for anything up to a hundred yards. I aimed as best I could at the tiger, but those who have done tiger-shooting know how small a mark this great brute offers when, crouched low, he steals along after his prey. He was visibly lessening the distance between himself and Provis, and would probably make his final rush in another moment or two. I aimed at a spot a few yards in advance where the path was comparatively level, so that I would be able to see the whole of the tiger's body, and immediately he appeared there, I fired.

Provis stopped a moment; then rushed forward exclaiming, 'Damn it, old man, stop that; your bullet pinged within an inch of my ear! Don't crack jokes in that way!' 'Hurry up! Hurry up, for God's sake! There is the tiger after you!' I gasped out; and hastily helped my friend into the machan beside me. We then looked out for the brute, but could see nothing of him. I felt sure of my shot, and declared he must be dead or dying behind one of the ruts. Provis was thoroughly scared when I told him of his narrow escape; and we both vowed we would never attempt tiger-shooting in that manner again. After waiting a quarter of an hour we fired several shots into the air. Waiting an hour and hearing nothing, we again discharged our pieces and then, re-loading carefully, descended and walked to where I last saw the tiger; but there was no tiger there. Feeling quite sure that we would recover him in the morning, we walked home and received quite an ovation from the natives when I told them that their arch-enemy was slain.

Next morning we carefully searched the ground; but although the mark where my bullet struck the ground and glanced off and the marks of Provis's shoes were distinct, there was not the slightest trace of a tiger's pug anywhere about. To this day I cannot be sure whether it was a tiger I fired at, or merely a phantom of my heated imagination. That the tiger was not dead we had sickening evidence a week later, when the head, arms and legs of a man were brought to us. The poor fellow had been killed the previous day at Ubrani, and the remnants of the tiger's meal were brought us to view, as a silent reproach for our want of success. Four months later, the one-eyed man-eater was shot by a native in his betel-garden and brought into Shimoga. There was no mistaking the brute, as one eye was completely gone. He was an enormous animal, of a fine bright yellow, certainly with the finest skin I have ever seen.

A VERY CURIOUS INCIDENT

KESRI SINGH

Colonel Kesri Singh was a celebrated game warden, hunter and forester who began his career with the game department of Gwalior state in the early twentieth century, and later served as conservator of forests in Rajasthan. Like most maharajas and princes of the time, the royals of Gwalior and Rajasthan made a fetish of hunting big game, especially tigers. Kesri Singh organised many successful tiger beats—for the maharajas and their guests, including George V and Mountbatten—but he appears to have been conflicted about hunting as spectacle and sport. He took pride in being a 'hunter of honour', and a sort of 'protector' of people terrorised or troubled by man-eaters and cattle-lifters. In the many books he wrote—where he often displays tremendous narrative flair—there are several instances where he watched big cats go about their business as he went about his, without feeling the urge to shoot. The following piece is an excerpt from One Man and a Thousand Tigers *(1959).*

[ODD incidents] are likely to befall anyone who spends a great deal of time looking for tigers.

I see from my records that it was in April 1943 that I went to Baswa to destroy a cattle-lifter reported to have attacked and killed several persons in the district. Baswa is a prosperous little place largely because it has a station on the main Jaipur-Delhi railway. But there is no motor road there and communications are not easy in the area round about. I therefore sent ahead a small advance party including a couple of riding camels. As soon as I could get away I followed them, and was met with the disagreeable news that there was no fresh information about the tiger from any quarter. The shikaris had not been able to pick up a fresh track or establish any sort of picture of the animal's normal habits.

It was in fact three days before I could get any sort of clue as to the tiger's present whereabouts. Then news came that he had killed a cow near a temple of Vishnu, at the foot of a large hill, about four miles east of where I had pitched camp. I set off at once on a camel and carefully inspected the site. There were no inhabited buildings in the vicinity of the temple which was surrounded by big shady trees and, on one side, by the remains of a mud wall that had no doubt once enclosed some sort of court or compound. Near the temple was a small cistern fed by a spring.

I found the remains of the cow about two hundred yards away; it had evidently been killed the previous night and was only half eaten. No one had seen or heard anything till the carcass was found in the morning. The place was served by a single priest who told me that fear of the tiger had for some time caused him to leave the temple long before dark and return well after daylight.

No pug-marks could be found in the hard ground near the kill, but after much trouble a few were discovered on the hillside. From these I concluded that after feeding, the tiger had gone over to the opposite slope where there was a good deal of cover. After this I rode round the area on another search for information, questioning everybody I could find. The only useful piece of knowledge I could glean was that the tiger, if he were in the neighbourhood of the temple, would be certain to drink at the spring. He had done so on several occasions.

Accordingly I bought a goat and returned to the temple. What was left of the cow was dragged near to the spring and the goat tied up in the shade nearby. The roof of the temple was flat, with a parapet about a foot high: it was plain that it would make a better place to shoot from than a machan in one of the trees. Some big stones were carried up and put on the parapet so as to form a kind of battlement and allow me to aim without exposing myself too obviously. Then, having sent off the shikaris with the camels in plenty of time before dusk, I settled down with a rug, rifle, thermos-flask and some sandwiches to await events.

I had brought a goat both because time was short and one was easily available, and because tigers are especially fond of goat-meat. Also, although the tiger was reported to be a powerful cattle-killer and no doubt capable of killing and tearing loose such a small animal very quickly, the bait was only fifteen yards from a particularly stable and convenient shooting post, and I was confident I should have time enough to knock him over if he would only be tempted.

About half-past nine I heard a sambar calling somewhere high on the hill, warning that a hunter was on the move. Ten minutes later by the luminous dial of my watch a jackal gave tongue, much nearer; and now the goat began to bleat intermittently. From this moment I should have kept every faculty concentrated on the scene below; but in fact my attention was almost immediately caught by something on the roof. I saw it moving on my left, out of the tail of my eye. It was a large, common rat. When I slowly turned my head to look at it, it came closer, so that at first I thought it must still be unaware of my presence and moved my hand sharply to scare it away. At this gesture it dodged back into the shadows, but after perhaps half a minute I became unpleasantly conscious that I was being watched from behind. Keeping my head below the level of the parapet I cautiously looked round, and there, sure enough, was the little humped form, quite near and looking almost silvery in the moonlight. I realized it was likely to distract my aim. The only things I had to throw at it were my cartridge bag and the thermos, and even the bag would have been impossibly noisy. While I was turning this absurd difficulty over in my mind and vainly longing for a stick, a fantastic thing happened. The rat, which had been keeping perfectly still, suddenly scuttled round till is was on my right and then made a rapid, squeaking dart at my hand which was on the edge of the rug, causing me to draw back and grab my cartridge bag.

It was ridiculous, shaming. There was I, with a weapon that would stop a rhinoceros, held at bay by a rodent weighing a few ounces. So much for the resourceful shikari. My sense of humour was not working; I was annoyed and, to be frank, curiously disquieted.

The rat would not go, but kept scuffling back and forth in the shadow under the parapet. It occurred to me that my handkerchief might frighten it away; animals are often startled by white objects. Circumspectly, I pulled it out and, holding it low, flapped it. The rat seemed unimpressed. But the next second I had forgotten its existence; there was the beginning of a loud bleat, abruptly choked, from below and immediately afterwards a loud twang, as of a parting rope. I was just in time to see a tiger slip from under the shadow of the trees, the white shape of the goat hanging from its mouth, and vanish over the mud wall.

When I drew back from the parapet there was no sign of the rat. Reckoning that there was still a chance the tiger would return to drink I decided to stay where I was and keep a strict look-out. But not even a jackal came to the dead cow and the rest of the night passed entirely without incident.

However, in the morning a surprise was waiting. Pugmarks of the tiger were plain in the dust round the place where the goat had been tied, and it was perfectly obvious they could not be the tracks of the man-killer. He was known to be a grown male and these, both from their size and the oblong rather than round impressions of the toes, could only have been left by a tigress.

Getting back to camp I was met by a party of peasants with the news I was dreading. While I had been waiting for him at the temple, the man-killer had broken into the communal cattle pen at a village some miles in the other direction and killed a good cow in full milk. Some of the men, desperate at the thought of loss, had tried to drive him off and one of them had been badly mauled. Far from pleased with life, I got back on my camel.

At the village my spirits began to rise a little. I found there was a good tree growing near the pen and soon had a machan put up in it. I also inspected the dead milker and gave orders for the carcass to be moved to a suitable spot outside the enclosure, about forty feet from the tree. Not much had been eaten by the disturbed tiger, and there seemed a good chance he might this time come back to his kill. Anyway, I knew of nowhere else to wait for him: a wandering tiger is always a chance quarry.

Late in the afternoon I returned to the village and climbed onto the machan. Everything went like clockwork. Just before nine o'clock the cattle thief stalked into the moonlight and after examining the kill and taking a good look round settled down to feed. Successful assaults on men had made him careless, or he would have been less easy about a carcass that had been shifted so far. As soon as his attention was engaged I shot him dead, got down from the machan, and leaving a shikari to skin him, returned to camp and bed in a much improved frame of mind.

More investigations round the temple area disclosed that the tigress that had escaped me quite often came to the spring to drink. She had never been known to take a domestic animal before and was very shy of human beings. I made no further attempt to shoot her. As for the rat, I have never seen one behave in such a way before or since, and do not propose to try and account for its behaviour here. However, I may add that though I am not a man of punctilious observance, I do not believe it was right to expose a live bait or shoot an animal at a shrine dedicated to the Preserver, and should not have done so had the motive been sport and not the urgent destruction of a man-killer. Certainly I am glad that providence prevented me killing without cause a beast that must have come in the first place only to drink at the temple spring.

LEOPARDS OF GABON

MARY KINGSLEY

In 1893, Mary Kingsley, aged thirty and recently released from the duty of caring for ailing parents used her modest inheritance to make a voyage to West Africa. She spent five months there, and returned in 1894 for a longer period. She was an unusual woman in many ways—travelling alone, wanting to study African culture, openly critical of missionaries for wanting to convert African people, although she did not reject the British imperial project entirely and believed in 'indirect rule'. Some of her books are considered classic studies of late-nineteenth-century African societies. Wildlife was not her primary interest, but Kingsley did have some interesting encounters with large animals in the wild, which she recounts with droll humour and a nice sense of drama, as in this excerpt from Travels in West Africa *(1897).*

I must say the African leopard is an audacious animal, although it is ungrateful of me to say a word against him, after the way he has let me off personally, and I will speak of his extreme beauty as compensation for my ingratitude. I really think, taken as a whole, he is the most lovely animal I have ever seen; only seeing him, in the one way you can gain a full idea of his beauty, namely in his native forest, is not an unmixed joy to a person, like myself, of a nervous disposition. I may remark that my nervousness regarding the big game of Africa is of a rather peculiar kind. I can confidently say I am not afraid of any wild animal—until I see it—and then—well, I will yield to nobody in terror; fortunately, as I say, my terror is a special variety; fortunately because no one can manage their own terror. You can suppress alarm, excitement, fear, fright, and all those small-fry emotions, but the real terror is as dependent on the inner make of you as the colour of your eyes, or the shape of your nose; and when terror ascends its throne in my mind I become preternaturally artful, and intelligent to an extent utterly foreign to my true nature, and save, in the case of close quarters with bad big animals, a feeling of rage against some unknown person that such things as leopards, elephants, crocodiles, & c., should be allowed out loose in that disgracefully dangerous way, I do not think much about it at the time. Whenever I have come across an awful animal in the forest and I know it has seen me, I take Jerome's advice, and instead of relying on the power of the human eye, rely upon that of the human leg and effect a masterly retreat in the face of the enemy. If I know it has not seen me, I sink in my tracks and keep an eye on it, hoping that it will go away soon. Thus, I once came upon a leopard.

I had got caught in a tornado in a dense forest. The massive, mighty trees were waving like a wheat-field in an autumn gale in England, and I dare say a field mouse in a wheat-field in a gale would have heard much the same uproar. The tornado shrieked like ten thousand vengeful demons. The great trees creaked and groaned and strained against it and their bush-rope cables groaned and smacked like whips, and ever and anon a thundering crash with snaps like pistol shots told that they and their mighty tree had strained and struggled in vain. The fierce rain came in a roar, tearing to shreds the leaves and blossoms and deluging everything. I was making bad weather of it, and climbing up over a lot of rocks out of a gully bottom where I had been half drowned in a stream, and on getting my head to the level of a block of rock I observed right in front of my eyes, broadside on, maybe a yard off, certainly not more, a big leopard. He was crouching on the ground, with his magnificent head thrown back and his eyes shut. His fore-paws were spread out in front of him and he lashed the ground with his tail, and I grieve to say, in face of that awful danger—I don't mean me, but the tornado—that depraved creature swore, softly, but repeatedly and profoundly. I did not get all these facts up in one glance, for no sooner did I see him than I ducked under the rocks, and remembered thankfully that leopards are said to have no power of smell. But I heard his observation on the weather, and the flip-flap of his tail on the ground. Every now and then I cautiously took a look at him with one eye round a rock-edge, and he remained in the same position. My feelings tell me he remained there twelve months, but my calmer judgment puts the time down at twenty minutes; and at last, on taking another cautious peep, I saw he was gone. At the time I wished I knew exactly where, but I do not care about that detail now, for I saw no more of him. He had moved off in one of those weird lulls which you get in a tornado, when for a few seconds the wild herd of hurrying winds seem to have lost themselves, and wander round crying and wailing like lost souls, until their common rage seizes them again and they rush back to their work of destruction. It was an immense pleasure to have seen the great creature like that. He was so evidently enraged and baffled by the uproar and dazzled by the floods of lightning that swept down into the deepest recesses of the forest, showing at one second every detail of twig, leaf, branch, and stone round you, and then leaving you in a sort of swirling dark until the next flash came; this, and the great conglomerate roar of the wind, rain and thunder, was enough to bewilder any living thing.

I have never hurt a leopard intentionally; I am habitually kind to animals, and besides I do not think it is ladylike to go shooting things with a gun. Twice, however, I have been in collision with them. On one occasion a big leopard had attacked a dog, who, with her family, was occupying a broken-down hut next to mine. The dog was a half-bred boarhound, and a savage brute on her own account. I, being roused by the uproar, rushed out into the feeble moonlight, thinking she was having one of her habitual turns-up with other dogs, and I saw a whirling mass of animal matter within a yard of me. I fired two mushroom-shaped native stools in rapid succession into the brown of it, and the meeting broke up into a leopard and a dog. The leopard crouched, I think to spring on me. I can see its great, beautiful, lambent eyes still, and I seized an earthen water-cooler and flung it straight at them. It was a noble shot; it burst on the leopard's head like a shell and the leopard went for the bush[.] Twenty minutes after, people began to drop in cautiously and inquire if anything was the matter, and I civilly asked them to go and ask the leopard in the bush, but they firmly refused. We found the dog had got her shoulder slit open as if by a blow from a cutlass, and the leopard had

evidently seized the dog by the scruff of her neck but owing to the loose folds of skin no bones were broken and she got round all right after much ointment from me, which she paid me for with several bites. Do not mistake this for a sporting adventure. I no more thought it was a leopard than that it was a lotus when I joined the fight. My other leopard was also after a dog. Leopards always come after dogs, because once upon a time the leopard and the dog were great friends, and the leopard went out one day and left her whelps in charge of the dog, and the dog went out flirting, and a snake came and killed the whelps, so there is ill-feeling to this day between the two.

TIGER TALES FROM BURMA

DAVID WILSON

A British forest officer posted in Burma in the early twentieth century, David Wilson published two books of real-life stories and anecdotes about tigers and other wildlife. Unusually for his times, Wilson was critical of the casual cruelty, bluster and exaggerated bravado of the average White hunter, and also the colonialist's complete belief in his own courage and the native's pusillanimity. (In one respect, alas, Wilson remains a man of his times, as we discover in his story about the young girls and the tigress. Although even here he could have done far, far worse.) The following are extracts from his book Anecdotes of the Big Cats and Other Beasts *(1910).*

The Old Men and the Tiger

THIS was told me in 1908 by Mr Thomson, who as District Magistrate had held an inquest at the time upon the tragedy; and his recollections have been verified and supplemented by Mr Webb, the present District Magistrate. The depositions have, in ordinary course, been destroyed; but the details that are still recoverable seem to be sufficient.

The time was 1900, and the scene was Zwettaw village, Thongwa township, not far from Rangoon. The old headman, U Myat Thin, described in confidential official registers which he never saw as 'an easy-going old Talaing' or native of Lower Burma, was sauntering outside the village about midday, watching his grandchildren, who were playing near him. Suddenly a tiger appeared and seized and carried away his grand-daughter. That kind of thing is done with the speed of thought; and Hercules himself, in the old man's place, could not have prevented the tiger getting the child. Probably Hercules himself, if unarmed, would have done no more than the old man did, namely, run into the village and shout for help.

But who was to help? Every man and woman fit for work was away in the fields. Only the old people and children were in the village. He took a spear from his house, and three other old men like himself did likewise. The four of them followed the tiger at once, and tracked and ran with such goodwill that they overtook him, though they were too late to save the child.

One of the finest traits of character which I have noticed in Burmese villagers is their readiness to fight to recover from a wild beast the body of any person it has killed. Let a European try to take a bone from a bulldog and he may be able to guess, faintly and distantly, at what these four old men were undertaking when they closed with a famishing tiger, to fight him for his freshly-killed food. They had no firearms, no missiles of any kind, not even bows and arrows. They had nothing to rely on but each other, as, with one spirit, they attacked him, thrusting at his vitals with their spears. The fight was too unequal. He killed one of them, and with a stroke of his paw he broke the shoulder of the grandfather, and so escaped away.

The news was sent to the men in the fields, and as soon as possible a new party took up the trail, including policemen with guns. They had not far to go. In the next field they found the tiger dead. He had been gored to death by a herd of buffaloes that had been peacefully grazing there when he came among them. If he had not been wounded they would probably not have attacked him, or he would not have lingered long enough to give them a chance. So the old men had not fought in vain.

A herdsman of experience has said to me: 'If the tiger was bleeding, the sight of his blood would make the buffaloes charge him.' That coincides with a red rag irritating a bull in England; but another herdsman said it was the smell, and several thought the wound made no difference. 'A buffalo will not stand to be eaten by a tiger, but at sight of one stampedes, either at him or away from him.' Very likely, indeed.

'I think the grandfather recovered,' continued Mr Thomson. 'I know I recommended a good reward and that it was paid.' It appears from the official registers that he was quite well before the end of the year. On 12th December 1900 the Assistant Commissioner felt bound to note, as a matter of business: 'The daily pilgrimage to the local Kyaung (a Buddhist monastery) is the end of his existence now, I think.' Why not? In the heroic days of Greece a time of prayer was deemed the fittest ending to a well-spent life.

It was not till 29th June 1908 that the registers tell of him what has some day to be told of us all 'Deceased. For successor see . . .'

So far as can be discovered, the brave old man paid no heed whatever to the rewards, or to what was thought about him. It was right to honour such gallantry in every possible way; but the deed was one no money could have purchased, and the story is one I like to tell whenever I hear anybody who knows no better talking of the 'cowardice of the Burmans'.

The Girl and the Tigress

This is a story that has been often told; and I confess I did not believe it when I heard it in 1895, in the district where it happened. Long afterwards, in 1908, Mr G. Tilly, who had been the District Superintendent of Police on the spot at the time, told me he held a local inquiry, and was so completely satisfied of the truth of it that he recommended the payment of a reward of R 100 to the girl, and the Deputy Commissioner and the Commissioner agreed with him, and the Chief Commissioner of Burma sanctioned the reward, which was paid.

The scene was Seiktha village on the Chindwin, an Upper Burman tributary of the Irrawaddy, in one of the districts that form the southern fringe of the mountains between Burma and Assam. One day in 1894 three nut-brown girls set out from Seiktha to cut firewood in the forest, making for a likely place they knew, a little south-east of their village. They carried one or two heavy knives or choppers, like butchers' cleavers, such as are common in Burman houses.

Now if there had only been a man with them, or even a big boy, he would certainly there and then, in going and coming, have walked in front, bearing a spear or dah, a big curved knife like a sword. What makes it needful to mention a thing so obvious to us who have lived there is that Englishwomen sometimes resent, as degrading to their sex, the Oriental custom that makes the man stalk in front; whereas a little reflection would show them, when familiar with plain facts of this kind, that there are reasons for it honourable to human nature. It is not as a master that a man, who is a man, precedes a woman, or goes into war, or business, or politics; but as a pioneer, protector, provider, and in short head servant…On this occasion there was no man at all, and in the absence of any natural protector it was 'go as you please.' A tigress in the bush saw her chance. The lightest-limbed and lightest-laden of the trio was a little girl, Mintha by name, who ran on in front. The tigress seized her and carried her away.

There is a lot, at times, in etymology. An Englishman who knows Burmese would tell you that Mintha means prince, or son of an official (min); but, as written in Burmese, without a long accent on the 'tha', and pronounced like an ordinary English word with the stress in front, the name Mintha has another modest meaning which you may discover from a dictionary, but can only with difficulty persuade a Burman to tell you. It means Better-than-an-Official, a name curiously recalling the kind of names that were common in England in the great days of Cromwell.

'We know what judges can be made to do,' said Selden, grimly.

'We know what officials are,' the Burmans have been saying for centuries; and they class them with thieves and plagues, perhaps with more emphasis today than ever before. So Mintha is an unpretentious name, and so common that the little girl who bore it had probably never thought of the meaning of it, and would certainly have referred you to her mother if you had asked her about it.

She was perhaps eleven years old, but small for that age, this brown little maiden whom they called 'Better-than-an-Official', and swift and silent like a dream the tigress stepped out and picked her up and carried her away between its teeth, as a cat does a little mouse.

Her older sister, Ngway Bwin, which means Silver-blossom, a girl on the verge of womanhood, about fourteen years old, was next behind her, and beheld her taken. She quickly turned to the third girl, Shway U or Grain-of-Gold, who happened at that moment to have a chopper in her hand; and, snatching the chopper, little Silver-blossom ran at the very top of her speed after the tigress. She overtook it, and lifting the big knife high above her head with both hands, she brought it down heavily on the animal's head. It dropped little Mintha, 'Better-than-an-Official', and stood as if it were stunned. It was easy to see the need of keeping it stunned. Silver-blossom knew that that was her only chance. So hammer, hammer, hammer, cut succeeding cut, the little Burmese maiden killed the tigress.

Grain-of-Gold was the only other person near. She always said, and says still (1909), that she did nothing but look on. The village headman reported, and still reports, that the animal, which was shown to everybody in 1894, was a full-grown tigress in the prime of life, measuring '8 cubits and 2 meiks'. A cubit, in rough village measures, is still the original cubit, from the elbow to the farthest finger-tip, and a 'meik' is the width of a clenched fist with the thumb standing out. So 8 cubits and 2 meiks can hardly be less than 11 or 12 feet; but the villagers measure along the curved outline of the body, so we may conclude the straight measurement was 8 or 9 feet.

The soft brown skin of Better-than-an-Official had been broken and she was a little hurt on the back of the neck and on one arm; but these injuries were so slight that it is likely the tigress meant to give its cubs the pleasure of playing with her, instead of which Better-than-an-Official, saved by her sister and quickly cured of her scratches, is now reported to be living at Kule village, Mingin township. The sister, Silver-blossom herself, was quite unhurt. She became, deservedly, the pride of the countryside, but 'died of a decline' ten years afterwards.

If her adventure appeared in a romance one would smile at the absurdity of the author who expected to be believed for a moment. Yet, after carefully questioning everybody concerned, Mr Tilly, who is a man of sense, believed it at the time and has never doubted it; and Mr Grant Brown, after a new local inquiry, believes it; and so do I. Let readers please themselves.

It may assist them to a right conclusion to remind them that Michelet has shown that Joan of Arc seems stranger to us than she really was because we are ignorant of history. Her performance was glorious for herself and France, one of the most glorious episodes in the history of the world; but all the same it was only the superlative of many similar doings of brave French women. Precisely in the same way it has to be remembered that, like hens emboldened to fly in the faces of dogs or boys in defence of chicks, many girls in charge of brothers or sisters have been known to surpass belief in their feats of devotion. So Silver-blossom was not odd in the sense of being peculiar. She was like other brave girls, only more so.

At the same time, it would be wrong to minimise what she did. It is the exact truth to say she expanded the range of human possibilities…

A pious Quaker's phrase would have been, 'God moved her.' If there is in English any better name for the Living Spirit of the Universe that surged in her heart and nerved her arm, it is not known to me. But, as a good Muslim Imam of my acquaintance once remarked to me, 'There are many names for God.'

Recovering the Corpse

The present Deputy Commissioner of Pyapon district, Burma (Major Nethersole, 1909), is my authority for this incident, which is selected as the most remarkable of several of its kind. He investigated it on the spot, and told me of it at the time. He himself gave as many days as he could spare to hunting the tiger concerned, which killed eight men in Pyapon district before it met its fate.

One of them was old Po An, the headman of Eyya village. 'Eyya' or 'Irra' is the first part of the name of our local Mississippi, the Irrawaddy, and the village is, in fact, at the mouth of the great water-way so called, though it is only one of many water-ways through which the mighty river mingles with the sea. In other words, the village is on the coast, and about the middle of the delta, between Rangoon and Bassein.

In the last week of 1908 Po An and his son, and a friend of his own age (about sixty), left home together to get bamboos. They went in a little boat, landed where they intended, entered the muddy woods and cut what they wanted, and started to carry the bamboos to their boat.

They had heard that there was a man-killing tiger 'somewhere thereabouts', but the Burman with a knife in his hand is not easily frightened in the forest. They made the mistake, which is the besetting sin of brave men and used to be called English, of despising the enemy, and did not even keep close together. In returning bamboo-laden, Po An lagged behind about forty yards, but nobody thought anything of that. His son and companion heard a noise in the jungle too, but did not think of it till a minute or two later, when they ceased to hear the sound of Po An behind, and shouted, 'Are you all right?' Receiving no reply they looked round. Not seeing him they laid down their burdens and retraced their steps, but had not far to go. In a glade through which they had come they saw the prostrate figure of Po An and the tiger standing over him.

They were only two men, and one of them was old, and they had no weapons but the big knives they had been using. But instantly they flourished their knives and moved forward, shouting and yelling as if they were the advance guard of an army of men.

The tiger, a big animal in the prime of life, looked up at them in deliberate surprise, and visibly hesitated. Then, as they approached, he moved aside, slowly and reluctantly, into cover, as if to watch what was going to happen and consider what to do.

The two men ran forward, snatched up the corpse and started for the boat, looking round continually, brandishing their knives and shouting, and seeing, or thinking they saw, those great eyes glaring at them through the bushes. They said they even heard the tiger following. Perhaps they did. Time after time they thought it was about to spring upon them, and faced towards the sound, real or imaginary, with knives uplifted and loud shouts of defiance. They reached the boat and got on board, but did not take time to untie the rope. They cut it and pushed off.

Next morning the elder of the two took Major Nethersole and another officer to the place, and there they saw the severed rope and the tracks of the tiger patrolling on the muddy banks. The tides had been such that the tracks must have been made after the men departed, and left no room for doubt that the tiger had come after them to the water's edge, and there lingered long, going up and down as if in a cage, and looking across the waters on which the men had disappeared.

It was several days before the son of Po An and his old friend discovered, as their excitement abated, how badly their nerves had been shaken. Their sleep began to be broken by hideous dreams.

That was more than three months ago. The tiger is dead now (April 1909). His skull and hide can be seen at Pyapon. But still, I believe, though now at greater and greater intervals, sometimes the one and sometimes the other of the two brave men is wakened by the nightmare of those awful eyes, and shrieks and shrieks to his neighbours to come and stay beside him.

THE KANCHINDA PANTHER

AUGUSTUS SOMERVILLE

Excerpted from the remarkable, now sadly forgotten, book At Midnight Comes the Killer *(1933), 'The Kachinda Panther' is told in the words of Somerville's friend, John Upshon. This is an incredible story of an encounter between a wounded panther and Upshon, who followed it into its cave and fought it with his bare hands.*

ON the south east of Peninsular India, and not far from the seafront, is a vast tract of land consisting mainly in forest-clad mountains, deep valleys and broad rivers, whose waters are fed by innumerable shallow streams, practically dry during the winter months, but rushing torrents during the rains. In these dense forests once roamed herds of elephants, bison, deer and buffalo, which, although sadly depleted in recent years, still provide some of the finest hunting for local sportsmen. This vast area during the period of British occupation was the sole property of the Raja of Mayurbhanj, who had his palace at Baripada. As the main revenue of the state came from timber, the Raja had built a light railway, a meter-gauge, from Rupsa on the main line to Talbund at its extreme end. It was on this line, at the little station

Betnoti, that I first met Mr John Upshon and his charming wife. Mr Upshon was at the time employed as a Permanent Way Inspector and the very nature of his duties compelled him to travel up and down this line frequently, so that there was no part of this dense forest, through which this line penetrated, that was not familiar to him.

It was while I was at Betnoti, enjoying the hospitality of this young couple, that I noticed the deep lacerations that Mr Upshon had on his chest and arms and on enquiry learned of the terrible experience he had had with a panther. The story he told me, which is true in every respect, I give in his own words.

It was on the 25 April 1955, he said, that the events I am about to narrate occurred. I remember the date well. It was my first wedding anniversary and we had arranged to have a few friends over and enjoy a pleasant evening. Imagine then my feelings when one of my trollymen, named Leppu, arrived at the bungalow to inform me that a leopard had killed a goat in the vicinity of one of our gang huts at Kanchinda. He further added that machans had been tied and every preparation made for sitting up that night. I am a keen shikari and the longing to take advantage of this excellent opportunity was irresistible, but I remembered the occasion and determined to forego the shoot, but as I told Leppu, I would not be able to come, my voice and face must have betrayed my disappointment. Now my wife is one of those women who have been blessed with the sublimest of all human virtues, an understanding mind. Instantly she countermanded the order and when I reminded her of the occasion, she brushed the objection aside. 'You will have an anniversary every year, John, but this panther will not wait. Besides it is your duty to your workmen to protect their property.' This last argument decided me and issuing immediate orders to get the car ready, I selected both my .405 rifle and my .12 bore and by 2 p.m. set out for Baripada, where the necessary petrol could only be obtained. Now Baripada is sixteen miles from my bungalow. The road is excellent and presents no difficulties, but at Baripada I discovered that I would have to travel another thirty-three miles to a small station called Banjriposi. The road was bad but not impassable and I arrived at Banjriposi within a couple of hours only to discover that my journey was not yet over as the 'kill' had occurred at a small station on this same line called Kanchinda. However, as it was getting dark I had no alternative but to set out immediately. The road to Kanchinda led through dense forest and was nothing more than a forest path, hacked out by wood-cutters and consisted in a succession of hollows and ruts and I would have to negotiate seven miles of this before reaching my destination. Eventually, just as night was falling I reached my gangmen's hut and proceeded across the fields to where the 'kill' was lying. The goat was an exceptionally large animal and judging from the way its throat had been lacerated, must have put up a determined fight before it was finally overcome. Very little of the carcass had been eaten and the chances of the animal returning that night were excellent.

Hurrying to the machan, which had been tied on the only tree overlooking the 'kill', I took up my position and as I was pretty sure that all our movements had been carefully noted by the panther, I instructed the gangmen to return to the hut, talking loudly but on no account to return should I fire.

Settling myself as comfortably as possible, I prepared for a long and tiresome vigil. There was no moon as darkness fell. Venus, her brightness undimmed by any rival star, hung like a jewel in the western sky. Slowly the forest sank into silence. An occasional night-jar called mournfully, while from the direction of the hut came the voices of the crewmen as they gathered round the fire. After a while even this died down and I was left in complete silence. I had noted the direction of the 'kill' carefully and strained my eyes watching the spot for evidence of the panther's return. Towards midnight, exhausted with the long drive and the strain of watching, I fell into a fitful doze, from which I was suddenly awakened by hearing a sharp crack from the direction of the 'kill'. With every faculty now thoroughly alert, I watched the spot where the goat was lying and after a time seemed to see a larger body worrying the carcass. In that uncertain light I could take no chances, so carefully aligning my sights I switched on my torch. In the brilliant beam I could see the panther distinctly. He was lying with his back to me, tearing at the stomach of the goat, but although I switched the torch, on and off, several times, he refused to turn and look at me. Lying as he was the narrow width of his body offered a most difficult target, and by switching my torch I had hoped to make him turn his head so that I could have sighted between his eyes, gleaming in the torch-light, for a head shot. There being no alternative, I laid down the rifle and took up the .12 bore, which I had loaded with L.G. Once again I depressed the switch and sighting along the middle of his spine, pressed the trigger. Simultaneously with the shot the panther bounded into the air and then made off across the fields in the direction of the forest. For a while I followed him with the torch, but never had an opportunity to fire again, and I was forced to admit I had either missed the animal completely or had only wounded him slightly.

From the direction of the hut I heard Leppu's voice enquiring if they should come; but I shouted back telling the men to wait till morning, as I had wounded the animal and it would be dangerous for them to come at that time.

Thereafter I tried to sleep but could not and it was with relief that with the first light of dawn I saw Leppu and the crewmen, reinforced by several villagers, coming towards me.

Later, examining the ground in the vicinity of the 'kill' we came on the blood trail and as the animal appeared to have bled freely I came to the conclusion that it must have been badly wounded and determined to take up the tracking at once, before the village cattle, wandering all over the area, obliterated the trail.

By this time it was getting quite light and after a hasty cup of coffee and a few sandwiches, we set out. With Leppu leading and carrying my rifle, I followed, with Kalia, another crewman and the rest of the party trailing behind.

The trail led directly through the forest and a large outcrop of rocks, standing like sentinels a short way up the hill. Here we came to a single rock, some ten feet high, which rose sheer out of the ground. Cracked in the centre and worn smooth by the action of wind and water was a large hole into which the animal had crawled. Hurrying round this rock we discovered that it was backed by an equally large rock that leaned over it, forming a large, natural cave. Of the two exits on either side, the one on the right showed that this had been the usual exit by which the animal left the cave, but careful survey all round showed no further signs of recent use.

'He is still inside, sahib,' Leppu shouted, 'Let us smoke him out.'

Acting on this advice we collected a large quantity of leaves and straw and thrust this into both entrances, as well as the crack in the rock. Being slightly damp the straw threw off dense clouds of smoke when lit, but although the men shouted and threw rocks into the cave, nothing emerged and after half-an-hour or so, when the fire had died down I determined that the animal had either sneaked out from some secret exit or had died in the cave.

'Leppu,' I informed my crewman, 'I am going inside the cave to have a look. The rest of you stand back and shout panther coming out.' But to this Leppu would not agree. 'If you are going in, sahib, I am coming with you,' and fired by his example Kalia announced his intention of coming with me as well. I tried to dissuade them but without success and it was finally decided that I would enter first, carrying the .12 bore, loaded with L.G. Kalia would come directly behind me carrying the torch as the cave was pitch dark within, while Leppu would bring up the rear with my rifle. The rest of the men would stand outside and warn us if the animal was escaping.

I can assure you I was not happy at the thought of entering that cave. It was against all my experience and my knowledge of the ways of wild animals and the thought that I was leading others into the same danger as myself was not very heartening. However, there was no way of backing out now. To have done so would have lowered me in the eyes of the men, who would immediately have concluded that I was afraid.

Holding the .12 bore carefully before me, I forced myself between the rocks at the entrance and entered. Once I was in the cave itself, I found a natural hollow, about four feet wide, ten feet long and sufficiently high to stand up in. Taking the torch from Kalia, who had followed immediately after me, I swung the beam round and saw that the floor on which we stood, was a foot or two lower than the entrance. About three feet from where we stood was a deep crevice in the rock, which ran the whole length of the cave to where the opposite entrance could be seen. Of the panther there was not a sign.

I was about to leave the cave when happening to cast the beam of the torch on the floor, I noticed a patch of blood at the very entrance to this crevice. Immediately I concluded that the animal had entered the cave, forced its way into the crevice and there died. Anxious to test the truth of my supposition, I stepped up to the entrance and was about to shine the torch into the cleft in the rocks, when I noticed a high spider crouched at the entrance, watching me. Now I have an inborn horror of these insects and would rather face a tiger than one of these creatures, so I handed the torch to Kalia, instructing him to shine the torch into the crevice, to see if the body of the panther was lying there. Advancing cautiously, Kalia did as he was told, but no sooner had the light entered the cleft in the rocks, than with a savage roar the panther was on him. Taken completely by surprise I had no opportunity to fire nor could I have done so without injuring the man as well, so I did the next thing automatically. As there was no room to swing the

gun, I jabbed the barrel into the panther's ribs with all my strength. In an instant it had released its victim and jumped back into the crevice.

Shouting to Leppu to help me lift the injured man, we soon got Kalia out of the cave and into the open, where I left Leppu to attend to his wounds, returning to retrieve my gun which had fallen to the ground in the melee.

As I entered the cave I discovered the torch, still alight, lying on the ground, while my gun lay a few feet away. Swiftly I entered and as swiftly returned to the entrance. With my legs halfway through, I turned to see if the panther was anywhere about and noticed the tip of his tail, which he was obviously holding erect, moving in the direction of the opposite exit from the cave. This gave me an idea. The exit was small and for a little while the panther would be silhouetted against the light. At that distance it was impossible to miss, so stepping back I levelled my gun and waited. What caused the animal to abandon the idea I do not know, but once he reached the end of the crevice, he paused a moment and then returned. The tables were now reversed and I was the target silhouetted against the light. The panther was taking no chances. He must have spotted me before he had traversed half the distance, for with a sudden roar, he raced along the passage and sprang. No sooner did his face appear, than I fired, but unable to raise the gun in that confined space, I fired from the hip and the L.G. intended for his face and chest, hit him in the stomach, and the next instant he was on me, burying his teeth in my right shoulder. One hundred and fifty pounds of bone and muscle is not easily supported and his charge flung me back against the rock. Fortunately I still retained my balance and bracing myself against the rock at my back, I struck out with all my strength at his head, using the butt of the gun to augment my blows. Partially stunned, he released his hold for an instant and I took advantage of this brief respite to force the gun between us, holding the barrel in one hand and the stock in the other, so as to form a barrier with which I was able to ward off his next attack. But my advantage was short-lived. With one vicious stroke of his paw, he severed the stock just below the trigger guard, wrenching the barrel out of my hand. I was now completely at his mercy. As he came in for the kill, I made one desperate lunge at his head, but succeeded only in forcing my hand into his gaping jaws and I felt his teeth slipping past the bones of my palm as he bit fiercely on my hand, but this also gave me a slight advantage. Seizing his tongue with my partially paralyzed fingers, I strove desperately to force my fist further and further down his throat. In this position he was unable to do me any further damage with his teeth, but his claws raked me unmercifully, tearing the shirt and coat from my shoulders. Fortunately for me, his hind legs were partially paralyzed from the two gun-shot wounds he had received or he would have disemboweled me. All this while, although I was myself unaware of it, I had been shouting to Leppu to shoot. It was now for the first time I saw this gallant fellow forcing his way into the cave. As he entered he cocked the hammer on my rifle and I distinctly heard the click as the hammer fell on the empty chamber and I realized with a sick feeling of despair, that I had forgotten to load the rifle. Leppu, I knew, was unable to work the bolt to force a cartridge from the magazine into the chamber and with that realization I probably went mad with fear, agony and frustration. Releasing the animal's tongue, I started lashing out wildly with hands and feet, in a frantic effort to drive the animal from me. By some lucky accident my boot drove straight into the gun-shot wound in his stomach and so great must have been the pain, that the panther fell back gasping with agony. This was my opportunity and seizing the rifle from Leppu, I wrenched open the bolt, driving a cartridge into the chamber and with my crippled hand presented the rifle in the direction of the panther and pulled the trigger. A good woman's prayers must have been my salvation that day, for the bullet crashed into the panther's body, hurling it to the ground and I fainted. I must have regained consciousness in a few minutes, for when I came to I discovered Leppu using the barrel of my rifle to prise open the panther's jaws, where in its death struggles it had bitten through the calf of my leg. Once free I wasted no time in getting out of the cave, but so weak had I become that Leppu had to practically carry me out. Once in the open a cup of the still warm coffee in my flask helped to revive me and tearing slips of cloth from Leppu's turban I bound my wounds as best I could and the men carried me back to the car.

Now you can imagine the quandary I was in. Once the excitement died down, reaction set in and I was trembling all over. My shoulder and right hand were lacerated and crippled and to make matters worse, blood from a scalp wound where the panther's claws had inflicted a nasty wound on my head, kept seeping down my forehead and entering my eyes. In this state I was obliged to drive my car down a country road, through ditches and nullahs and around fallen logs, a distance of seven miles to the main road. How I ever completed this nightmare journey I have no idea. I must have blacked out on several occasions for when I came to it was to find Leppu clinging desperately to the wheel to prevent me from going off the road. However, at last we made it and arriving at Banjriposi, I drove to the only dispensary the town boasted. Here I was patched up, the meagre resources of this dispensary being wholly inadequate for the job, and returned to the car for the thirty mile drive to Baripada.

But here I came up against a real obstacle. The Doctor would not hear of it. 'Mr Upshon,' he exclaimed, 'you are in a state of shock. You have lost a lot of blood and you are physically unfit to undertake a thirty-mile drive. Wait here and I will make other arrangements to drive you in.'

An old Sikh driver who happened to be at Banjriposi, awaiting some minor repairs to his truck, came up just at this time and hearing the discussion, very sportingly offered to drive the car to Baripada.

At the Baripada Hospital I received expert attention and sixteen stitches. Four hours later I was back at my bungalow at Betnoti, where my wife, although considerably upset when she heard of my narrow escape, promptly had me removed to the Railway Hospital at Kharagpur, from whence I returned three weeks later, perfectly cured.

The panther's skin now hangs in the place of honour in my hall and whenever I look at it I am filled with a deep sense of respect for a very brave animal, who gallantly defended his home and his life against a weaker but far better equipped foe.

THE PANAR MAN-EATER

JIM CORBETT

The Panar leopard, along with the Champawat tiger (also shot by Corbett), was one of the earliest man-eating felines to be reported by the Government of India. It was believed to have killed over four hundred people.

WHILE I was hunting the Champawat man-eater in 1907, I heard of a man-eating leopard that was terrorizing the inhabitants of villages on the eastern border of Almora district. This leopard, about which questions were asked in the House of Commons, was known under several names and was credited with having killed four hundred human beings. I knew the animal under the name of the Panar man-eater, and I shall therefore use this name for the purpose of my story.

No mention is made in government records of man-eaters prior to the year 1905 and it would appear that until the advent of the Champawat tiger and the Panar leopard, man-eaters were unknown in Kumaon. When therefore these two animals—who between them killed eight hundred and thirty-six human beings—made their appearance, the Government was faced with a difficult situation for it had no machinery to put in action against them and had to rely on personal appeals to sportsmen. Unfortunately there were very few sportsmen in Kumaon at that time who had any inclination for this new form of sport which, rightly or wrongly, was considered as hazardous as Wilson's solo attempt—made a few years later—to conquer Everest. I myself was as ignorant of man-eaters as Wilson was of Everest and that I succeeded in my attempt, where he apparently failed in his, was due entirely to luck.

When I returned to my home in Naini Tal alter killing the Champawat tiger I was asked by the Government to undertake the shooting of the Panar leopard. I was working hard for a living at the time and several weeks elapsed before I was able to spare the time to undertake this task, and then just as I was ready to start for the outlying area of Almora district in which the leopard was operating, I received an urgent request from Berthoud, the Deputy Commissioner of Naini Tal, to go to the help of the people of Muktesar where a man-eating tiger had established a reign of terror. After hunting down the tiger, an account of which I have given, I went in pursuit of the Panar leopard.

As I had not previously visited the vast area over which this leopard was operating, I went via Almora to learn all I could about the leopard from Stiffe, the Deputy Commissioner of Almora. He kindly invited me to lunch, provided me with maps, and then gave me a bit of a jolt when wishing me goodbye by asking me if I had considered all the risks and prepared for them by making my will.

My maps showed that there were two approaches to the affected area, one via Panwanaula on the Pithoragarh road, and the other via Lamgara on the Dabidhura road.

I selected the latter route and after lunch set out in good heart—despite the reference to a will—accompanied by one servant and four men carrying my luggage. My men and I had already done a stiff march of fourteen miles from Khairna, but being young and fit we were prepared to do another long march before calling it a day.

As the full moon was rising we arrived at a small isolated building which, from the scribbling on the walls and the torn bits of paper lying about, we assumed was used as a school. I had no tent with me and as the door of the building was locked I decided to spend the night in the courtyard with my men, a perfectly safe proceeding for we were still many miles from the man-eater's hunting grounds. This courtyard, which was about twenty feet square, abutted on the public road and was surrounded on three sides by a two-foot-high wall. On the fourth side it was bounded by the school building.

There was plenty of fuel in the jungle behind the school and my men soon had a fire burning in a corner of the courtyard for my servant to cook my dinner. I was sitting with my back to the locked door, smoking, and my servant had just laid a leg of mutton on the low wall nearest the road and turned to attend to the fire, when I saw the head of a leopard appear over the wall close to the leg of mutton. Fascinated, I sat motionless and watched—for the leopard was facing me—and when the man had moved away a few feet the leopard grabbed the meat and bounded across the road into the jungle beyond. The meat had been put down on a big sheet of paper, which had stuck to it, and when my servant heard the rustle of paper and saw what he thought was a dog running away with it he dashed forward shouting, but on realizing that he was dealing with a leopard and not with a mere dog he changed direction and dashed towards me with even greater speed. All white people in the East are credited with being a little mad—for other reasons than walking about in the midday sun—and I am afraid my good servant thought I was a little more mad than most of my kind when he found I was laughing, for he said in a very aggrieved voice, 'It was your dinner that the leopard carried away and I have nothing else for you to eat.' However, he duly produced a meal that did him credit, and to which I did as much justice as I am sure the hungry leopard did to his leg of prime mutton.

Making an early start next morning, we halted at Lamgara for a meal, and by evening reached the Dol Dak Bungalow on the border of the man-eater's domain. Leaving my men at the bungalow I set out the following morning to try to get news of the man-eater. Going from village to village, and examining the connecting footpaths for leopard pug-marks, I arrived in the late evening at an isolated homestead consisting of a single stone-built slate-roofed house, situated in a few acres of cultivated land and surrounded by scrub jungle. On the footpath leading to this homestead I found the pug-marks of a big male leopard.

As I approached the house a man appeared on the narrow balcony and, climbing down a few wooden steps, came across the courtyard to meet me. He was a young man, possibly twenty-two years of age, and in great distress. It appeared that the previous night while he and his wife were sleeping on the floor of the single room that comprised the house, with the door open for it was April and very hot, the man-eater climbed on to the balcony and getting a grip of his wife's throat started to pull her head-foremost out of the room. With a strangled scream the woman flung an arm round her husband who, realizing in a flash what was happening, seized her arm with one hand and placing the other against the lintel of the door, for leverage, jerked her away from the leopard and closed the door. For the rest of the night the man and his wife cowered in a corner of the room, while the leopard tried to tear down the door. In the hot unventilated room the woman's wounds started to turn septic and by morning her suffering and fear had rendered her unconscious.

Throughout the day the man remained with his wife, too frightened to leave her for fear the leopard should return and carry her away, and too frightened to face the mile of scrub jungle that lay between him and his nearest neighbour. As day was closing down and the unfortunate man was facing another night of terror he saw me coming towards the house, and when I had heard his story I was no longer surprised that he had run towards me and thrown himself sobbing at my feet.

A difficult situation faced me. I had not up to that time approached Government to provide people living in areas in which a man-eater was operating with first-aid sets, so there was no medical or any other kind of aid nearer than Almora, and Almora was twenty-five miles away. To get help for the woman I would have to go for it myself and that would mean condemning the man to lunacy, for he had already stood as much as any man could stand and another night in that room, with the prospect of the leopard returning and trying to gain entrance, would of a certainty have landed him in a mad-house.

The man's wife, a girl of about eighteen, was lying on her back when the leopard clamped its teeth into her throat, and when the man got a grip of her arm and started to pull her back, the leopard—to get a better purchase—drove the claws of one paw into her breast. In the final struggle the claws ripped through the flesh, making four deep cuts. In the heat of the small room, which had only one door and no windows and in which a swarm of flies were buzzing, all the wounds in the girl's throat and on her breast had turned septic, and whether medical aid could be procured or not, the chances of her surviving were very slight; so, instead of going for help, I decided to stay the night with the man. I very sincerely hope that no one who reads this story will ever be condemned to seeing and hearing the sufferings of a human being, or of an animal, that has had the misfortune of being caught by the throat by either a leopard or a tiger and not having the means—other than a bullet—of alleviating or of ending the suffering.

The balcony which ran the length of the house, and which was boarded up at both ends, was about fifteen feet long and four feet wide, accessible by steps hewn in a pine sapling. Opposite these steps was the one door of the house, and under the balcony was an open recess four feet wide and four feet high, used for storing firewood.

The man begged me to stay in the room with him and his wife but it was not possible for me to do this, for, though I am not squeamish, the smell in the room was overpowering and more than I could stand. So between us we moved the firewood from one end of the recess under the balcony, clearing a small space where I could sit with my back to the wall. Night was now closing in, so after a wash and a drink at a nearby spring I settled down in my corner and told the man to go up to his wife and keep the door of the room open. As he climbed the steps the man said, 'The leopard will surely kill you, Sahib, and then what will I do?' 'Close the door,' I answered, 'and wait for morning.'

The moon was two nights off the full and there would be a short period of darkness. It was this period of darkness that was worrying me. If the leopard had remained scratching at the door until daylight, as the man said it had, it would not have gone far and even now it might be lurking in the bushes watching me. I had been in position for half an hour, straining my eyes into the darkening night and praying for the moon to top the hills to the east, when a jackal gave its alarm call. This call, which is given with the full force of the animal's lungs, can be heard for a very long distance and can be described as 'pheaon, pheaon', repeated over and over again as long as the danger that has alarmed the jackal is in sight. Leopards when hunting or when approaching a kill move very slowly, and it would be many minutes before this one—assuming it was the man-eater—covered the half mile between us, and even if in the meantime the moon had not risen it would be giving sufficient light to shoot by, so I was able to relax and breathe more freely.

Minutes dragged by. The jackal stopped calling. The moon rose over the hills, flooding the ground in front of me with brilliant light. No movement to be seen anywhere, and the only sound to be heard in all the world was the agonized fight for breath of the unfortunate girl above me. Minutes gave way to hours. The moon climbed the heavens and then started to go down in the west, casting the shadow of the house on the ground I was watching. Another period of danger, for if the leopard had seen me he would, with a leopard's patience, be waiting for these lengthening shadows to mask his movements. Nothing happened, and one of the longest nights I have ever watched through came to an end when the light from the sun lit up the sky where, twelve hours earlier, the moon had risen.

The man, after his vigil of the previous night, had slept soundly and as I left my corner and eased my aching bones—only those who have sat motionless on hard ground for hours know how bones can ache—he came down the steps. Except for a few wild raspberries I had eaten nothing for twenty-four hours, and as no useful purpose would have been served by my remaining any longer, I bade the man goodbye and set off to rejoin my men at the Dol Dak Bungalow, eight miles away, and summon aid for the girl. I had only gone a few miles when I met my men. Alarmed at my long absence they had packed up my belongings, paid my dues at the Dak Bungalow, and then set out to look for me. While I was talking to them the Road Overseer, whom I have mentioned in my story of the Temple tiger, came along. He was well mounted on a sturdy Bhootia pony, and as he was on his way to Almora he gladly undertook to carry a letter from me to Stiffe. Immediately on receipt of my letter Stiffe dispatched medical aid for the girl, but her sufferings were over when it arrived.

It was this Road Overseer who informed me about the human kill that took me to Dabidhura, where I met with one of the most interesting and the most exciting shikar experiences I have ever had. After that experience I asked the old priest of the Dabidhura temple if the man-eater had as effective protection from his temple as the tiger I had failed to shoot, and he answered, 'No, no, Sahib. This shaitan (devil) has killed many people who worshipped at my temple and when you come back to shoot him, as you say you will, I shall offer prayers for your success morning and evening.'

2

No matter how full of happiness our life may have been, there are periods in it that we look back to with special pleasure. Such a period for me was the year 1910, for in that year I shot the Muktesar man-eating tiger and the Panar man-eating leopard, and in between these two—for me—great events, my men and I set up an all-time record at Mokameh Ghat by handling, without any mechanical means, five thousand five hundred tonnes of goods in a single working day.

My first attempt to shoot the Panar leopard was made in April 1910, and it was not until September of the same year that I was able to spare the time to make a second attempt. I have no idea how many human beings were killed by the leopard between April and September, for no bulletins were issued by Government and beyond a reference to questions asked in the House of Commons no mention of the leopard—as far as I am aware—was made in the Indian press. The Panar leopard was credited with having killed four hundred human beings, against one hundred and twenty-five killed by the Rudraprayag leopard, and the fact that the former received such scant publicity while the latter was headline news throughout India was due entirely to the fact that the

Panar leopard operated in a remote area far from the beaten track, whereas the Rudraprayag leopard operated in an area visited each year by sixty thousand pilgrims ranging from the humblest in the land to the highest, all of whom had to run the gauntlet of the man-eater. It was these pilgrims, and the daily bulletins issued by the Government, that made the Rudraprayag leopard so famous, though it caused far less human suffering than the Panar leopard.

Accompanied by a servant and four men carrying my camp kit and provisions, I set out from Naini Tal on 10 September on my second attempt to shoot the Panar leopard. The sky was overcast when we left home at 4 a.m. and we had only gone a few miles when a deluge of rain came on. Throughout the day it rained and we arrived at Almora, after a twenty-eight-mile march, wet to the bone. I was to have spent the night with Stiffe, but not having a stitch of dry clothing to put on I excused myself and spent the night at the Dak Bungalow. There were no other travellers there and the man in charge very kindly put two rooms at my disposal, with a big wood fire in each, and by morning my kit was dry enough for me to continue my journey.

It had been my intention to follow the same route from Almora that I had followed in April, and start my hunt for the leopard from the house in which the girl had died of her wounds. While I was having breakfast a mason by the name of Panwa, who did odd jobs for us in Naini Tal, presented himself. Panwa's home was in the Panar valley, and on learning from my men that I was on my way to try to shoot the man-eater he asked for permission to join our party, for he wanted to visit his home and was frightened to undertake the journey alone. Panwa knew the country and on his advice I altered my plans and instead of taking the road to Dabidhura via the school where the leopard had eaten my dinner, I took the road leading to Pithoragarh. Spending the night at the Panwa Naula Dak Bungalow, we made an early start next morning and after proceeding a few miles left the Pithoragarh road for a track leading off to the right. We were now in the man-eater's territory where there were no roads, and where the only communication was along footpaths running from village to village.

Progress was slow, for the villages were widely scattered over many hundreds of square miles of country, and as the exact whereabouts of the man-eater were not known it was necessary to visit each village to make inquiries. Going through Salan and Rangot pattis (patti is a group of villages), I arrived late on the evening of the fourth day at Chakati, where I was informed by the headman that a human being had been killed a few days previously at a village called Sanouli on the far side of the Panar river. Owing to the recent heavy rain the Panar was in flood and the headman advised me to spend the night in his village, promising to give me a guide next morning to show me the only safe ford over the river, for the Panar was not bridged.

The headman and I had carried on our conversation at one end of a long row of double-storied buildings and when, on his advice, I elected to stay the night in the village, he said he would have two rooms vacated in the upper storey for myself and my men. I had noticed while talking to him that the end room on the ground floor was untenanted, so I told him I would stay in it and that he need only have one room vacated in the upper storey for my men. The room I had elected to spend the night in had no door, but this did not matter for I had been told that the last kill had taken place on the far side of the river and I knew the man-eater would not attempt to cross the river while it was in flood.

The room had no furniture of any kind, and after my men had swept all the straw and bits of rags out of it, complaining as they did so that the last tenant must have been a very dirty person, they spread my groundsheet on the mud floor and made up my bed. I ate my dinner—which my servant cooked on an open fire in the courtyard—sitting on my bed, and as I had done a lot of walking during the twelve hours I had been on my feet, it did not take me long to get to sleep. The sun was just rising next morning, flooding the room with light, when on hearing a slight sound in the room I opened my eyes and saw a man sitting on the floor near my bed. He was about fifty years of age, and in the last stage of leprosy. On seeing that I was awake this unfortunate living death said he hoped I had spent a comfortable night in his room. He went on to say that he had been on a two days' visit to friends in an adjoining village, and finding me asleep in his room on his return had sat near my bed and waited for me to awake.

Leprosy, the most terrible and the most contagious of all diseases in the East, is very prevalent throughout Kumaon, and especially bad in Almora district. Being fatalists the people look upon the disease as a visitation from God, and neither segregate the afflicted nor take any precautions against infection. So quite evidently, the headman did not think it necessary to warn me that the room I had selected to stay in had for years been the home of a leper. It did not take me long to dress that morning, and as soon as our guide was ready we left the village.

Moving about as I have done in Kumaon I have always gone in dread of leprosy, and I have never felt as unclean as I did after my night in that poor unfortunate's room. At the first stream we came to I called a halt, for my servant to get breakfast ready for me and for my men to have their food. Then, telling my men to wash my groundsheet and lay my bedding out in the sun, I took a bar of carbolic soap and went down the stream to where there was a little pool surrounded by great slabs of rock. Taking off every stitch of clothing I had worn in that room, I washed it all in the pool and, after laying it out on the slabs of rock, I used the remainder of the soap to scrub myself as I had never scrubbed myself before. Two hours later, in garments that had shrunk a little from the rough treatment they had received, I returned to my men feeling clean once again, and with a hunter's appetite for breakfast.

Our guide was a man about four feet six inches tall with a big head crowned with a mop of long hair; a great barrel of a body, short legs, and few words. When I asked him if we had any stiff climbing to do, he stretched out his open hand, and answered, 'Flat as that.' Having said this he led us down a very steep hill into a deep valley. Here I expected him to turn and follow the valley down to its junction with the river. But no. Without saying a word or even turning his head he crossed the open ground and went straight up the hill on the far side. This hill, in addition to being very steep and overgrown with thorn bushes, had loose gravel on it which made the going difficult, and as the sun was now overhead and very hot, we reached the top in a bath of sweat. Our guide, whose legs appeared to have been made for climbing hills, had not turned a hair.

There was an extensive view from the top of the hill, and when our guide informed us that we still had the two high hills in the foreground to climb before reaching the Panar river, Panwa, the mason, who was carrying a bundle containing presents for his family and a great coat made of heavy dark material, handed the coat to the guide and said that as he was making us climb all the hills in Kumaon he could carry the coat for the rest of the way. Unwinding a length of goat hair cord from round his body the guide folded up the coat and strapped it securely to his back. Down and up we went, and down and up again, and then away down in a deep valley we saw the river. So far we had been going over trackless ground, without a village in sight, but we now came on a narrow path running straight down to the river. The nearer we got to the river the less I liked the look of it. The path leading to the water and up the far side showed that there was a ford here, but the river was in flood and the crossing appeared to me to be a very hazardous one. The guide assured us, however, that it was perfectly safe to cross, so removing my shoes and stockings I linked arms with Panwa and stepped into the water. The river was about forty yards wide and from its broken surface I judged it was running over a very rough bed. In this I was right, and after stubbing my toes a few times and narrowly avoiding being washed off our feet, we struggled out on the far bank.

Our guide had followed us into the river and on looking back, I saw that the little man was in difficulties. The water which for us had been thigh deep was for him waist deep and on reaching the main stream, instead of bracing his back against it and walking crab fashion, he very foolishly faced up-stream with the result that he was swept over backwards and submerged under the fast-running current. I was barefoot and helpless on the sharp stones, but Panwa—to whom sharp stones were no obstacle—threw down the bundle he was carrying and without a moment's hesitation sprinted along the bank to where fifty yards farther down, a big slab of rock jutted into the river at the head of a terrifying rapid. Running out on to this wet and slippery rock Panwa lay down, and as the drowning man was swept past, grabbed him by his long hair and after a desperate struggle drew him on to the rock. When the two men rejoined me—the guide looking like a drowned rat—I complimented Panwa on his noble and brave act in having saved the little man's life, at great risk to his own. After looking at me in some surprise Panwa said, 'Oh, it was not his life that I wanted to save, but my new coat that was strapped to his back.' Anyway, whatever the motive, a tragedy had been averted, and after my men had linked arms and crossed safely I decided to call it a day and spend the night on the riverbank. Panwa, whose village was five miles farther up the river, now left me, taking with him the guide, who was frightened to attempt a second crossing of the river.

3

Next morning we set out to find Sanouli, where the last human kill had taken place. Late in the evening of that day we found ourselves in a wide open valley, and as there were no human habitations in sight, we decided to spend the night on the open ground. We were now in the heart of the man-eater's country and after a very unrestful night, spent on cold wet ground, arrived about midday at Sanouli. The inhabitants of this small village were overjoyed to see us and they very gladly put a room at the disposal of my men, and gave me the use of an open platform with a thatched roof.

The village was built on the side of a hill overlooking a valley in which there were terraced fields, from which a paddy crop had recently been harvested. The hill on the far side of the valley sloped up gradually, and a hundred yards from the cultivated land there was a dense patch of brushwood, some twenty acres in extent. On the brow of the hill, above this patch of brushwood, there was a village, and on the shoulder of the hill to the right another village. To the left of the terraced fields the valley was closed in by a steep grassy hill. So, in effect, the patch of brushwood was surrounded on three sides by cultivated land, and on the fourth by open grass land.

While breakfast was being got ready, the men of the village sat round me and talked. During the second half of March and the first half of April, four human beings had been killed in this area by the man-eater. The first kill had taken place in the village on the shoulder of the hill, the second and third in the village on the brow of the hill, and the fourth in Sanouli. All four victims had been killed at night and carried some five hundred yards into the patch of brushwood, where the leopard had eaten them at his leisure, for—having no firearms—the inhabitants of the three villages were too frightened to make any attempt to recover the bodies. The last kill had taken place six days before, and my informants were convinced that the leopard was still in the patch of brushwood.

I had purchased two young male goats in a village we passed through earlier that day, and towards evening I took the smaller one and tied it at the edge of the path of brushwood to test the villager's assertion that the leopard was still in the cover. I did not sit over the goat, because there were no suitable trees nearby and also because clouds were banking up and it looked as though there might be rain during the night. The platform that had been placed at my disposal was open all round, so I tied the second goat near it in the hope that if the leopard visited the village during the night it would prefer a tender goat to a tough human being. Long into the night I listened to the two goats calling to each other. This convinced me that the leopard was not within hearing distance. However, there was no reason why he should not return to the locality, so I went to sleep hoping for the best. There was a light shower during the night and when the sun rose in a cloudless sky every leaf and blade of grass was sparkling with raindrops and every bird that had a song to sing was singing a joyful welcome to the day. The goat near my platform was contentedly browsing off a bush and bleating occasionally, while the one across the valley was silent. Telling my servant to keep my breakfast warm, I crossed the valley and went to the spot where I had tied up the smaller goat. Here I found that, some time before the rain came on, a leopard had killed the goat, broken the rope, and carried away the kill. The rain had washed out the drag-mark, but this did not matter for there was only one place to which the leopard could have taken his kill, and that was into the dense patch of brushwood.

Stalking a leopard, or a tiger, on its kill is one of the most interesting forms of sport I know of, but it can only be indulged in with any hope of success when the conditions are favourable. Here the conditions were not favourable, for the brushwood was too dense to permit of a noiseless approach. Returning to the village, I had breakfast and then called the villagers together, as I wanted to consult them about the surrounding country. It was necessary to visit the kill to see if the leopard had left sufficient for me to sit over and, while doing so, I would not be able to avoid disturbing the leopard. What I wanted to learn from the villagers was whether there was any other heavy cover, within a reasonable distance, to which the leopard could retire on being disturbed by me. I was told that there was no such cover nearer than two miles, and that to get to it the leopard would have to cross a wide stretch of cultivated land.

At midday I returned to the patch of brushwood and, a hundred yards from where he had killed it, I found all that the leopard had left of the goat—its hooves, horns, and part of its stomach. As there was no fear of the leopard leaving the cover at that time of day for the jungle two miles away, I tried for several hours to stalk it, helped by bulbuls, drongos, thrushes, and scimitar-babblers, all of whom kept me informed of the leopard's every movement. In case any should question why I did not collect the men of the three villages and get them to drive the leopard out on to the open ground, where I could have shot it, it is necessary to say that this could not have been attempted without grave danger to the beaters. As soon as the leopard found he was being driven towards open ground, he would have broken back and attacked anyone who got in his way.

On my return to the village after my unsuccessful attempt to get a shot at the leopard, I went down with a bad attack of malaria and for the next twenty-four hours I lay on the platform in a stupor. By the evening of the following day the fever had left me and I was able to continue the hunt. On their own initiative the previous night my men had tied out the second goat where the first had been killed, but the leopard had not touched it. This was all to the good, for the leopard would now be hungry, and I set out on that third evening full of hope.

On the near side of the patch of brushwood, and about a hundred yards from where the goat had been killed two nights previously there was an old oak tree. This tree was growing out of a six-foot-high bank between two terraced fields and was leaning away from the hill at an angle that made it possible for me to walk up the trunk in my rubber-soled shoes. On the underside of the trunk and about fifteen feet from the ground there was a branch jutting out over the lower field. This branch, which was about a foot thick, offered a very uncomfortable and a very unsafe seat for it was hollow and rotten. However, as it was the only branch on the tree, and as there were no other trees within a radius of several hundred yards, I decided to risk the branch.

As I had every reason to believe—from the similarity of the pug-marks I had found in the brushwood to those I had seen in April on the path leading to the homestead where the girl was killed—that the leopard I was dealing with was the Panar man-eater, I made my men cut a number of long blackthorn shoots. After I had taken my seat with my back to the tree and my legs stretched out along the branch, I made the men tie the shoots into bundles and lay them on the trunk of the tree and lash them to it securely with strong rope. To the efficient carrying out of these small details I am convinced I owe my life.

Several of the blackthorn shoots, which were from ten to twenty feet long, projected on either side of the tree; and as I had nothing to hold on to, to maintain my balance, I gathered the shoots on either side of me and held them firmly pressed between my arms and my body. By five o'clock my preparations were complete. I was firmly seated on the branch with my coat collar pulled up well in front to protect my throat, and my soft hat pulled down well behind to protect the back of my neck. The goat was tied to a stake driven into the field thirty yards in front of me, and my men were sitting out in the field smoking and talking loudly.

Up to this point all had been quiet in the patch of brushwood, but now, a scimitar-babbler gave its piercing alarm call followed a minute or two later by the chattering of several white-throated laughing thrushes. These two species of birds are the most reliable informants in the hills, and on hearing them I signalled to my men to return to the village. This they appeared to be very glad to do, and as they walked away, still talking loudly, the goat started bleating. Nothing happened for the next half-hour and then, as the sun was fading off the hill above the village, two drongos that had been sitting on the tree above me, flew off and started to bait some animal on the open ground between me and the patch of brushwood. The goat while calling had been facing in the direction of the village, and it now turned round, facing me, and stopped calling. By watching the goat I could follow the movements of the animal that the drongos were baiting and that the goat was interested in, and this animal could only be a leopard.

The moon was in her third quarter and there would be several hours of darkness. In anticipation of the leopard's coming when light conditions were not favourable, I had armed myself with a twelve-bore double-barrelled shot gun loaded with slugs, for there was a better chance of my hitting the leopard with eight slugs than with a single rifle bullet. Aids to night shooting, in the way of electric lights and torches, were not used in India at the time I am writing about, and all that one had to rely on for accuracy of aim was a strip of white cloth tied round the muzzle of the weapon.

Again nothing happened for many minutes, and then I felt a gentle pull on the blackthorn shoots I was holding and blessed my forethought in having had the shoots tied to the leaning tree, for I could not turn round to defend myself and at best the collar of my coat and my hat were poor protection. No question now that I was dealing with a man-eater, and a very determined man-eater at that. Finding that he could not climb over the thorns, the leopard, after his initial pull, had now got the butt ends of the shoots between his teeth and was jerking them violently, pulling me hard against the trunk of the tree. And now the last of the daylight faded out of the sky and the leopard, who did all his human killing in the dark, was in his element and I was out of mine, for in the dark a human being is the most helpless of all animals and—speaking for myself—his courage is at its lowest ebb. Having killed four hundred human beings at night, the leopard was quite unafraid of me, as was evident from the fact that while tugging at the shoots, he was growling loud enough to be heard by the men anxiously listening in the village. While this growling terrified the men, as they told me later, it had the opposite effect on me, for it let me know where the leopard was and what he was doing. It was when he was silent that I was most terrified, for I did not know what his next move would be. Several times he had nearly unseated me by pulling on the shoots vigorously and then suddenly letting them go, and now that it was dark and I had nothing stable to hold on to, I felt sure that if he sprang up he would only need to touch me to send me crashing to the ground.

After one of these nerve-racking periods of silence the leopard jumped down off the high bank and dashed towards the goat. In the hope that the leopard would come while there was still sufficient light to shoot by, I had tied the goat thirty yards from the tree to give me time to kill the leopard before it got to the goat. But now, in the dark, I could not save the goat—which being white, I could only just see as an indistinct blur—so I waited until it had stopped struggling and then aimed where I thought the leopard would be and pressed the trigger. My shot was greeted with an angry grunt and I saw a white flash as the leopard went over backwards, and disappeared down another high bank into the field beyond.

For ten or fifteen minutes I listened anxiously for further sounds from the leopard, and then my men called out and asked if they should come to me. It was now quite safe for them to do so, provided they kept to the high ground. So I told them to light pine torches, and thereafter carry out my instructions. These torches, made of twelve to eighteen inches long splinters of resin-impregnated pinewood cut from a living tree, give a brilliant light and provide the remote villages in Kumaon with the only illumination they have ever known.

After a lot of shooting and running about, some twenty men each carrying a torch left the village and, following my instructions, circled round above the terraced fields and approached my tree from behind. The knots in the ropes securing the blackthorn shoots to the tree had been pulled so tight by the leopard that they had to be cut. After the thorns had been removed men climbed the tree and helped me down, for the uncomfortable seat had given me cramps in my legs.

The combined light from the torches lit up the field on which the dead goat was lying, but the terraced field beyond was in shadow. When cigarettes had been handed round I told the men I had wounded the leopard but did not know how badly, and that we would return to the village now and I would look for the wounded animal in the morning. At this, great disappointment was expressed. 'If you have wounded the leopard it must surely be dead by now. There are many of us, and you have a gun, so there is no danger.' At least let us go as far as the edge of the field and see if the leopard has left a blood trail.' After all arguments for and against going to look for the leopard immediately had been exhausted, I consented against my better judgement to go as far as the edge of the field, from where we could look down on the terraced field below.

Having acceded to their request, I made the men promise that they would walk in line behind me, hold their torches high, and not run away and leave me in the dark if the leopard charged. This promise they very willingly gave, and after the torchers had been replenished and were burning brightly we set off, I walking in front and the men following five yards behind.

Thirty yards to the goat, and another twenty yards to the edge of the field. Very slowly, and in silence, we moved forward. When we reached the goat—no time now to look for a blood trail—the farther end of the lower field came into view. The nearer we approached the edge, the more of this field became visible, and then, when only a narrow strip remained in shadow from the torches, the leopard, with a succession of angry grunts, sprang up the bank and into full view.

There is something very terrifying in the angry grunt of a charging leopard, and I have seen a line of elephants that were staunch to tiger turn and stampede from a charging leopard; so I was not surprised when my companions, all of whom were unarmed, turned as one man and bolted. Fortunately for me, in their anxiety to get away they collided with each other and some of the burning splinters of pine—held loosely in their hands—fell to the ground and continued to flicker, giving me sufficient light to put a charge of slugs into the leopard's chest.

On hearing my shot the men stopped running, and then I heard one of them say, 'Oh, no. He won't be angry with us, for he knows that this devil has turned our courage to water.' Yes, I knew, from my recent experience on the tree, that fear of a man-eater robs a man of courage. As for running away, had I been one of the torchbearers I would have run with the best. So there was nothing for me to be angry about. Presently, while I was making believe to examine the leopard, to ease their embarrassment, the men returned in twos and threes. When they were assembled, I asked, without looking up, 'Did you bring a bamboo pole and rope to carry the leopard back to the village?' 'Yes,' they answered eagerly, 'we left them at the foot of the tree.' 'Go and fetch them,' I said, 'for I want to get back to the village for a cup of hot tea.' The cold night-wind blowing down from the north had brought on another attack of malaria, and now that all the excitement was over I was finding it difficult to remain on my feet.

That night, for the first time in years, the people of Sanouli slept, and have since continued to sleep, free from fear.

MR IYER'S BRUSH WITH A TIGER

A. WIMBUSH

Wimbush was a forest officer posted in the Nilgiris in the 1920s and early '30s. This account of an unusual, tragi-comic episode first appeared in The Indian Forester, *the world's oldest surviving forestry journal.*

THE following unusual incident occurred at Iskagundam on July 19, 1928, in the Nallamalai Hills of Kurnool district in the Madras Presidency, where the writer was camping with Rao Sahib K.R. Venkataramana Iyer Avergal, Conservator of Forests, and Messrs. B.K. Roy and S. Raghunatha Rao, the District Forest Officers of South and West Kurnool divisions.

Mr Venkataramana Iyer was occupying one room in the forest rest house, whilst the writer occupied the other, the two District Officers being in tents close by. About 7.30 p.m., Mr Venkataramana Iyer was doing some office work by the light of a petrol lantern in his room whilst the other three officers were talking in the adjoining room. Suddenly, Mr Venkataramana Iyer appeared at the door in a state of some excitement, saying that a tiger had just walked into his room.

The statement sounded singular if true, but investigation as to whether [some] 'pi dog' had passed through his room or was still there seemed to be indicated. A rifle was standing handy, so after loading it, more as a sign of respect for Mr Venkataramana Iyer's veracity than with any expectation of using it, two of the officers proceeded to investigate through the door leading on to the back veranda which, luckily, was propped open, about nine inches, by means of a stone. That truth is stranger than fiction was proved by the unmistakable fact that a tiger was underneath the office table, diagonally opposite to the back door. It was examining the window behind the table which, though open, was protected by bars. The tiger did not present a perfect shot owing to the fact that it was partly screened by the office chair and a table leg.

However, the petrol lamp gave a good light. A few inches of shoulder, though not the neck, were clearly visible. A shot was, accordingly, taken which was followed by a brief moment of pandemonium, after which all was still.

The pandemonium resulted in the extinction of the petrol lamp and, as was found afterwards, the disposal of most of the Conservator's office work. A fairly lengthy consultation then ensued as to what was to be done next. All concerned were extremely anxious to have dinner, but the feeling that the tiger might also be in the same state ruled out any idea of asking the servants to take the dishes backwards and forwards between the kitchen and the house.

The supposition was that the tiger was dead, so the only natural thing to do seemed to be to try to verify this supposition. Fortunately, another petrol lamp was available, so one officer with the rifle and another with the lamp approached the door and peered in. No tiger was to be seen, so with a walking-stick the brick which was preventing the door from opening more than about nine inches was pushed further in. As the door opened, a tiger's tail became visible on the floor. As the tail did not move, the door was pushed further open with some confidence. It immediately became apparent that the tail belonged to a live tiger which was squatting on its haunches more or less behind the opening door.

This presented a quandary which led to a discussion as to what on earth had ever induced the officers to join the Forest Service. Something, however, had to be done, so after considering all possibilities, including that of making a hole in the thatched roof, it was decided to go and fetch a crowbar from the Ranger's camp close by and make a hole in the mud wall separating the two rooms. This decision was given effect to, but before the crowbar arrived the fatuity of the proposed procedure became apparent and the idea was dropped in favour of making a hole in the roof. Consequently, a ladder and an electric torch were obtained and a Forest Guard very shortly had the hole made, whilst the back and front doors were kept under observation.

The Guard, after examining the room by the aid of the torch, and after making several loud enquiries of the tiger as to whether it was dead or not, called for an officer to come up on the roof with the rifle. On arrival up aloft the officer was able to see the tiger, apparently dead, lying with its head resting against the corner of the room.

However, the officer, realizing that a tiger killed twice is better than one not killed at all, put in another shot, whereupon the tiger, which was not dead at all, proceeded to expire somewhat leisurely. The party then hauled the animal, which proved to be an extremely emaciated tigress, measuring 8 ft. 2 in., on to the veranda and forthwith enjoyed a well-earned dinner.

During the process of skinning, which took place immediately after dinner, it was found that the tigress had a bullet wound full of maggots in her stomach, as well as having one of the smaller pads on a back foot badly lacerated. The first shot of the evening had broken her near shoulder to pulp, the bullet having emerged from the base of the neck towards the front.

Mr Venkataramana Iyer, who, in retreating from his office table in the first instance, had actually brushed against the tigress, found, on returning to his room, that the letter which he had been writing was bespattered with blood.

With this satisfactorily sanguinary ending to a somewhat unique experience, the writer retired to rest at 4.30 in the morning, having pegged out the tiger skin, washed off the innumerable ticks resulting from the skinning, and recorded the events of the night whilst they were still very fresh in his memory.

FAILURES

MRS W.W. BAILLIE

Excerpted from the closing pages of Days and Nights of Shikar *(see 'The First Panther').*

I went again a year or two later to shoot in the Central Provinces, or to try to shoot I should say, as everything I did went wrong and there was nothing but disappointments and disasters, though I *saw* some tigers; in fact, things went so badly for me that I wrote some sad verses on grief and disaster which I set to (banjo) music, in a very minor key and sang Adagio, molto lamentoso, con-all-the-expression-I-could-put-into-it when feeling at my lowest.

The ship going out to Bombay was terribly crowded, but that of course was the same misfortune for everybody. There were nearly five hundred children, and parents to match, and there was no room to sit on deck with any comfort. Being so crowded together should have kept us warm, but it was very cold the early part of the voyage.

On landing in Bombay neither of my servants was there to meet me as they had promised: Govind was too ill to come at all and Jiwan, the old cook, only met me a week later. I went to my agents to ask for my letters which were to tell me where I was to go and shoot, but by some mistake they had all been forwarded to England. After many quips and quirks (whatever they may be) I fell on my feet, and some kind friends in Nagpur took pity on me, arranged everything for me and started me off on my shoot. I had had hinges put on my wooden boxes so that they might be handy for the servants to open and shut, as they often had to pack quickly for a march, but the customs people, after rummaging in them, had hammered many nails in, especially on the hinge side, instead of replacing the screws, so it was with difficulty that we could open them at all, and then with everlasting damage to the hinges.

The first camp I went to was on a high-road where roamed a tiger whose custom was to spring on a bullock being driven along in a passing cart, and drag it off. The tiger always chose a dark night, and of course the cartmen were able to do nothing to prevent it except to give up travelling on moonless nights on that part of the road that ran through jungle. I often had a try for him, but he was always too wary. I drove through his piece of hunting ground one night, but the cartmen were in such a panic of fear that they shouted and galloped their bullocks all the way, although I was ready with the loaded rifle, so the tiger had no chance of getting his dinner. I could not get beaters in this jungle, and as the tiger had killed a calf near a village, I sat up, meaning only to wait a few hours, as there was a very poor moon. It was getting low in the sky and I could scarcely see, so I called for the shikaris, who were waiting at a distance, to come and put the ladder up for me to climb down. I called again; no answer but the eternal silence, the beautiful starry silence of the Indian jungle at night, broken only occasionally by the cry of peafowl or deer or night birds. Then I whistled for the men, then I yelled—which broke the beautiful silence unpleasantly—but could not make them hear, so I lay down in the machan to sleep. I was soon awakened—after all this noise too—by the gentle rustle of a leaf, then the crackling of bones, and I suppose the tiger was there, but the moon was setting and some clouds—which had no business to be there at all at that time of the year—blew over and obscured what little moon there was, so there was no tiger for me that night, as he was away before dawn.

Then a much sadder thing happened: a very fine tiger came out one afternoon, to my amazement, in daylight, before the sun had set, a thing I had never seen before and probably never shall again, and I was not able to get a shot! That was most tantalizing. The place was quite lonely, far away in the jungle, and the bullock that had been killed was lying partly covered and hidden by bushes. There was a very convenient tree near it for the machan, and forest in front and on both sides of it, but behind was a wide open grass glade. We were rather late and hurried in putting up the machan, but I complained that the tree was very open behind me as there were no branches there and no leaves to hide me, so that from the rear I was very much exposed to the view of any animal coming from the open bit of grassland. The shikari said that the tiger was sure to come by way of the jungle in front, looked rather scornful at my poor ignorance and asked *what* tiger would come walking out in the open when he could steal along hidden paths. Of course it was much more likely he should come through the trees and scrub, but I told him that all the same I must really have a few branches tied up behind me. He said there was very little time; chopping boughs and then fixing them up would make so much noise, and that the tiger who might be coming at that minute would be sure to see or hear and be frightened away. I found we were making more noise talking, though in whispers, and arguing about it all than perhaps it was worth, so, against my better judgment, I gave in and the men went off.

I had to keep a lookout on all sides at once and it was not so very long before the tiger appeared from the open, rather behind me on my right. He was forty yards away and walked along boldly, and if I had dared to move I should have had a beautiful shot at him, but I dared not wink an eye. I could see him over my shoulder as he came quite near; he stopped for a short time and then came and stood behind me, not venturing at once up to the kill in front. I could not see him at all now, as I did not dare to turn my head and only knew he was there by an occasional soft purring that he made. There we both were, within a few yards of each other, waiting, waiting, and he must have stood there for half an hour to judge by the sun. I sat deadly still, hoping every second to see him walk out in front from under my tree. At last, as I had heard no purring for a long time, I turned my head very slightly and quite silently I thought. The tiger was away at a gallop long before I could swing round or bring the rifle up to my shoulder. I ought not to have stirred, so I dare say this was all my own fault, but he was frightened away and never came back to the place: such a chance as it was to miss!

Another time as I sat watching over a kill a tiger came but never showed himself. I knew of his presence by the swearing and chattering of many monkeys that were there. They had all been busy eating berries that grew on low bushes around, and some of them were on the ground, when I saw them suddenly starting to swing themselves up trees. I heard the tiger make a dash at something with a snarl and a low growl, and following this was the rush away of monkeys who were scolding and using abusive language. The tiger was certainly very angry about something, so were the monkeys, so was I: the monkeys swore, I swore (in undertones), and the tiger simply cursed. One baby monkey grew very much excited and chattered in a funny, shrill little voice, trying its hardest to imitate its parents. Perhaps the monkeys gave me away by making the tiger look up, as after prowling round for a long time he went away without my catching so much as a glimpse of him, and afterwards we saw the tracks of where he had been wandering about in the sandy nullah. He was supposed to be a man-eater that had killed a boy a short time before near this spot.

My tent had been pitched, unknowingly, in a hotbed of scorpions, and the boy was constantly finding one or two as he swept it out in the morning. I found one in my slipper, but luckily dropped it before I put my foot inside, when this beast ran out. When we changed camp there were still scorpions lying hidden in the folds of the tent and in my boxes, and it was a marvel that no one was stung.

After several more disappointments with the tigers in those jungles I went to another district to shoot, with hopes of better luck. The march out was very hilly and the road very bad, but I had a glorious pair of bullocks that tore along, shaving corners and bumping down into rocky streams. They did their twenty miles in about six hours and, as usual, I reached the place where we were to camp long before the servants and kit. A forest officer and his mother were in camp there and very kindly gave me tea and dinner. They had a fox terrier and a monkey, and on my arrival the monkey was told to make its salaam; it came up rather shyly and kissed my foot and then went and sat with its arms round the terrier's neck: they seemed to be great friends.

The next march took us to the shooting ground, so I gave up the sportive bullocks that had brought me along so well, and rode a good little chestnut pony that I had hired, called Thomas. There was a tiger kill one night and the calf was half eaten; the remainder was carefully and neatly covered up, and completely hidden, with dead bamboo leaves which the tiger had raked together so that it really looked as if he had every intention of coming back, but I had no luck that time. After some days he killed again in a different place which was a very good one to beat, *if* we could get enough coolies. Nanur, the guard, had ordered men the day before to be ready to beat in case there should be a kill, as we should not have time to collect them in one morning. They came, I saw, but the tiger conquered, as he had a good dinner and escaped unharmed. It was an ideal place to beat, a valley with hills all round and a nullah running straight up to my tree, down which I could see a long way. There was an open stretch covered with thick high grass on my left, and it looked unlikely that the tiger would try to go through that, but men were placed in trees along the edge of it to stop him if he should want to break through there. After the beat began I saw the stops climbing down from their trees and moving about, and I watched them grouping together and going off to the top of a small hill, to be out of the tiger's way! I could not of course shout to them to stay where they were, on account of making any noise. There were two tigers in the beat; one broke away through the side at the start, so Nanur said afterwards, and the other came briskly trotting along in the nullah straight for me. This really looked hopeful. He came steadily on until within eighty yards, then suddenly turned, jumped up the nullah bank and disappeared into the long grass, towards the trees the stops should have been in. That was the last I saw of the tiger, and there was no movement in, or waving of, the grass as he passed through it to show his whereabouts. He went near the men in trees on the hill and they did not attempt to turn him, though they made plenty of noise and great demonstrations to try and turn a poor scared deer that ran past them—this against orders of course!—there was a great difference between that and the stern silence with which the tiger was let by. It was most annoying, and one might as well beat for a tiger down Piccadilly as with these sort of men, though the remainder were doing their best.

When everything I tried went so wrong for me I began to feel that I really was 'Champion, in this Scheme of Frustration', as I remember *Punch* once neatly put it. I must own, though rather against my will, as it tends to spoil the record for 'Champion', that I had shot a good tiger in the first district, though without an incident worth recording, and now, soon after my unhappy beat, when sitting up over a calf that had been killed by these same two tigers, I shot the tigress that came out just at dusk.

The shikari and guards came with torches after hearing the shots, and I went back to camp with them, leaving the dead tigress lying there until next day. In the morning when we went to bring the tigress in we found that the tiger had come and had been feasting on the calf, only a few yards from his poor dead mate who lay stretched there. I decided on another night's sitting up; the remains of the two-days-old kill, as it was in the hot weather, were impossible to sit over for obvious reasons, so they were dragged away for the vultures to finish and a small buffalo calf was tied in its place. There was no moon, so I could only hope for a shot before dark or one at dawn. I saw or heard nothing in the evening, and the calf, I think, spent a happy and peaceful night, lying down and sleeping. A little before dawn I heard a sambur give its warning call, and soon afterwards the sound of a short heavy rush of some animal and a roar. There was no sound of a struggle, no other noise of any kind, and the calf was killed—the whole thing took perhaps two seconds. It was quite dark and I could see nothing below, but by the sounds following I think the tiger was drinking the blood. He did not settle down to eat at once, but I could hear him wandering round, and he stood for a time in the place the dead tigress had been lying, which had been taken back to camp in the morning. There was a little swish, swish of the long grass as he came through it, back to the kill where he now began to feed. There seemed to be a faint shadow moving, but nothing that I could really distinguish; and which was tiger and which was the dead calf I could not make out. I waited and waited, longing for a streak of dawn which would *not* come. I thought I should be foolish to shoot in the dark when probably a few minutes more would give me a fair shot: I looked up at the sky and the stars were certainly fading. Come dawn! It never dawned so slowly before. There was just a faint streak of grey, my rifle was at my shoulder, but when I picked it up I found that a small fork of white paper I had fastened most carefully, as I thought, to the foresight to give me a guide for a night shot, had gone, torn away I suppose by a branch or something it must have brushed against. I gave one more glance up at the stars and then looked down on the tiger. I saw a shadowy white thing, his face and whiskers, and I think he was looking up at me, but he was off and away before I could pull the trigger and I fired into the grass that he vanished into. I think I missed and we found no blood tracks when the men came, nor could we find the bullet mark in the ground.

When we got back to camp we found that the useful little pony, Thomas, had disappeared. He was always allowed to graze in the fields, watched over by a small boy who had the charge of him and my calves. The boy had let him graze away into the jungle out of his sight and was afraid, I think, to tell of it at once when he could not find him, so that some little time elapsed before a search was made. Men were sent out in all directions to look for him and he was tracked through the jungle for some miles in the direction of his home forty miles away—then all trace was lost. He had a rope round his neck with a long end dragging, and I was much afraid he might get entangled among trees and be starved to death. The police made all inquiries at the neighbouring villages and also at his home, but they could hear nothing of him, and they said it was not possible for him to have been stolen without their getting information. We never heard of the pony again; the shikaris said he must have been killed by a tiger, but I lived in hopes of hearing news of him for a long time. It was a sad, unsatisfactory end to poor Thomas and a great loss to me. The owner wrote to say that the pony had never come back, and he asked for the price of him, plus ten rupees, which he charged 'for the pony's death, on account of the fright it gave him!'

On leaving this camp we made a night march to a place where there was a small bungalow to put up in, which was cooler than a tent in these hot days. Jiwan came to say that everything was ready if I would come and get in my cart. I found there were no ropes for the luggage, and none of it had been tied on. The men in this part of the country make very strong ropes of thinly split bamboo which they twist up in their hands, and I had often sat and watched in admiration the making of them; so ropes were sent for from the village, the things tied on and then there was more delay: the cartmen had thought fit to go off to eat their food! After some time they came back and the bullocks were yoked. One of my pair jumped about, went off with a rush, nearly upset the cart and then broke away and bolted. It took an hour to find another, as the guard said we must not put the runaway bail in again, he was such a badmash. At last we started in bright moonlight and got along well for a time. We had to go down a long steep hill which led after a very sudden turn into the wide rocky bed of a dry nullah. I was in the leading cart and after many bumps and jolts got safe over and up the other side. Then there were sounds of a cart and oxen rushing down the steep road, great shouting among the men, and down raced the bullocks much too fast to be able to turn at the sudden bend; more shouts and yells at the bullocks, then a bump and a crash, and after that dead silence. My cartman jumped out and ran back and I followed him. One of the carts lay upset on its side, wheels off, all the boxes and luggage strewn about, and two men lying as if they were dead, having been shot off the top of the loaded cart on which they had been perched, on to the rough rocks. Several other men were scrambling on to their legs and the oxen apparently were none the worse. The jumble of broken cart, overturned kit and disabled men made a sad weird picture among the black rocks and under the shadow of trees.

I went up to one man who was lying very still and saw that it was poor old Jiwan. I spoke to him and it was a great relief to hear him able to give an answer; he half tried to rise when I came, but could not move, and I told him to lie still. He said he had been thrown from the top of the cart on to his side and hip and that his back was broken. He looked desperately pale and ghastly in the moonlight that showed in flecks through the trees. The sepoy was the other man that was hurt, he was lying against a rock with a big box across his legs and was groaning now and then. None of the cartmen were much hurt, they had been running with the cart and trying to hold it back. We were fortunately near a village and the men went up to fetch a charpai to carry Jiwan there. We lifted him on to it; his back was not broken, but he could scarcely move. He was taken up and laid on a bed of straw in the veranda of the kotwal's house; and the charpai went back for the sepoy, as it was the only one they had, so they said. There was nothing I could do for them after I had seen them (un) comfortably settled, and they did not want brandy or anything I could give them, so I went down to finish my night in the cart.

In the morning Jiwan and the sepoy were both terribly stiff and in great pain, though the cook was much the worse of the two: he said I could do him no good, the kotwal would look after them, and they would sooner be left to lie still and follow me when they were able if I would send a cart back for them, so I took the guard and my small boy and went on the last few miles to the bungalow. On the way I saw a tiger sitting lazily out in the open—a wide grassy glade several hundred yards away—sunning himself. He had not seen us and I let the driver go on a short distance to where we were hidden from him, meaning to stop and run up the hill above him to try and get a shot, but two of the men behind me had seen him too, and stood looking and pointing at him from where he could see them, so the tiger got up slowly, looked at them for some little time and then sauntered away through the grass and was finally lost to sight among the trees. I suppose that was the same tiger that eluded me in the early dawn; I often tried for him again but never got him.

I rather wondered how I was to live after poor Jiwan's accident; the boy knew nothing about cooking. I thought perhaps I could boil an egg (if I could get one), or porridge, or a potato, though the only time I had ever tried to cook a potato the bottom of the saucepan fell out; anyway, it was much worse for Jiwan than for me. A Mussulman overseer who lived a mile away heard about the accident and came to help me. He was very good and sent me cooked food for some days, and then sent his own cart, with a thick bed of straw in it, to bring the cook and sepoy when they were fit to travel. The boy and I unpacked the cracked and broken boxes and found that a bottle of chutney and also one of lime-juice had survived the disaster! But the chutney, I found next day, was a seething mass of drowned or struggling cockroaches that had found their way in through a hole in the cork.

Poor Jiwan *would* come the first minute that he was able, he had a miserable drive and had to be lifted out of the cart and laid on a charpai; I made him some tea and put something to eat near him which he might not touch, because of his Brahmin caste, but I knew that when I had gone and no one was looking, he would not be able to resist the tea at any rate. He was a wonderful old man and managed to crawl about somehow and would persist in cooking my food however bad he felt. The sepoy was much better and able to walk.

There was no more sport after this: the Forest Guard, Nanur, who had been a soldier and fought and was wounded at Armentieres, I think he said, was down with the fever; the shikari had a dreadfully swelled face and toothache and could do nothing; several of the village men were ill; and I damaged my foot and could not get about. For several weeks we had a very sad camp, one of the calves, used as baits, died, and Jiwan grew thinner every day and had constant fever. I shot a peacock so that he might have some soup, but I think he was too ill to eat. The monotony was broken one evening by a bear visiting the camp; it came close up to the cook-house and Nanur came running to fetch me, but by the time I got there some clever man had lighted a flaring torch, to show me the bear! he said; in reality he was so much frightened he dare not wait in the dark until I came, so of course the glare had driven the bear away.

We managed to tie up for the tiger once more when the shikari was sufficiently recovered. I sat in a tree all night and a violent storm came on, so that I had to pull a rug over me and put a waterproof sheet on the top, quite covering me and a multitude of sins, and I slept. Invariably I wake at the first streak of dawn when sleeping under the sky, but because I had this wretched rug over my head I slept ten minutes too long. A distant noise woke me, I think it was the rumble of a cart on the road not far away. I sat up and *there* was the tiger, who seemed to have just come to the kill. He also, I think, had heard the cart, as he was standing looking in its direction; he was gone before I could get hold of the rifle, and it was all my own stupid fault.

When so many things went wrong I had to console myself with the thought of some philosopher's story—I forget who—of ancient days, which ran something like this: All the people in a certain country were suffering under so many troubles that they could bear it no longer; so each one took his pack of sorrows on his back and went off to the market to sell or exchange it. There was much bargaining and haggling and, as each found there was no one worse off than himself, every one went home again with his own burden!

We made all preparations to start back for the railway and home. Storms were beginning, and the rains expected, and we hurried our marches back, as we had a river to cross which the guard said might soon become flooded.

The first march we travelled straight on all one night and day and, as there was no other prospect of a wash, I bathed in the river when we came to it. The stretch of sand that had to be walked over was so hot and burning from the sun it nearly blistered my feet, and then there was deep black mud to wade through before getting into deep water, so for purposes of cleanliness I don't think the bath was an improvement! I tried to persuade Jiwan to go into hospital until he felt better, but he was anxious to go back to his home and friends, so went off at once by train, and I have heard since that he has quite recovered…

A PHOTOGRAPHER ANNOYS A TIGER

F. W. CHAMPION

Champion came to India in 1913, when he was barely twenty, and stayed in the country till 1947, working for most of this period with the Imperial Forest Service. He became a passionate conservationist and one of the world's first wildlife photographers. He was fiercely critical of hunting as sport and preferred 'shooting' with a camera—his photographs of tigers, especially those taken at night—using cameras triggered with tripwires and equipped with a flashlight—are classic and much sought-after images today. Champion inspired several hunter-conservationists, including Jim Corbett, to take up wildlife photography. This piece is excerpted from a longer essay first published in the anthology Big Game Encounters *(1936), edited by Stanley Jepson.*

THERE are some people who claim that big-game photography is much more dangerous than big-game shooting, but I am of the opinion that on the average such is not really the case. My reason for this statement which, being a photographer myself, I suppose I should not make, is that I hold the view that most wild animals want only to be left alone, and they will leave you alone.

The photographer does not, or should not, wound or harry his subjects, so that in most cases the animals have no cause to bear him ill-will; but when animals are pursued and wounded they naturally show resentment and become much more dangerous than they are in their normal and undisturbed state. In the case of a really good shot very few animals are wounded without being killed almost at once, so that the danger is no greater—indeed, it is often less—because it is possible to shoot at greater ranges than are satisfactory for the production of really good photographs. But many good sportsmen are not such accurate shots, and, in such cases, they often 'ask for trouble', and the possibility of this 'trouble' is really what appeals to them in big-game shooting. There are unfortunately a few, an increasing number it would seem, who are content with potting tigers from motor-cars or safe machans, and yet who talk a lot about the danger of big-game 'hunting', when there is really no danger whatever involved in their kind of hunting.

As regards big-game photography, for the ordinary man it tends to be on the average, for the reasons I have given above, somewhat less dangerous than the more sporting forms of shooting, but it all depends upon the individual. If one likes to creep up to tiger kills on foot and unarmed in the daytime and to try to take photographs at close range of angry and disturbed tigers, one can certainly claim that one is indulging in a really dangerous form of sport, because in most cases the kills will be in thick cover among which it is possible to take photographs only at a range of ten yards or less. Clambering about steep and dangerous precipices burdened with a heavy camera trying to photograph the sheep and goats of the Himalayas is also dangerous, as is stalking wild elephants to close ranges...As regards myself, I make no claims to being a particularly brave man, and now-a-days, as a married man with a wife and children dependent upon me, I have to be more careful than perhaps I used to be. Even so, I still get my tense moments and thrills[.]

I [remember] two thrills that I have had in recent years, one with a tiger and the other with a musth wild elephant. I sometimes set automatic flashlight traps over tiger kills and the tiger episode occurred in such a case. I would mention in passing that I use auto-photography partly because I became so riddled with malaria as a result of sitting up all night in the jungle that I had to give it up, partly because I couldn't spare the time, and partly because it is possible in certain cases to obtain artistic pictures with its use which are quite unobtainable in any other way, although auto-photography really needs no apology and is just as dangerous or undangerous (except as regards malaria) as sitting in a machan to shoot. Anyhow, what happened in this particular case was as follows.

--

I obtained a kill by a particularly fine tiger subsequently shot by Mr (now Sir) W.L. Stampe and measuring over ten feet between pegs and I set my automatic flashlight traps over the kill in the usual way, requiring about two hours' silent work on foot at the kill, with the tiger hanging about all the time.

I then left the kill for the night and returned in the morning on foot and with no weapon, to see what had happened. On reaching the spot I found that the tiger had returned and had removed the kill without firing my flashlight in a way which seemed to me quite impossible.

I was so astonished that, without thinking what I was doing, I silently followed the drag, accompanied by my Garhwali orderly, Mahendra Singh, up a steep slope culminating in a small plateau. On reaching the plateau we found that the drag went round a big rock, so we went round the rock too, and suddenly blundered right on the kill with the tiger in possession! The distance could not have been more than five or six yards and the tiger had apparently been so engrossed in his meal that he hadn't heard us coming.

As we turned the corner, however, he suddenly looked up and immediately crouched with a horrible snarl, lashing his tail from side to side and ready to spring at any moment. The situation was critical and it really looked as though our number was up this time. We had no rifle. The tiger had been suddenly disturbed and was obviously very angry.

Retreat was very difficult either for the tiger or for us. But instinctively we both did the only possible thing in such circumstances and 'froze', staring the tiger straight in the eyes. This continued for a minute or so, the tiger snarling and lashing his tail and we standing motionless with our hearts beating like sledge-hammers. Then we began gradually to move backwards inch by inch, hoping that the tiger wouldn't notice that we were moving.

The snarls increased.

We stopped, fearing the worst. But as opportunity offered, we continued our almost imperceptible retreat, until finally with sighs of relief we disappeared behind the rock.

The tiger did not follow and we beat a hasty retreat! This was, I think, one of the nearest things I have ever had, as the slightest sudden movement on our part would have precipitated an attack which we could never have met, with no weapon between us.

Anyhow, 'All's well that ends well,' but I shall always remain thankful that I had a staunch man with me, who instantly realized without being told—indeed, there was no opportunity to speak!—what was the only chance of escaping from a really critical situation.

I think that most shikaris will agree that this sudden meeting with an angry tiger would have been a tense moment, even if I had been armed with a heavy rifle. Without a rifle at all, 'tense' hardly describes the situation.

I would emphasize that I do not bear this tiger any grudge. After all, we all feel cross sometimes and there was ample excuse for the animal's actions. The tiger was hungry and was suddenly startled and cornered at close quarters. He really behaved very well, for he merely cursed me and told me to get out, whereas other tigers in such circumstances might well have preferred giving punishment first and abuse afterwards!

A PANTHER HUNT

EHA

Edward Hamilton Aitken, better known by his pen-name EHA, was born in Satara (in present-day Maharashtra) in 1851 and lived in India all his life, but for his final two years, spent in Edinburgh. A civil servant by profession, he was a keen naturalist and a founding member of the Bombay Natural History Society (BNHS). Over thirty years he explored the jungles around Khargoda, Ratnagiri, Bombay and the Konkan, where he was posted, and wrote about birds, insects, rodents (the smaller the creatures, the greater his interest in them), and only occasionally about big animals, as in the account that follows. His writings on nature, remarkable as much for his knowledge as for his humour, were popular in his day and were collected and published as books, among them, The Naturalist on the Prowl, The Tribes on My Frontier, The Common Birds of Bombay. *EHA preferred studying live nature rather than specimens collected for the purpose—in one of his autobiographical sketches he writes, 'I carried my gun and rifle with me... They served to keep up my character as a sportsman, and did not often require to be cleaned.'*

I have never in my life written a tale of sport, or a narrative of personal adventure, but I have read a good many, and I think

I know how the thing should be done, so I will turn aside from the peaceful course of [my other] papers and endeavour to give an account of what befell me not long ago.

My friend H and I had just arrived at an out-worn little town, which had once been a place of some importance, and about sunset, having disposed of urgent work and dismissed our clerks, we went out for a stroll round a fine old fort in the middle of the plain to the east of the town. My friend had three dogs, rowdy little beasts, supposed to be fox-terriers, and I had a respectable and respected old spaniel, which acted as their guide, philosopher and friend. These accompanied us. As we neared the dark old fort, a pair of great Fish Owls came out of it and flew past us. I remembered finding their nest, nearly two years ago, in a large hollow tree just inside the gate. There was one young one, a goblin in yellow down, with eyes as large as a rupee, and so plentifully stocked with vermin that I made all the haste I could to restore him to his parents and wash my hands of him. I mentioned to H that the natives in the town say that there is generally a small panther in the fort. H ridiculed the idea and insinuated that my shikari, Banawat Beg, had been playing on my credulity. H is naturally disputatious, and I have always had a strong, innate passion for the truth, so we were on the borders of an argument, when H started and exclaimed, 'What is that?'

I listened and heard a distant sound like the sawing of wood. 'A panther,' I answered, not in the spirit of controversy, but because it really was uncommonly like the voice of a panther. However, it was not repeated, and H thought it must be some night bird; so we went on our way. As we got round to the east of the fort the walls loomed dark and grand against the western sky, and stopping to admire them, I noticed a stone, or some other object, very like the head and ears of a large cat, on the top of the mound just under the walls. 'Look there,' I said in jest, 'do you now see the panther inspecting us?' H replied, 'I do.' And at that instant the object moved. 'By the Accountant-General,' cried H, 'it is a panther! What shall we do? It will be down on the dogs.'

In truth, the situation was not a pleasant one. We could not move five yards from where we stood without losing sight of the beast against the black wall, and then he would be at liberty to stalk us in the darkness and take his pick of the dogs. Of course he would take Moses, who is fleshy and tender. We held a hurried council and decided that H should make for the high road as fast as he could, with the dogs, while I should remain where I was and mount guard on the panther. As H went away, I saw the beast raise himself and look longingly after the receding figure and the dogs: then he turned and looked at me. He clearly saw that he was being watched and cursed me in his heart, but dared not advance.

Giving my friend time to get safe away, I began to think what I should do. It was nearly dark now, and I felt that I could not walk home with that blackguard watching me. So I walked slowly towards him, but he did not move. I stopped and shouted at the pitch of my voice, but he gave no sign. I advanced again till I seemed to be within fifty yards of him, but still the round head with two ears remained motionless against the sky. That head looked very large at this distance. At last I took up a stone and threw it with all my might. It fell just in front of the brute, and in an instant he sprang to his feet and jumped into the fort ditch. Then I got myself home as fast as I could, and found that H had tied up the dogs and gone out again to look for me.

Next morning, we visited the place and could see plainly where the panther, coming down from one of the bastions into the ditch, had made a path through the long grass. We could also trace his course up the side of the ditch to the mound on top of which he had stopped to reconnoitre the plain when we first noticed him. Much against the better judgment of our shikaris, we determined at once to beat the fort for him.

Before going any further with my story, it is necessary to give a short description of the place. The fort is built on ground very little higher than the surrounding plain, so that it never owed any strength to its situation; but all that the art of the times could do was done to make up for this disadvantage. Its walls were of solid masonry, very thick and of great height, and at intervals there were strong bastions and towers. There were two strong gates, an outer and an inner, with flanking towers. A deep moat and mound surrounded the whole. Inside, a remarkably fine well supplied the garrison with water, while a temple and a mosque helped them to think that their religious needs were satisfied also. Such was the fort before time took it in hand. Now great trees of the fig tribe tower above the wall, while their roots straggle and sprawl over the masonry, separating and dislodging the massive stones. The 'hyssop on the wall', rank grasses and pendant masses of creeping plants, make it difficult to see the fortifications from without. Within, aromatic shrubs, thorn bushes and fruit trees, tied together with the stinging cowitch, make it difficult to walk in any direction, while gigantic mango and tamarind trees throw a gloomy shade over the whole. It was simply insanity to attempt to beat for a dangerous beast in such a place, and we must have been infatuated to think of it. Surely it was a case of *quem dei perdere volunt priusquam dementant*, if ever there was one.

As I have said, both our shikaris were opposed to the plan, but when we insisted on it, they carried out our wishes loyally. They were two of the most remarkable men whom it has been my lot to meet, and very unlike each other. Tajoob Khan, my friend's lieutenant, was a large-boned, tall man of black complexion, with small beard parted in the middle; silent, cool and self-contained, almost phlegmatic until danger kindled him. He was dressed in a green shikar suit and wore in his belt a dearly beloved hunting knife, with which he had once saved his master's life and killed a tiger, burying it to the hilt in the brute's heart. His grateful master had the trusty blade fitted with a new, richly chased handle, bearing an inscription in Arabic characters to commemorate the event; and Tajoob Khan will never part with that weapon till he parts with life. My man, Banawat Beg, was fair-skinned, small and spare, but supple as a cat. He was dressed in a suit of plain khaki, and wore on his head a small cap with flaps to pull over his ears when the wind blew cold. I never saw a native so restless in mind and body as little Banawat Beg. He had an eye like a hawk, and appeared to know every beast, bird and tree in the jungle.

It would be difficult to say which of these men had been present at the death of most tigers, and there was a good deal of jealousy between them, but for once they were fully agreed as to the only practicable way of beating the fort. This was to divide it into two halves by a line of men armed with tom-toms and crackers, and beat down one half first and the other after. We got plenty of men without difficulty, for almost everyone in the town had to avenge the death of a fine goat or a favourite dog; but the tom-toms had all been engaged for a marriage at the house of a wealthy vakeel and we could not get one. But Banawat Beg, always fertile in resource, went to the coppersmith's lane and hired a hundred kettles and large handis, which when struck with hollow bamboos made an abominable din. As soon as we could get into suitable trees, the beat began, with the usual yelling and shouting so familiar to every shikari. Above all I could hear the sonorous voice of Tajoob Khan, challenging the panther to show his base visage and taunting him about certain scandals affecting the characters of his mother and aunts.

Suddenly the word 'bagh' (tiger or panther) rang out in the shrill tone of Banawat Beg and silenced everyone, and I could hear a heavy animal coming down at a brisk trot. The men with the kettles and crackers dropped their apparatus and went up the nearest trees like squirrels. Fortunately, one man tried to take his kettle up with him, but it slipped from his grasp and fell upon a large stone just in front of the beast, causing him to double back.

The beaters now began to advance again, and soon I descried the spotted form of a large panther slinking under the bush towards H, who was well posted over a piece of open ground, across which the panther would have to pass. He did so at a gentle trot, and H fired both barrels, but without effect. Then the beast started off at full speed in my direction. The bushes were so dense that I could not get a glimpse of him, but the noise he made among the fallen leaves let me guess his course exactly, and glancing ahead, I marked a small opening, not more than three inches wide, among the leaves of a thick corrinda bush, behind which I felt sure he would pass. I was right. For a moment his body darkened the hole, and I fired. A scuffle in the grass told me that the brute was in the throes of death. Reloading, I approached cautiously, and what was my disgust to see a huge hyena lying on the ground, shot through the heart. Yet I could have sworn that its skin was spotted when I first caught sight of it. Not one of us is secure against the dominion of the imagination over the senses.

The beat was taken up again, but nothing rose except a small jungle cat, which I stopped with a bullet through the head. After giving each of the kettle-wallas a little bamboo baksheesh for his cowardice, we beat the other side of the fort, but found nothing. Where was the panther? The general opinion appeared to be that our panther was indeed a hyena, but Tajoob Khan, coming up, silenced that by showing the head of a goat which he had found in the temple, still fresh and bleeding. 'A hyena,' he said, 'would have eaten the head first.' Suddenly Banawat Beg whispered, 'Dekkho,' and raising our eyes to a tower just above us, we beheld a large round face looking at us over the parapet. I raised my gun, and it disappeared.

What was to be done next? It would be madness to attempt to clamber up into the tower, even if it were possible. Banawat Beg solved the difficulty. 'Throw up a cracker,' he said. So a large Chinese cracker was lighted and slung into the tower. A moment's pause, then bang, bang, bang went the cracker, and in an instant, without a sound, an enormous panther cleared the parapet and landed in our midst from a height of twenty feet. We all, without exception, fell flat on our backs. It was the most ludicrous sight I ever saw. There we were, lying on the ground, looking at this great tom cat, with its back arched, its tail erect, its ears thrown back, and its whiskers standing out fiercely. It stood so for a moment, then, with a snarl, bounded away through the thicket. We were up and after it in a moment, laughing outright in our excitement. The incident had changed all our feelings and banished thoughts of danger.

We traced the beast to a dense patch of cactus, and taking our stand at one end, sent the beaters to the other. Out he came like greased lightning, as they say in America. H fired both barrels, but missed him. I could not fire for fear of hitting the beaters. The sport now became more like rabbit-shooting than anything else. From bush to bush the brute rushed, and the pop of my friend's gun was heard every minute. Tajoob Khan did not like this sort of thing and tried to restrain H, but he knocked down Tajoob Khan. I tried what I could do, but it was useless. He was too excited to listen to reason. Dreading the risk to my friend of wounding the panther in such circumstances, I waited for the chance of a sure shot. At last the panther passed me, and bounding over a high bush, gave a chance. I fired at him in mid-air, aiming for the heart; but the sun was in my eyes, and I only grazed his back. I had done just what I feared. His snorts and snarls told too plainly that he was getting very angry. At last he took refuge in a recess in the walls, and arching his back, stood at bay, with a very ugly look in his face.

H was in full pursuit, far ahead of us all. Frantically I shouted to him to be cautious, but it was too late. An excellent shot with either gun or rifle, and naturally fearless, he had lost his head. From less than twenty yards he fired both barrels at once. With a fearful roar I saw the brute dart out upon him. H sprang up a tree, for he was as nimble as a monkey; but got stuck in a fork about ten feet from the ground, and with horror I saw the panther spring upon him and bury his claws in his shoulders. The panther's own weight dragged him slowly down, while his claws ploughed through my poor friend's back. He fell to the ground, that brute, only to spring again. Twice and thrice the sickening process was repeated. I aimed at the panther's spine, just behind the shoulder, and pulled the trigger. My last ball cartridge missed fire! Catching a kettle from the hand of a beater, I rushed to within three yards of the brute and discharged it at him with all my force. It struck him full on the head and must have half stunned him, for he rushed sulkily under the old archway again.

Then I looked up for my friend. He was reduced to ribbons. Shreds of cloth and long strips of skin and flesh floated promiscuously upon the wind, which now began to howl through the branches of the trees. Madness took possession of me. I had fired my last ball, but I remembered how Sir Samuel Baker, in the same predicament, dropped a charging buffalo with a handful of small change. So I dived my hand into my pocket. There was no money there, only a penknife with a blade at each end. This would do. Anything would do. I took a cartridge loaded with small shot and drove one blade into it, so that the other blade pointed outwards, then putting it into my right barrel, I advanced towards the panther. 'Now do the same to me. Ha! Ha!' I cried, like an exultant maniac. The brute arched his back and prepared to spring. Then I fired. When the smoke cleared away, he was lying motionless on the ground. One blade and half the handle of the penknife stood out of his right eye, the other blade was in his brain. Fiercely I said to the men '*Utthao*,' and left him. Then we collected the shreds of my poor friend, and putting them into a coolie's basket, wended our way home in stern silence.

The panther was found to measure exactly seven feet and one inch, but the measurement was worthless, as poor H had cut off nearly the whole of the brute's tail with his first shot.

It is not usually done, but I may mention that the events narrated in the second part of this story never really happened, because we wisely decided not to beat for the panther, but to sit up for him over a live goat. We did so, but it was a very tame affair compared with the adventure which I have described. And after all, you cannot limit a shikari's adventures to things that have actually happened. It would rob the sporting world of half its best books, and many a sportsman hero of half his reputation. However, I promise not to do it again.

RECORDS OF SLAUGHTER

The following excerpts from two books on hunters and hunting remind us what shikar really was—often, bloodlust dressed up as 'sport'—and how it was celebrated and rewarded. Frederick Selous, the most famous of the 19th-century 'great White hunters' who is the subject of one of the books, for instance, has been glorified in popular literature and cinema for decades and received honours from the British colonial government. To this day, all the romanticizing masks the truth that Selous was a brutal, self-mythologizing professional hunter, poacher (for ivory) and mercenary. Primarily an elephant slaughterer, he killed hundreds of other animals as well, although his 'haul' of lions was considered 'modest'.

I. From *Big Game Shooting Records* (1932) by Edgar Barclay

'THERE is a romance and a devilishness about a tiger possessed by no other Indian animal.' So says Major-General A. E. Wardrop, and doubtless ninety-nine men out of every hundred, who have shot big game in India, will agree with him.

Tigers may be hunted with a line of elephants, the rifles either shooting from howdahs or from positions towards which the animals are driven; or they may be driven by beaters on foot. They are also shot by sitting up over a 'kill' or 'bait' or by watching for their arrival at pools where they are known to drink. In some parts where the cover is so continuous as to make driving impracticable, tigers are surrounded with nets and shot from outside or inside. Tiger shooting on foot is a most dangerous form of sport and though not usually systematically followed, it is sometimes resorted to.

Though the range of the tiger includes the Caucasus, Northern Persia, the Malay Peninsula, Sumatra, Java, Manchuria, Korea, etc., they are by no means plentiful in most of these countries and all the largest bags have been made within the Indian Empire.

The most productive tiger shoot appears to have occurred on the occasion of His Majesty the King's [George V] visit to Nepal in 1911. I take the following details of the wonderful sport enjoyed from Major-General Nigel Woodyatt's delightful book, *My Sporting Memories*:

> King George arrived in the Nepalese Tarai on 18th December, and killed two tigers on that date. With the exception of Sunday the 24th, His Majesty shot every day, leaving for Calcutta on the evening of 28th December. The total bag of King George and his suite was: tiger, 39; rhino, 18; bear, 4; barking deer, 11. On 20th December, in the Chitawan Valley, the day's bag amounted to: tiger, 7; bear, 2; rhinoceros, 2.

So far as I know, this day's bag of 7 tigers has only once been exceeded and that was in 1897 in the same country.

I quote 'The Field' of 5th June, 1897, for the details of the shoot in question:

> The shoot organised for Sir Baker Russell in Nepal during the last week of April by the kind permission of Sir Bir Sham Sher, Prime Minister of Nepal, appears to have been quite a phenomenal one in those parts. Unfortunately Sir Baker was himself unavoidably prevented from attending it, but the remainder of his party, which consisted of Colonel Garbott, C.O. of the 2nd Bengal Lancers; Major Ellis, R.E.; Major Bewicke-Copley (Sir Baker's military secretary); Major Smith-Dorrien; and Capt Browne Clayton, were lucky enough to secure twenty-three tigers, four cubs, and four leopards in fourteen days, besides a large quantity of various kinds of deer and birds.

Another bag of 7 tigers as the result of a single day's shooting was made by the Maharajah of

Cooch Behar's party in February, 1907. The following is the Maharajah's own description of the day's sport:

> The big shoot commenced on the 18th at Saralbhanga River. Our party consisted of Their Excellencies the Karl and Countess of Minto, Lady Eileen Elliot, Adam, Dunlop Smith, Crooke-Law, Bulkeley, Mackenzie, Graham, Rajey, Hammond, Lyall, Perrie, Sujey and myself. The first day was a glorious one. Before lunch we had three tigers padded and bagged another four in the afternoon, making in all seven tigers.

On the 16th of March, 1903, the Maharajah and his party, which at that time included Lord and

Lady Lonsdale, had another great day. Shooting the Reserves on the Jorai nullah, 5 tigers were bagged within twelve minutes, and on two separate occasions in 1902 the day's bag included

4 tigers. Between 1871 and 1907, 365 tigers were killed on the domains of the Maharajah of Cooch Behar, and it is interesting to note that during the same period the total number of leopards killed amounted to 311.

A notable bag to one rifle was made by Mr. R. P. Cobbold in the Central Provinces in 1897. Between March 1st and June 1st, Mr. Cobbold shot 11 tigers, 3 panthers, 4 buffaloes, 2 bison, 4 bears, 2 sambar and cheetah, making a total of 26 head of big game. The tigers were all obtained by driving and it is noteworthy that no animal wounded escaped. Mr. Cobbold was shooting with a .577 by Holland and Holland.

It is impossible to say definitely who has killed the greatest number of tigers. Of that great hunter, Sir Henry Ramsay, General Woodyatt says: 'I do not think he knew how many tiger he had shot. Probably several hundreds, and he never sat up for a tiger, if he could help it.' Mangal Khan, an Indian gentleman in the United Provinces, informed Sir John Hewett in 1921 or 1922 that he had seen over 900 tigers killed. Concerning Mangal Khan, General Woodyatt Writes: 'His ancestral home (he is a big land-holder) is in Pilibhit in the U.P. and the name he gave it is Sherpur (tiger town). A grand sportsman he is too. He has been known to clap his hands in order to turn a tiger to some other stop.'

Lieut-Colonel A. E. Ward, a mighty hunter with a vast knowledge of Indian game, and several of the Indian Princes must also have shot enormous numbers of tigers. H.H. the Maharajah of Bikaner is said to have shot 143 tigers up to the year 1930, and other men, though probably not very many, have killed over a hundred. But certainly one of the most noted tiger-hunters of modern times was Colonel Faunthorpe.

Col. Faunthorpe will always be remembered as one of the greatest figures in the annals of Indian sport. He excelled as a hog-hunter and as an all-round horseman and judge of horseflesh, whilst as a big game hunter and rifle shot, and particularly as a howdah shot, it is doubtful if he ever had a superior in India...In 1901 he was given charge of the district of Bahraich in Oudh where he enjoyed excellent shooting in the vast forests bordering on Nepal, and later he was posted to the Naini Tal district, which area included some of the finest tiger country in Northern India, and whilst there he organized many big shoots for distinguished visitors.

On being transferred to Muzaffamagar in 1905, Faunthorpe found himself in a district the ravines of which harboured a great number of panthers. With the assistance of the local Banjaras, who were first-rate men at tracking the panthers, he was most successful with these animals. Whenever a panther had been located word was sent to Faunthorpe, who immediately galloped to the spot; the Banjaras's dogs were then put into the panther's lair with a view to making it bolt, thus giving Faunthorpe the chance of a shot. This was carried out with such success that in a little over a year he is believed to have shot nearly a hundred panthers.

In 1907 he was appointed to Kheri and he subsequently enjoyed such big game shooting as falls to the lot of very few men in India. The exact number of tigers that Faunthorpe killed does not appear to be definitely known, but it is stated in that excellent biographical sketch which appeared in 'The

Hoghunter's Annual' that 'the number that he shot must be over three hundred'.

Faunthorpe's skill with the rifle was of a quite exceptional order. To be able to stand on the seat of a howdah and wait for the rush of a stag through a thinner patch of jungle, where a fleeting glance of its head might be obtained, and then to kill it with a shot through the neck at some 200 yds., is an accomplishment that few men would attempt with the slightest hope of success, but Faunthorpe has been known to do it. Not only was he brilliant as a lightning-shot at moving targets, but, if circumstances demanded, he was equally capable of infinite patience in firing, even with his game in full view. The following instance quoted from General Wardrop's classic, *Modern Pig-sticking*, well illustrates his capacity in this respect. Faunthorpe was beating for a well-known tigress whose mate had been killed by General Wardrop and a brother officer some years before. 'She dodged the line for hours, but, getting bored, climbed on to a stack of grass bundles…Faunthorpe aimed at her for about two minutes while his elephant swayed; at last he got a bead he was satisfied with, and knocked her over, stone dead, at a distance of over 200 yards.'

Before the War, Faunthorpe commanded the United Provinces Horse and at the outbreak of hostilities in 1914 he was on leave in England…On his return to India he became Commissioner at Lucknow and much of his spare time was then spent in conjunction with Arthur S. Vernay collecting specimens for the Natural History Museums of Chicago and New York. For the furtherance of this object he was placed on special duty, and in 1922-23 the Vernay-Faunthorpe Expedition was carried out. With the assistance of the Government of India, the Ruling Princes, and Local Governments, this expedition was a great success and a representative collection of the big game animals of India, Burma and Nepal was obtained.

In connection with this work Col. Faunthorpe also shot some lions in the Gir country in Kathiawar and he is one of the very few men who have ever done so. Mr G M. Dyott, FRGS, who accompanied the expedition as photographer, obtained some excellent cinematograph pictures for use in the Museum Lecture Hall.

II. From *Life of Frederick Courtney Selous* (1919), by John Guille Millais:

[Frederick] Selous has always been regarded by the British public as the first lion-hunter of all time...[but] being as truthful as he was modest, he always entirely disclaimed any great prowess as a lion-hunter and said what was true, that many men had killed a far greater number of lions than himself. It was only on particular occasions like the last adventure described that he went out of his way to shoot lions that had become troublesome and dangerous, but at all times he never declined a fight when he was lucky enough to meet lions, whether he was himself afoot or accompanied by dogs. If he had wished to make a great bag of lions, doubtless he could have done so; but he never wished to pose as a lion-hunter like Jules Gerard and others, and so his total bag was modest. Actually, he himself shot thirty-one lions and assisted in the destruction of eleven others [.]

The title, therefore, of being 'the greatest lion-hunter' even if we admit the desirability of using superlatives seems to belong to the man or men who by perfectly fair means and taking risks the same as Selous himself did have shot the greatest number of lions. Wherefore, I give a few particulars.

As Selous himself has said, probably the greatest lion-hunter within his experience of South Africa was Petrus Jacobs, who killed in his life chiefly with the assistance of dogs well over one hundred lions, and was himself badly mauled when he was over seventy-three years of age.

Probably the greatest all-round hunter of African game now living is William Judd, now a professional hunter in British East Africa. In South and East Africa he has killed forty-eight lions and been in at the death of forty-three others. In giving me these particulars, he says: 'I have never had any really narrow squeaks from lions with the exception of the time I was out with Selous on the Gwasin Guishu plateau.' It may be remarked that this immunity is due to the fact that he is a magnificent shot. He considers the buffalo a far more dangerous opponent.

A. B. Percival, Game Warden, is said to have shot fifty lions during his residence in British East Africa. In Somaliland, hunting almost exclusively for lions, Colonel Curtis in one season killed twenty-seven, and in the same time Colonel Paget and Lord Wolverton nearly as many. Captain Mellis also in one season accounted for twenty-one lions, and several other British sportsmen have killed twenty in one trip in that part of Africa.

What a man does and what he could actually do in the way of lion-killing is perhaps beside the question. A great lion-hunter like Sir Alfred Pease, both an admirable shot and a superb horseman, has only killed fourteen lions and joined in eleven 'partnerships', but this in no way represents the number of lions he *could* have killed had he wished to do so. Being of an unselfish disposition it was ever his pleasure, since he had killed all the specimens he wanted, to give his friends who were anxious to shoot lions every opportunity of doing so. In fact, on many occasions, at his farm on the Kapiti Plains, he himself rounded up the lions for other men to kill, and simply looked on standing ready in case of trouble. 'Lions were so plentiful at my place on the Athi,' he writes, 'that one party killed in one day (1911-12) fourteen lions. I have often spared a fine lion to give a guest a chance, and have never seen him again. The finest lion I ever saw was an enormous black-maned fellow. I prevented my son-in-law from firing at him, as I wished President Roosevelt to get him during his stay with me. Subsequently, I think a German got his skin; but in reality, I believe H.D. Hill killed him after a German party and the Brothers Hill had fought a great battle with him near Lukania.'

Sir Alfred then goes on to give particulars of the astounding performances of the Brothers Harold D. Hill and Clifford Hill, who if they wished it, which they probably do not, are justly entitled to the right of being called the first of modern lion-hunters.

> 'Harold Hill managed my farm in British East Africa for several years. He told me a year ago that he had, since he had been there, 1906-15, on my farms of Theki and Katanga, and on his own and his brother's farms, Katelembo and Wami, himself killed one hundred and thirty-six lions. I think this figure will include a very great number of what I should call "partnerships". His brother Clifford must have killed as many or more than Harold, for he has done more actual hunting. Clifford

> Hill acted as professional hunter to many "safaris" but you could absolutely rely on any statement he made, although it is not likely that he believed, himself, in counting heads of game killed. I should not be surprised if these two brothers have not been in at the death of over three hundred lions during their residence in East Africa.
>
> 'Some years ago Lord Delamere had, I think, killed between fifty and sixty lions. Many of these (over twenty) were killed in Somaliland. Some of these were "ridden" and others may have been killed at night, but Delamere was, nevertheless, a keen and fearless hunter.'

Commenting on the different methods of hunting lions in Somaliland and British East Africa, Sir Alfred says: 'The Somaliland method of hunting (i.e. following a fresh spoor on hard ground till the lion was viewed) was, in my opinion, the best test of skill and sporting qualities, since you tracked and did the whole thing on your own initiative. Personally, I enjoyed most the B.E.A. work. You saw much more of the beasts, and I loved galloping and rounding them up for others to kill as much as I enjoyed anything in my whole life.'

Paul Rainey's methods of hunting lions with a large pack of hounds can hardly come into the true category of lion-hunting where risks are taken. The dogs, it is true, were often killed or wounded; but as a friend who had taken part in these hunts remarked, 'It was just like rat -hunting, and about as dangerous.' It is true that one man, George Swartz (formerly a German waiter at the Norfolk Hotel, Nairobi), was killed in one of these hunts, but the accident was singular. Swartz was a very bold fellow and moved close in in thick bush when the dogs had a lion at bay one day in the Kedong in 1912. The lion 'broke bay', and either intentionally charged Swartz or ran over to him by chance as he worked the cinema-camera. The beast gave the man one bite in the stomach and then left him, but the unfortunate fellow died shortly afterwards of his wounds. Paul Rainey claims to have killed over two hundred lions with his dogs.

It has always been the custom amongst hunters that he who draws first blood from any animal even if it is only a scratch is entitled to the beast when subsequently killed. It is a good law on the whole, but there are many instances where it is scarcely justified, that is to say, when the first shooter has done little beyond slightly injuring the animal and the second hunter has stood 'all the racket', and killed the beast at the risk of his life. Here is such an example given to me by Sir Alfred Pease:

'I lent my rifle (a .256 Mannlicher) to a friend, also my horse to gallop and round up a lion, whilst I kept watch on a bush where another had hidden, not being able owing to dongas to get round him. My friend soon jumped off and fired two or three shots at the first lion, which worked round and came and lay down under a thin thorn-bush less than a hundred yards from my position. I then went towards the bush and the lion charged me. I fired twice at about sixty and fifteen yards, and the beast, a very fine black-maned lion, fell dead to my second barrel.

'My friend now came up, and to my disgust said excitedly, "My lion!" I said, "Mine, I think?" He said, "No; I had first blood!" I had no idea the lion had been hit, but when we examined him there was a .256 hole in his back ribs. I was rather sore, as I had stood the racket; but it was the rule. I killed the second lion in a quarter of an hour. We did not quarrel, however, and he gave my daughter the skin of the first lion, which was nice of him.'

SHOOTING A CUB

JAMES INGLIS

Inglis, an indigo planter in the Terai region along the Bihar-Nepal border, was a flamboyant, colourful and sometimes contradictory man. His opinion of the 'heathen natives' was often outrageous even for his time, but he appears to have done good work as famine commissioner of Bhagalpur during the Bihar famine of 1874. As a hunter he comes across in his own writing as a man with a juvenile passion for murder and mayhem. In this appalling account, an extract from Tent Life in Tiger Land *(1892), his friends and he are like a nasty teen gang in the jungles of the Awadh region of North India.*

I have been out after tiger on foot but on few occasions. One was in the sal jungles in Oudh. A neighbour of mine, a most intimate and dear friend, whom I had nicknamed the 'General', and a young friend, Fullerton, were with me. A tigress and cub were reported to be in a dense patch of nurkool jungle, on the banks of the creek which divided the General's cultivation from mine. The nurkool is a tall, feathery-looking cane, very much relished by elephants. It grows in dense brakes, and generally in damp, boggy ground, affording complete shade and shelter for wild animals, and is a favourite haunt of pig, wolf, tiger, and buffalo.

We had only one elephant, the use of which Fullerton had got from a neighbouring Babu. It was not a staunch animal, so we put one of our men in the howdah, with a plentiful supply of bombs, a kind of native firework, enclosed in a clay case, which burns like a huge squib, and sets fire to the jungle. Along with the elephant we had a line of about one hundred coolies, and several men with drums and tom-toms. Fullerton took the side nearest the river, as it was possible the brute might sneak out that way, and make her escape along the bank. The General's shikari remained behind, in rear of the line of beaters, in case the tigress might break the line, and try to escape by the rear. My Gomasta [clerk], the General, and myself, then took up positions behind trees all along the side of the glade or dell in which was the bit of nurkool jungle.

It was a small basin, sloping gently down to the creek from the sal jungle, which grew up dark and thick all around. A margin of close sward, as green and level as a billiard-table, encircled the glade, and in the basin the thick nurkool grew up close, dense, and high, like a rustling barrier of living green. In the centre was the decaying stump of a mighty forest monarch, with its withered arms stretching out their bleached and shattered lengths far over the waving feathery tops of the nurkool.

The General and I cut down some branches, which we stuck in the ground before us. I had a fallen log in front of me, on which I rested my guns. I had a naked khukri ready to hand, for we were sure that the tigress was in the swamp, and I did not know what might happen. I did not half like this style of shooting, and wished I was safely seated on the back of my faithful old Bhaugulpore elephant. The General whistled as a sign for the beat to begin. The coolies dashed into the thicket. The stately elephant slowly forced his ponderous body through the crashing swaying brake. The rattle of the tom-toms and rumble of the drums, mingled with the hoarse shouts and cries of the beaters, the fiery rush of sputtering flame, and the loud report as each bomb burst, with the huge volumes of blinding smoke, and the scent of gunpowder that came on the breeze, told us that the bombs were doing their work. The jungle was too green to burn; but the fireworks raised a dense sulphurous smoke, which penetrated among the tall stems of the nurkool, and by the waving and crashing of the tall swaying canes, the heaving of the howdah, with the red pugree of the peon, and the gleaming of the staves and weapons, we could see that the beat was advancing.

As they neared the large withered tree in the centre of the brake, the elephant curled up his trunk and trumpeted. This was a sure sign there was game afoot. We could see the peon in the howdah leaning over the front bar, and eagerly peering into the recesses of the thicket before him. He lit one of the bombs, and hurled it right up against the bole of the tree. It hissed and sputtered, and the smoke came curling over the reeds in dense volumes. A roar followed that made the valley ring again. We heard a swift rush. The elephant turned tail, and fled madly away, crashing through the matted brake that crackled and tore under his tread. The howdah swayed wildly, and the peon clung tenaciously on to the top bar with all his desperate might. The mahout, or elephant-driver, tried in vain to check the rush of the frightened brute, but after repeated sounding whacks on the head he got him to stop, and again turn round. Meantime the cries and shouting had ceased, and the beaters came pouring from the jungle by twos and threes, like the frightened inhabitants of some hive or antheap.

Some in their hurry came tumbling out headlong; others, with their faces turned backwards to see if anything was in pursuit of them, got entangled in the reeds, and fell prone on their hands and knees. One fellow had just emerged from the thick cover, when another terrified compatriot dashed out in blind unreasoning fear close behind him. The first one thought the tiger was on him. With one howl of anguish and dismay he fled as fast as he could run, and the General and I, who had witnessed the episode, could not help uniting in a resounding peal of laughter, that did more to bring the scared coolies to their senses than anything else we could have done.

There was no doubt now of the tiger's whereabouts. One of the beaters gave us a most graphic description of its appearance and proportions. According to him it was bigger than an elephant, had a mouth as wide as a coal scuttle, and eyes that glared like a thousand suns. From all this we inferred that there was a full-grown tiger or tigress in the jungle. We re-formed the line of beaters, and once more got the elephant to enter the patch. The same story was repeated. No sooner did they get near the old tree, than the tigress again charged with a roar, and our valiant coolies and the chicken-hearted elephant vacated the jungle as fast as their legs could carry them. This happened twice or thrice. The tigress charged every time, but would not leave her safe cover. The elephant wheeled round at every charge, and would not show fight. Fullerton got into the howdah, and fired two shots into the spot where the tigress was lying.

He did not apparently wound her, but the reports brought her to the charge once more, and the elephant, by this time fairly tired of the game, and thoroughly demoralised with fear, bolted right away, and nearly cracked poor Fullerton's head against the branch of a tree.

We could plainly see, that with only one elephant we could never dislodge the tigress, so making the coolies beat up the patch in lines, we shot several pig and a hog-deer, and adjourned for something to eat by the bank of the creek. We had been trying to oust the tigress for over four hours, but she was as wise as she was savage, and refused to become a mark for our bullets in the open. After lunch we made another grand attempt. We promised the coolies double pay if they roused the tigress to flight. The elephant was forced again into the nurkool very much against his will, and the mahout was promised a reward if we got the tigress. The din this time was prodigious, and strange to say they got quite close up to the big withered tree without the usual roar and charge. This seemed somewhat to stimulate the beaters and the old elephant. The coolies redoubled their cries, smote among the reeds with their heavy staves, and shouted encouragement to each other. Eight in the middle of the line, as it seemed to us from the outside, there was then a fierce roar and a mighty commotion. Cries of fear and consternation arose, and forth poured the coolies again, helter skelter, like so many rabbits from a warren when a weasel or ferret has entered the burrow. Right before me a huge old boar and a couple of sows came plunging forth. I let them get on a little distance from the brake, and then with my 'Express' [rifle] I rolled over the boar and one of his companions and just then the General shouted out to me, 'There's the tiger!'

I looked in the direction of his levelled gun, and there at the edge of the jungle was a handsome, half-grown tiger cub, beautifully marked, his tail switching angrily from side to side, and his twitching retracted lips and bristling moustache drawn back like those of a vicious cat, showing his gleaming polished fangs and teeth.

The General had a fine chance, took a steady aim, and shot the young savage right through the heart. The handsome young tiger gave one convulsive leap into the air and fell on his side stone dead. We could not help a cheer, and shouted for Fullerton, who soon came running up. We got some coolies together, but they were frightened to go near the dead animal, as we could plainly hear the old vixen inside snarling and snapping, for all the world like an angry terrier. We heard her half-suppressed growl and snarl. She was evidently in a fine temper. How we wished for a couple of staunch elephants to hunt her out of the cane. It was no use, however, the elephant would not go near the jungle again. The coolies were thoroughly scared, and had got plenty of pork and venison to eat, so did not care for anything else. We collected a lot of tame buffaloes, and tried to drive them through the jungle, but the coolies had lost heart, and would not exert themselves; so we had to content ourselves with the cub, and very reluctantly had to leave the savage mother alone. I never saw a brute charge so persistently as she did. She always rushed forward with a succession of roars, and was very wary and cunning. She never charged home, she did not even touch the elephant or any of the coolies, but evidently trusted to frighten her assailants away by a bold show and a fierce outcry.

We went back two days after with five elephants, which with great difficulty we had got together, and thoroughly beat the patch of nurkool, killed a lot of pig and a couple of deer, shot an alligator, and destroyed over thirty of its eggs, which we discovered on the bank of the creek; and returning in the evening shot a nilghai and a black buck, but the tigress had disappeared. She was gone, and we grumbled sorely at our bad luck.

THE CHARGE OF THE TIGRESS

DAVID WILSON

An episode from Burma, circa 1909:

[THERE is] an episode in the 'Shikar Book' of C.W. Allan about a tigress, which for various reasons may be transcribed:

'...14th April. I started up to inspect the Banbwebin fire line—accompanied by my wife, an Indian and two Burmans...After we had gone about five miles up the path, we heard bamboos being broken. The Burmans said there must be a herd of wild elephants feeding on the flowered bamboos. I thought they might possibly be bison or a rhinoceros, so walked on to see what they really were. The Indian was walking ahead of me, and I was following, looking down the side of the hill from which the sound of the bamboos being broken came, when Barhan, the Indian peon, stopped and said 'Bagh' (tiger). I looked up and saw the tiger crossing the path about sixty paces ahead of me, so had a quick shot at it. On which it turned round and came down the hill straight at me...My wife, who was just behind me, on seeing it come down the hill, called out, 'It is coming!'

It came on, and when [it was] less than thirty paces from me I fired the second barrel and knocked it over. After receiving the shot it fell and lay on the ground, trying to drag itself towards us...It put its head up and snarled and showed its teeth....The Burmans, who were very excited, kept on saying, 'Give it another shot, quick, or it will get up and go for us!' So after a bit I put in another cartridge and walked up a few paces and gave it a bullet in the chest and finished it off.

'After giving it a shot in the chest I walked round and got above it, and then approached cautiously with my gun at the ready to give it another shot if necessary; but after throwing a clod or two of earth at it, and finding that it did not move, I walked up and pulled its tail, and when I found that it was dead I called out to my wife, who was close by all the time, and she came up.

'We found it to be a tigress—measuring eight feet and five inches as she lay. The first shot had missed and the second caught her at the point of the shoulder. On looking at my gun, I found that the 200 yards leaf-sight had got pushed up, and that had made me shoot high. I was carrying the gun in my right hand, but holding it across my back, and in pulling it forward in a hurry, the leaf-sight had got pushed up, and I did not notice it in the excitement of the moment...

'Maung Nita, one of the Burmans who was with me, said, "Sir, if you had not finished her with the second shot we would all have been lying kicking on the ground."

'As three men were not able to lift her, my wife rode back to our camp and called other eight men, and they slung [the tigress] on poles and carried her into camp.

'On dissecting the tigress, I found that she had nothing in her stomach and appeared to have had no food for some time. She was evidently out shikaring (hunting), and was after the animals that I had heard breaking bamboos.'

—

In a private letter to me at the time, Mr Allan Wrote, 'Had I missed the second shot she would have had us…She was very angry. She was hungry and meant business. On opening her we found that she had evidently not had a meal for some days.'

This illustrates a truth which is often forgotten by us. The big beasts live from hand to mouth, like improvident working men. A dog may bury a bone, a tiger return to a kill, and a leopard has been known to put half a corpse or an unfinished bit of venison up a tree for security. But beyond the next meal they never look. It is only the insects of the universe, like ants and bees, or such animals as squirrels, that practise thrift. Hence arose the Jewish proverb about considering the ways of the ant in order to be wise. There is no such lesson to be learned from the cat. One can be sorry for the tigress all the same. Think of her empty stomach, and perhaps hungry cubs in her lair; and then this big, strong Englishman, with his diabolical machinery in his hand, molesting her as she was stalking the wild cattle. 'She meant business,' said he. Of course she did. Did anyone think she was hunting for amusement?

No matter now! Her body lies inert enough, a subject for their inquisitive knives[.]

Put yourself in the skin of that tigress, if you can. Think what a gunshot means to a wild beast, and consider how, when fired at, she 'faced the music' in the real sense of that phrase, and went 'straight at the guns', as gallantly as the Light Brigade at Balaklava. As even the enemy notes—'After receiving the shot, it fell and lay on the ground, trying to drag itself towards us…It put its head up and snarled and showed its teeth.' Was she not like the glorious Englishman, who, when his legs were cut away, still fought upon his stumps? Did any hero of Homer's ever surpass that sorely-stricken tigress? Could any living creature have done more? And yet there are men to be found who call the big cats cowards! I never heard Mr Allan do that, nor any other man of sense who knew them well at first hand.

No wonder tigers flourished in the days of old. It is the invention of gunpowder, and then of breechloaders, that has handicapped them hopelessly. The long guerilla war between them and us has lasted for scores of millenniums; but the end is now in sight. Let us not libel the brave that are doomed to disappear. Let us not rail at the conquered. If they were fierce and strong, they were not cruel. As Nature made them, so they filled their function. They came, and chased, and conquered, impelled by hunger: and now that their hour has come they are going away. The day is at hand when the big wild cats shall all be as completely extinct as the vanished giants that wallowed in the primeval slime.

THE TEMPLE TIGER

JIM CORBETT

To conclude this section of real-life encounters, one of Corbett's most famous stories, and arguably his best.

IT is not possible for those who have never lived in the upper reaches of the Himalayas to have any conception of the stranglehold that superstition has on the people who inhabit that sparsely populated region. The dividing line between the superstitions of simple uneducated people who live on high mountains, and the beliefs of sophisticated educated people who live at lesser heights, is so faint that it is difficult to determine where the one ends and the other begins. If therefore you are tempted to laugh at the credulity of the actors in the tale I am going to tell, I would ask you to pause for a moment and try to define the difference between superstition as exemplified in my tale, and your beliefs in the faith you have been brought up in.

Shortly after the Kaiser's war, Robert Bellairs and I were on a shooting trip in the interiors of Kumaon and we camped one September evening at the foot of Trisul, where we were informed that eight hundred goats were sacrificed each year to the demon of Trisul. With us we had fifteen of the keenest and the most cheerful hillmen I have ever been associated with on a shikar. One of these men, Bala Singh, a Garhwali, had been with me for years and had accompanied me on many expeditions. It was his pride and pleasure when on shikar to select and carry the heaviest of my loads and, striding at the head of the other men, enliven the march with snatches of song. Around the campfire at night the men always sang part-songs before going to sleep, and during that first night, at the foot of Trisul, the singing lasted longer than usual and was accompanied by clapping of hands, shouting, and the beating of tin cans.

It had been our intention to camp at this spot and explore the country around for baral and thar, and we were very surprised as we sat down to breakfast next morning to see our men making preparations to strike camp. On asking for an explanation we were told that the site we had camped on was not suitable: that it was damp; that the drinking water was bad; that fuel was difficult to get; and, finally, that there was a better site two miles away.

I had six Garhwalis to carry my luggage and I noticed that it was being made up into five head-loads, and that Bala Singh was sitting apart near the campfire with a blanket over his head and shoulders. After breakfast I walked over to him, and noted as I did so that all the other men had stopped work and were watching me very intently. Bala Singh saw me coming and made no attempt to greet me, which was very unusual, and to all my questions he returned the one answer—that he was not ill. That day we did our two-mile march in silence, Bala Singh bringing up the rear and moving like a man who was walking in his sleep, or who was under the influence of drugs.

It was now quite apparent that whatever had happened to Bala Singh was affecting the other fourteen men, for they were performing their duties without their usual cheerfulness, and all of them had a strained and frightened look on their faces. While the 40-lb tent Robert and I shared was being erected, I took my Garhwali servant Mothi Singh—who had been with me for twenty-five years—aside and demanded to be told what was wrong with Bala Singh. After a lot of hedging and evasive answers I eventually got Mothi Singh's story, which, when it came, was short and direct. 'While we were sitting round the campfire last night and singing,' Mothi Singh said, 'the demon of Trisul entered Bala Singh's mouth and he swallowed him.' Mothi Singh went on to say that they had shouted and beaten tin cans to try to drive the demon out of Bala Singh, but that they had not succeeded in doing so, and that now nothing could be done about it.

Bala Singh was sitting apart, with the blanket still draped over his head. He was out of earshot of the other men, so, going over to him, I asked him to tell me what had happened the previous night. For a long minute Bala Singh looked up at me with eyes full of distress, and then in a hopeless tone of voice he said: 'Of what use is it, Sahib, for me to tell you what happened last night, for you will not believe me.' 'Have I ever,' I asked, 'disbelieved you?' 'No,' he said, 'no, you have never disbelieved me, but this is a matter that you will not understand.' 'Whether I understand it or not,' I said, 'I want you to tell me exactly what happened.' After a long silence Bala Singh said: 'Very well, Sahib, I will tell you what happened. You know that in our hill-songs it is customary for one man to sing the verse, and for all the other men present to join in the chorus. Well, while I was singing a verse of one of our songs last night the demon of Trisul jumped into my mouth, and though I tried to eject him, he slipped down my throat into my stomach. The other men saw my struggle with the demon, for the fire was burning brightly, and they tried to drive him away by shouting and beating tin cans; but,' he added with a sob, 'the demon would not go.' 'Where is the demon now?' I asked. Placing his hand on the pit of his stomach, Bala Singh answered with great conviction, 'He is here, Sahib, here; I can feel him moving about.'

--

Robert had spent the day prospecting the ground to the west of our camp and had shot a thar, of which he had seen several. After dinner we sat long into the night reviewing the situation. We had planned for, and looked forward to, this shoot for many months. It had taken Robert seven days' and me ten days' hard walking to reach our shooting ground, and on the night of our arrival Bala Singh had swallowed the demon of Trisul. What our personal opinions were on this subject did not matter, but what did matter was that every man in camp was convinced that Bala Singh had a demon in his stomach, and they were frightened of him and were shunning his company. To carry on a month's shoot under these conditions was not possible, and Robert very reluctantly agreed with me that the only thing to be done was for me to return to Naini Tal with Bala Singh, while he carried on with the shoot alone. So next morning I packed up my things, and after an early breakfast with Robert, set off on my ten-day walk back to Naini Tal.

Bala Singh, a perfect specimen of a man of about thirty years of age, had left Naini Tal full of the joy of life; now he returned silent, with a strained look in his eyes, and with the appearance of one who had lost all interest in life. My sisters, one of whom had been a medical missionary, did all they could for him. Friends from far and near came to visit him, but he just sat at the door of his house, never speaking unless spoken to. The civil surgeon of Naini Tal, Colonel Cooke, a man of great experience and a close friend of the family, came to visit Bala Singh at my request. His verdict after a long and painstaking examination was that Bala Singh was in perfect physical condition, and that he could ascribe no reason for the man's apparent depression.

A few days later I had a brainwave. There was in Naini Tal at that time a very eminent Indian doctor and I thought if I could get him to examine Bala Singh and, after he had done so, tell him about the demon and persuade him to assure Bala Singh that there was no demon in his stomach, he would be able to cure him of his trouble, for in addition to being a Hindu, the doctor was himself a hillman. My brainwave, however, did not work out as I had hoped and anticipated, for as soon as he saw the sick man the doctor appeared to get suspicious and when in reply to some shrewd questions he learnt from Bala Singh that the demon of Trisul was in his stomach, he stepped away from him hurriedly and turning to me said, 'I am sorry you sent for me, for I can do nothing for this man.'

There were two men from Bala Singh's village in Naini Tal. Next day I sent for them. They knew what was wrong with Bala Singh for they had come to see him several times, and at my request they agreed to take him home. Provided with funds the three men started on their eight-day journey next morning. Three weeks later the two men returned and made their report to me.

Bala Singh had accomplished the journey without any trouble. On the night of his arrival home, and while his relatives and friends were gathered around him, he had suddenly announced to the assembly that the demon wanted to be released to return to Trisul, and that the only way this could be accomplished was for him to die. 'So,' my informants concluded, 'Bala Singh just lay down and died, and next morning we assisted at his cremation.'

Superstition, I am convinced, is a mental complaint similar to measles in that it attacks an individual or a community while leaving others immune. I therefore do not claim any credit for not contracting, while living on the upper reaches of the Himalayas, the virulent type of superstition that Bala Singh died of. But though I claim I am not superstitious, I can give no explanation for the experience I met with at the bungalow while hunting the Champawat tiger and the scream I heard coming from the deserted Thak village. Nor can I give any explanation for my repeated failures while engaged in one of the most interesting tiger hunts I have ever indulged in, which I shall now relate.

2

No one who has visited Dabidhura is ever likely to forget the view that is to be obtained from the Rest House built near the summit of 'God's Mountain' by one who, quite evidently, was a lover of scenery. From the veranda of the little three-roomed house, the hill falls steeply away to the valley of the Panar river. Beyond this valley, the hills rise ridge upon ridge until they merge into the eternal snows which, until the advent of aircraft, formed an impenetrable barrier between India and her hungry northern neighbours.

A bridle-road running from Naini Tal, the administrative headquarters of Kumaon, to Loharghat, an outlying subdivision on her eastern border, passes through Dabidhura, and a branch of this road connects Dabidhura with Almora. I was hunting the Panar man-eating leopard—about which I shall tell you later— in the vicinity of this latter road when I was informed by a road overseer, on his way to Almora, that the leopard had killed a man at Dabidhura. So to Dabidhura I went.

The western approach to Dabidhura is up one of the steepest roads in Kumaon. The object the man who designed this road had in view was to get to the top by the shortest route possible, and this he accomplished by dispensing with hairpin bends and running his road straight up the face of the eight-thousand-foot mountain. After panting up this road on a hot afternoon in April, I was sitting on the veranda of the Rest House drinking gallons of tea and feasting my eyes on the breathtaking view, when the priest of Dabidhura came to see me. When two years previously I had been hunting the Champawat man-eater, I had made friends with this frail old man, who officiated at the little temple nestling in the shadow of the great rock that had made Dabidhura a place of pilgrimage, and for whose presence in that unusual place I shall hazard no guess. When passing the temple a few minutes earlier I had made the customary offering which had been acknowledged by a nod by the old priest who was at his devotions. These devotions finished, the priest crossed the road that runs between the temple and the Rest House and accepting a cigarette sat down on the floor of the veranda with his back against the wall for a comfortable chat. He was a friendly old man with plenty of time on his hands, and as I had done all the walking I wanted to that day, we sat long into the evening chatting and smoking.

From the priest I learnt that I had been misinformed by the road overseer about the man alleged to have been killed at Dabidhura the previous night by the man-eater. The alleged victim, a herdsman on his way from Almora to a village south of Dabidhura, had been the priest's guest the previous night. After the evening meal the herdsman had elected, against the priest's advice, to sleep on the chabutra (platform) of the temple. Round about midnight, when the rock was casting a shadow over the temple, the man-eater crept up and, seizing the man's ankles, attempted to drag him off the platform. Awakening with a yell, the man grabbed a smouldering bit of wood from the nearby lire, and beat off the leopard. His yell brought the priest and several other men to his rescue and the combined force drove the animal away. The man's wounds were not serious, and after they had received rough-and-ready treatment at the hands of the bania, whose shop was near the temple the herdsman continued his journey.

On the evidence of the priest I decided to remain at Dabidhura. The temple and the bania's shop were daily visited by men from the surrounding villages. These men would spread the news of my arrival and—knowing where I was to be found—I would immediately be informed of any kills of human beings, or of animals, that might take place in the area.

As the old priest got up to leave me that evening I asked him if it would be possible for me to get some shooting in the locality, for my men had been without meat for many days and there was none to be purchased at Dabidhura. 'Yes,' he answered, 'there is the temple tiger.' On my assuring him that I had no desire to shoot his tiger he rejoined with a laugh, 'I have no objection, Sahib, to your *trying* to shoot this tiger, but neither you nor anyone else will ever succeed in *killing* it.' And that is how I came to hear of the Dabidhura temple tiger, which provided me with one of the most interesting shikar experiences I have ever had.

3

The morning following my arrival at Dabidhura I went down the Loharghat road to see if I could find any trace of the man-eater, or learn anything about it in the village adjoining the road, for the leopard was alleged to have gone in that direction after its attack on the man at the temple. On my return to the Rest House for a late lunch I found a man in conversation with my servant. This man informed me he had learnt from the priest that I wanted to do some shooting and he said he could show me a jarao—the hillman's name for sambar—with horns as big as the branches of an oak tree. Hill sambar do on occasions grow very fine horns—one had been shot in Kumaon some time previously with horns measuring forty-seven inches—and as a big animal would not only provide my men with meat but would also provide a meat ration for all at Dabidhura, I told the man I would accompany him after lunch.

Some months previously I had been to Calcutta on a short visit, and one morning walked into Manton's, the gunmaker's shop. On a glass showcase near the door was a rifle. I was looking at the weapon when the manager, who was an old friend of mine, came up. He informed me that the rifle, a .275 by Westley Richards, was a new model which the makers were anxious to introduce on the Indian market for hill shooting. The rifle was a beauty and the manager had little difficulty in persuading me to buy it on the understanding that if it did not suit me I would be at liberty to return it. So when I set out with my village friend that evening to shoot his jarao with horns as big as the branches of an oak tree, I was carrying my brand-new rifle.

To the south of Dabidhura the hill is less steep than it is to the north and we had proceeded in this direction through oak and scrub jungle for about two miles when we came to a grassy knoll with an extensive view of the valley below. Pointing to a small patch of grass—surrounded by dense jungle—on the left-hand side of the valley, my guide informed me that the jarao came out to graze on this patch of grass morning and evening. He further informed me that there was a footpath on the right-hand side of the valley which he used when on his way to or from Dabidhura, and that it was from this path he was accustomed to seeing the jarao. The rifle I was carrying was sighted to five hundred yards and guaranteed to be dead accurate, and as the distance between the path and the jarao's feeding ground appeared to be only about three hundred yards, I decided to go down the path and wait for a shot.

While we had been talking I had noticed some vultures circling to our left front. On drawing my companion's attention to them he informed me there was a small village in a fold of the hill in that direction and suggested that the vultures were possibly interested in some domestic animal that had died in the village. However, he said we would soon know what had attracted the birds, for our way lay through the village. The 'village' consisted of a single grass hut, a cattle shed, and an acre or so of terraced fields from which the crops had recently been cut. In one of these fields, separated from the hut and cattle shed by a ten-foot wide rainwater channel, vultures were tearing the last shreds of flesh from the skeleton of some large animal. A man walked out of the hut as we approached and, after greeting us, asked where I had come from and when I had arrived. On my telling him that I had come from Naini Tal to try to shoot the man-eating leopard and that I had arrived at Dabidhura the previous day, he expressed great regret at not having known of my arrival. 'For you could then,' he said, 'have shot the tiger that killed my cow.' He went on to tell me that he had tethered his fifteen head of cattle in the field, on which the vultures were pulling about the skeleton, the previous night, to fertilize it, and that during the night a tiger had come and killed one of the cows. He had no firearms and as there was no within reach to whom he could appeal to shoot the tiger, he had gone to a village where a man lived who had the contract for collecting hides and skins in that area. This man had removed the hide of the cow two hours before my arrival, and the vultures had then carried out their function. When I asked the man whether he had known that there was a tiger in the locality and, if so, why he had tethered his cattle out in the open at night, he surprised me by saying there had always been a tiger on the Dabidhura hill, but that up to the previous night it had never molested cattle.

As I moved away from the hut the man asked me where I was going and when I told him I was going to try to shoot the jarao on the far side of the valley, he begged me to leave the jarao alone for the present and to shoot the tiger. 'My holding is small and the land poor, as you can see,' he said, 'and if the tiger kills my cows, on which I depend for a living, my family and I will starve.'

While we had been talking, a woman had come up the hill with a gharra of water on her head, followed a little later by a girl carrying a bundle of green grass and a boy carrying a bundle of dry sticks: four people living on an acre or so of poor land and a few pints of milk—for hill cattle give little milk—sold to the bania at Dabidhura. Little wonder, then, that the man was so anxious for *me* to shoot the tiger.

The vultures had destroyed the kill. This did not matter, however, for there was no heavy cover near the field where the tiger could have lain up and seen the vultures at their work, so he would be almost certain to return, for he had not been disturbed at his feed the previous night. My guide was also keen on my trying to shoot the tiger in preference to his jarao, so, telling the two men to sit down, I set off to try to find out in which direction the tiger had gone, for there were no trees on which I could sit near the field, and it was my intention to intercept the tiger on its way back. The hill was criss-crossed with cattle paths but the ground was too hard to show pug-marks, and after circling round the village twice I eventually tried the rainwater channel. Here on the soft damp ground I found the pug-marks of a big male tiger. These pug-marks showed that the tiger had gone up the channel after his feed, so it was reasonable to assume that he would return the same way. Growing out of the bank, on the same side of the channel as the hut and about thirty yards from it, was a gnarled and stunted oak tree smothered by a wild rose creeper. Laying down the rifle, I stepped from the bank on to the tree, which was leaning out over the channel, and found there was a reasonably comfortable seat on the top of the creeper.

Rejoining the two men at the hut I told them I was going back to the Rest House for my heavy rifle, a double-barrelled .500 express using modified cordite. My guide very sportingly offered to save me this trouble, so after instructing him I sat down with the villager at the door of his hut and listened to the tales he had to tell of a poor but undaunted man's fight against nature and wild animals, to keep a grass roof above his head. When I asked him why he did not leave this isolated place and try to make a living elsewhere, he said simply, 'This is my home.'

The sun was near setting when I saw two men coming down the hill towards the hut. Neither of them had a rifle, but Bala Singh—one of the best men who ever stepped out of Garhwal, and of whose tragic death some years later I have already told you—was carrying a lantern. On reaching me Bala Singh said he had not brought my heavy rifle because the cartridges for it were locked up in my suitcase and I had forgotten to send the key. Well, the tiger would have to be shot with my new rifle, and it could not have a better christening.

—

Before taking my seat on the tree I told the owner of the hut that my success would depend on his keeping his two children, a girl of eight and a boy of six, quiet, and that his wife would have to defer cooking the evening meal until I had shot the tiger, or until I decided the tiger was not coming. My instructions to Bala Singh were to keep the inmates of the hut quiet, light the lantern when I whistled, and then await my further orders.

The vesper songs of the multitude of birds in the valley were hushed as the red glow from the setting sun died off the hills. Twilight deepened and a horned owl hooted on the hill above me. There would be a short period of semi-darkness before the moon rose. The time had now come, and the inmates of the hut were as silent as the dead. I was gripping the rifle and straining my eyes on the ground under me when the tiger, who had avoided passing under my tree, arrived at his kill and was angry at what he found. In a low muttering voice he cursed the vultures who, though they had departed two hours earlier, had left their musky smell on the ground they had fouled. For two, three, possibly four minutes he continued to mutter to himself, and then there was silence. The light was getting stronger. Another few minutes and the moon rose over the brow of the hill, flooding my world with light. The bones picked clean by the vultures were showing white in the moonlight, and nowhere was the tiger to be seen. Moistening my lips, which excitement had dried, I gave a low whistle. Bala Singh was on the alert and I heard him ask the owner of the hut for a light from the fire. Through the crevices of the grass hut I saw a glimmer of light, which grew stronger as the lantern was lit. The light moved across the hut and Bala Singh pulled open the door and stood on the threshold awaiting my further orders. With the exception of that one low whistle, I had made no sound or movement from the time I had taken my seat on the tree. And now, when I looked down, there was the tiger standing below me, in brilliant moonlight, looking over his right shoulder at Bala Singh. The distance between the muzzle of my rifle and the tiger's head was about five feet, and the thought flashed through my mind that the cordite would probably singe his hair. The ivory foresight of my rifle was on the exact spot of the tiger's heart—where I knew my bullet would kill him instantaneously—when I gently pressed the trigger. The trigger gave under the pressure, and nothing happened.

Heavens! How incredibly careless I had been. I distinctly remembered having put a clip of five cartridges in the magazine when I took my seat on the tree, but quite evidently when I pushed the bolt home it had failed to convey a cartridge from the magazine into the chamber, and this I had omitted to observe. Had the rifle been old and worn it might still have been possible to rectify my mistake. But the rifle was new and as I raised the lever to draw back the bolt there was a loud metallic click, and in one bound the tiger was up the bank and out of sight. Turning my head to see how Bala Singh had reacted, I saw him step back into the hut and close the door.

There was now no longer any need for silence and as Bala Singh came up at my call, to help me off the tree, I drew back the bolt of the rifle with the object of unloading the magazine and, as I did so, I noticed that the extractor at the end of the bolt held a cartridge. So the rifle had been loaded after all and the safety-catch off. Why then had the rifle not fired when I pulled the trigger? Too late, I knew the reason. One of the recommendations stressed by Manton's manager when showing me the rifle was that it had a double pull off. Never having handled a rifle with this so-called improvement, I did not know it was necessary, after the initial pull had taken up the slack, to pull the trigger a second time to release the striker. When I explained the reason for my failure to Bala Singh, he blamed himself, 'For', said he, 'if I had brought your heavy rifle *and* the suitcase this would not have happened.' I was inclined to agree with him at the time, but as the days went by I was not so sure that even with the heavy rifle I would have been able to kill the tiger that evening.

4

Another long walk next morning, to try to get news of the man-eater, and when I returned to the Rest House I was greeted by a very agitated man who informed me that the tiger had just killed one of his cows. He had been grazing his cattle on the far side of the valley from where I sat the previous evening, when a tiger appeared and killed a red cow that had calved a few days previously. 'And now,' he said, 'the heifer calf will die, for none of my other cows are in milk.'

Luck had been with the tiger the previous evening but his luck could not last indefinitely, and for the killing of this cow he would have to die, for cattle are scarce in the hills and the loss of a milch cow to a poor man was a serious matter. The man had no anxiety about the rest of his small herd, which had stampeded back to his village, so he was willing to wait while I had a meal. At 1 p.m. we set out, the man leading, I on his heels, and two of my men following with material for making a machan.

From an open patch of ground on the hillside my guide pointed out the lay of the land. His cattle had been grazing on a short stretch of grass a quarter of a mile below the ridge, when the tiger, coming up from the direction of the valley, had killed his cow. The rest of the herd had stampeded up the hill and over the ridge to his village, which was on the far side. Our shortest way was across the valley and up the other side, but I did not want to risk disturbing the tiger, so we skirted round the head of the valley to approach from above the spot where the cow had been killed. Between the ridge over which the cattle had stampeded and the spot where they had been grazing was more or less open tree jungle. The tracks of the running animals had bitten deep into the soft loamy earth, and it was easy to follow these tracks back to where they had started. Here there was a big pool of blood with a drag-mark leading away from it. The drag led across the hill for two hundred yards to a deep and well-wooded ravine with a trickle of water in it. Up this ravine the tiger had taken his kill.

The cow had been killed at about 10 a.m. on open ground, and the tiger's first anxiety would have been to remove it to some secluded spot where it would be hidden from prying eyes. So he had dragged it up the ravine and, after depositing it in a place he knew of, he had, as his pug-marks showed, gone down the ravine into the valley below. In an area in which human beings and cattle are moving about, it is unwise to predict where a tiger will be lying up, for the slightest disturbance may make him change his position. So, though the pug-marks led down the ravine, the three men and I very cautiously followed the drag up the ravine.

Two hundred yards below the ridge along which we had come, rainwater had scooped out a big hole in the hillside. Here the ravine started. The hole, which at the upper end had a sheer drop into it of fifteen feet, had been made many years previously and was now partly overgrown with oak and ash saplings ten to twelve feet tall. Between these saplings and the fifteen-foot drop was a small open space on which the tiger had deposited his kill. I could sympathize with the owner of the cow when he told me with tears in his eyes that the fine animal that lay dead before us had been bred by him and that it was a special favourite. No portion of the animal had been touched, the tiger having evidently brought it here to eat at his leisure.

A place had now to be found in which to sit. There were several big oak trees on either side of the ravine, but none overlooked the kill and all of them were unclimbable. Thirty yards below the kill and on the left-hand side of the ravine was a small stout holly tree. The branches were growing out at right angles to the trunk, and six feet above ground there was a strong enough branch for me to sit on and another on which to rest my feet. The three men protested strongly against my sitting so close to the ground. However, there was no other suitable place for me to sit, so the holly tree it would have to be. Before sending the men away I instructed them to go to the hut where I had been the previous evening, and to wait there until I called to them, or until I joined them. The distance across the valley was about half a mile and though the men would not be able to see either me or the kill, I was able to see the hut through the leaves of the holly tree.

The men left me at 4 p.m. and I settled down on the holly branch for what I anticipated would be a long wait, for the hill faced west and the tiger would probably not be on the move much before sundown. To the left my field of vision—through the holly leaves—extended down the ravine for fifty yards. In front I had a clear view into the ravine, which was about ten feet deep and twenty feet wide, and of the hill facing me on which there were outcrops of rock but no trees. To the right I had a clear view up to the ridge but I could not see the kill, which was hidden by the thick growth of saplings. Behind me was a dense thicket of ringals which extended down to the level of my tree and further helped to mask the kill. The tiger after depositing his kill in the hole, made by rainwater, had gone down the ravine and it was reasonable to assume that when he returned he would come by the same route. So I concentrated all my attention on the ravine, intending to shoot the tiger when he was at right angles to me. That I could kill him at that short range I had no doubt whatsoever and to make quite sure of getting in a second shot, if it was necessary, I cocked both hammers of my rifle.

There were sambar, kakar, and langur in the jungle and a great number of pheasants, magpies, babblers, thrushes, and jays, all of which call on seeing a member of the cat family, so I thought I would receive ample warning of the tiger's coming. But here I was wrong, for without having heard a single alarm call, I suddenly heard the tiger at his kill. After going down the ravine, possibly for a drink, the tiger had skirted round the thicket of ringals and approached his kill without passing me. This did not worry me unduly for tigers are restless at a kill in daylight, and I felt sure that sooner or later the tiger would show up on the open ground in front of me. He had been eating for about fifteen minutes, tearing off great chunks of flesh, when I caught sight of a bear coming along the crest of the hill from left to right. He was a great big Himalayan black bear, and was strolling along as though it did not matter to him how long he took to get from here to there. Suddenly he stopped, turned facing downhill, and lay flat. After a minute or two he raised his head, snuffed the wind, and again lay flat. The wind, as always in daylight in the hills, was blowing uphill and the bear had got the scent of flesh and blood, mingled with the scent of tiger. I was a little to the right of the kill, so he had not got my scent. Presently he got to his feet and, with the bent legs and body held close to the ground, started to stalk the tiger.

It was a revelation to me in animal stalking to see that bear coming down the hill. He had possibly two hundred yards to go and though he was not built for stalking, as tigers and leopards are, he covered the distance as smoothly as a snake and as silently as a shadow. The nearer he got the more cautious he became. I could see the lip of the fifteen-foot drop into the hole, and when the bear got to within a few feet of this spot he drew himself along with belly to ground. Waiting until the tiger was eating with great gusto, the bear very slowly projected his head over the lip of the hole and looked down, and then as slowly drew his head back. Excitement with me had now reached the stage when the whole of my body was trembling, and my mouth and throat were dry.

On two occasions I have seen Himalayan bears walk off with tigers' kills. On both occasions the tigers were not present. And on two occasions I have seen bears walk up to feeding leopards and, after shooing them off, carry the kills away. But on this occasion the tiger—and a big male at that—was present at his kill and, further, he was not an animal to be shooed away like a leopard. At the back of my mind was the thought that surely this bear would not be so foolish as to try to dispossess the king of the jungle of his kill. But that was just what the bear appeared to intend doing, and his opportunity came when the tiger was cracking a bone. Whether the bear had been waiting for this moment I do not know; anyway, while the tiger was crunching the bone, the bear drew himself to the edge and, gathering his feet under him, launched himself into the hole with a mighty scream. The object of the scream I imagine was to intimidate the tiger, but so far from having this effect it appeared to infuriate him, for the bear's mighty scream was answered by an even mightier roar from the tiger.

Fights in the wild are very rare and this is only the second case I know of different species of animals fighting for the sake of fighting and not for the purpose of one using the other as food. I did not see the fight, for the reasons I have given, but I heard every detail of it. Waged in a hollow of restricted area the sound was terrifying and I was thankful that the fight was a straight one between two contestants who were capable of defending themselves, and not a three-cornered one in which I was involved. Time stands still when every drop of blood racing through a rapidly beating heart is tingling with excitement. The fight may have lasted three minutes, or it may have lasted longer. Anyway, when the tiger considered he had administered sufficient chastisement he broke off the engagement and came along the open ground in front of me at a fast gallop, closely followed by the still screaming bear. Just as I was aligning the sights of my rifle on the tiger's left shoulder he turned sharp to the left and leaping the twenty-foot-wide ravine, landed at my feet. While he was still in the air I depressed the muzzle of the rifle and fired, as I thought, straight into his back. My shot was greeted with an angry grunt as the tiger crashed into the ringals behind me. For a few yards he carried on and then there was silence; shot through the heart and died in his tracks, I thought.

A .500 modified cordite rifle fired anywhere makes a considerable noise, but here, in the ravine, it sounded like a cannon. The detonation, however, had not the least effect on the maddened bear. Following close on the heels of the tiger he did not attempt to leap the ravine, as the tiger had done. Storming down one bank he came up the other straight towards me. I had no wish to shoot an animal that had the courage to drive a tiger off his kill, but to have let that screaming fury come any nearer would have been madness, so, when he was a few feet from me, I put the bullet of the left barrel into his broad forehead. Slowly he slid down the bank on his stomach, until his haunches met the opposite bank.

Where a moment earlier the jungle had resounded with angry strife and the detonations of a heavy rifle, there was now silence, and when my heart had resumed its normal beat, my thoughts turned to a soothing smoke. Laying the rifle across my knees I put both hands into my pockets to feel for cigarette case and matches. At that moment I caught sight of a movement on my right and, turning my head, saw the tiger unhurriedly cantering along on the open ground over which he had galloped a minute or two earlier and looking not at me, but at his dead enemy.

I know that in relating these events as they occurred, sportsmen will accuse me of rank bad shooting and gross carelessness. I have no defence to make against the accusation of bad shooting, but I do not plead guilty to carelessness. When I fired, as I thought, into the tiger's back, I was convinced I was delivering a fatal wound, and the angry response followed by the mad rush and sudden cessation of sound were ample justification for thinking the tiger had died in his tracks. My second shot had killed the bear outright so there was no necessity—while I was still on the tree—to reload the rifle before laying it across my knees.

Surprise at seeing the tiger alive and unhurt lost me a second or two, and thereafter I acted quickly. The rifle was of the under-lever model; the lever being held in position by two lugs on the trigger guard. This made the rapid loading of the rifle difficult, and, further, the spare cartridges were in my trousers' pocket; easy to get at when standing up, but not so easy when sitting on a thin branch. Whether the tiger knew the bear was dead, or whether he was just keeping an eye on it to avoid a flank attack, I do not know. Anyway, he carried on across the face of the steep hill at a slow canter and had reached a spot forty yards away—which I can best describe as eleven o'clock—and was passing a great slab of rock when, with only one barrel loaded, I put up the rifle and fired. At my shot he reared up, fell over sideways, made a bad landing, scrambled to his feet, and cantered on round the shoulder of the hill with his tail in the air. The nickel-cased soft-nosed bullet with steel base had struck the rock a few inches from the tiger's face and the blowback had thrown him off his balance but had done him no harm.

After a quiet smoke I stepped down from the holly tree and went to have a look at the bear, who, I found, was even bigger than I had at first thought. His self-sought fight with the tiger had been a very real one, for blood from a number of deep cuts was seeping through the thick fur on his neck and in several places his scalp was torn right down to the bone. These wounds in themselves would have mattered little to a tough animal like a bear, but what did matter and what had annoyed him was the injury to his nose. All males resent being struck on the nose, and not only had the bear been struck on that tender spot but insult had been added to injury by his nose being torn in half. Reason enough for him to have chased the tiger with murder in his eyes, and for him to have ignored the report of my heavy rifle.

There was not sufficient time for me to call up my men to skin the bear, so I set off to collect them at the hut and get back to the Rest House before nightfall, for somewhere in that area there was a man-eater. My men, and the dozen or so villagers who had collected at the hut, were too intent on gazing across the valley to observe my approach, and when I walked in among them, they were dumb with amazement. Bala Singh was the first to recover speech, and when I heard his story I was not surprised that the assembled men had looked at me as one returned from the dead. 'We advised you,' Bala Singh said, 'not to sit so close to the ground, and when we heard your first scream, followed by the tiger's roar, we were convinced that you had been pulled out of the tree and that you were fighting for your life with the tiger. Then, when the tiger stopped roaring and you continued to scream, we thought the tiger was carrying you away. Later we heard two reports from your rifle, followed by a third, and we were greatly mystified, for we could not understand how a man who was being carried away by a tiger could fire his rifle. And while we were consulting with these men what we should do, you suddenly appeared and we became speechless.' To men keyed-tip and listening for sounds from where a tiger was being sat up for, the scream of a bear could easily be mistaken for the scream of a human being, for the two are very similar and at a distance would not be distinguishable from one another.

Bala Singh got a cup of tea ready for me while I told the men about the fight they had heard and about the bear I had shot. Bear's fat is greatly valued as a cure for rheumatism, and the men were delighted when I told them I did not want the fat and that they could share it with their friends. Next morning I set out to skin the bear, accompanied by a crowd of men who were anxious not only to get a share of the fat but also to see the animal that had fought a tiger. I have never measured or weighed a bear but have seen quite a few, and the one I skinned that morning was the biggest and the fattest Himalayan bear I have ever seen. When the fat and the other prized parts of the bear had been divided, a very happy throng of men turned their faces to Dabidhura, and the happiest and the most envied of all was Bala Singh who proudly carried, strapped to his back, the bear's skin I had given him.

The tiger did not return to finish his interrupted meal, and by evening the vultures had picked clean the bones of the cow and the bear.

5

Skinning a bear encased in fat is a very messy job, and as I plodded back to the Rest House for a hot bath and a late breakfast I met a very agitated forest guard, whose headquarters were at Dabidhura. He had been at an outlying beat the previous night and on his return to Dabidhura that morning had heard at the bania's shop about the bear I had shot. Being in urgent need of bear's fat for his father, who was crippled with rheumatism, he was hurrying to try to get a share of the fat when he ran into a herd of stampeding cattle, followed by a boy who informed him that a tiger had killed one of his cows. The forest guard had a rough idea where the cattle had been grazing when attacked by the tiger, so while Bala Singh and the other men carried onto Dabidhura I set off with him to try to find the kill. Uphill and downhill we went for two miles or more until we came to a small valley. It was in this valley that the forest guard thought the cow had been killed.

There had been an auction of condemned stores at the Gurkha depot at Almora a few days previously, and my companion had treated himself to a pair of army boots many sizes too big for his feet. In these he had clumped ahead of me until we came to the lip of the valley. Here I made him remove his boots and when I saw the condition of his feet I marvelled that a man who had gone barefoot all his life had, for the sake of vanity, endured such torture. 'I bought big boots,' he told me, 'because I thought they would shrink.'

The boat-shaped valley, some five acres in extent, was like a beautiful park dotted over with giant oak trees. On the side from which I approached it the ground sloped gently down and was free of bushes, but on the far side the hill went up more steeply with a few scattered bushes on it. I stood on the lip of the valley for a few minutes scanning every foot of ground in my field of vision without seeing anything suspicious, and then went down the grassy slope followed by the forest guard, now walking silently on bare feet. As I approached the flat ground on the floor of the valley I saw that the dead leaves and dry twigs over a considerable area had been scratched together, and piled into a great heap. Though no part of the cow was visible I knew that under this pile of dead matter the tiger had hidden his kill, and very foolishly I did not inform my companion of this fact, for he told me later that he did not know that tigers were in the habit of hiding their kills. When a tiger hides his kill it is usually an indication that he does not intend lying up near it, but it is not safe to assume this always. So, though I had scanned the ground before entering the valley, I again stood perfectly still while I had another look.

A little beyond the piled-up leaves and twigs the hill went up at an angle of forty-five degrees, and forty yards up the hillside there was a small clump of bushes. As I was looking at these I saw the tiger, who was lying on a small bit of flat ground with his feet towards me, turn over and present his back to me. I could see part of his head, and a three-inch wide strip of his body from shoulder to hindquarters. A head shot was out of the question, and nothing would be gained by inflicting a flesh wound. I had the whole afternoon and evening before me and as the tiger would be bound to stand up sooner or later, I decided to sit down and wait on events. As I came to this decision I caught sight of a movement on my left, and on turning my head saw a bear coming stealthily up the valley towards the kill, followed by two half-grown cubs. The bear had evidently heard the tiger killing the cow and after giving the tiger time to settle down—as I have done on many occasions—she was now coming to investigate, for unless they have a special reason bears do not move about at midday. Had I been standing on the lip of the valley, instead of a few feet from the kill, I believe I should have witnessed a very interesting sight, for on finding the kill, which with their keen scent they would have had no difficulty in doing, the bears would have started to uncover it. This would have awakened the tiger and I cannot imagine that he would have relinquished his kill without a fight, and the fight would have been worth seeing.

The forest guard, who all this time had been standing quietly behind me seeing nothing but the ground at his feet, now caught sight of the bears and exclaimed in a loud voice, 'Dekko Sahib, bhalu, bhalu.' The tiger was up and away in a flash, but he had some twenty yards of open ground to cover, and as I aligned my sights on him and pressed the trigger the forest guard, under the impression that I was facing in the wrong direction, grabbed my arm and gave it a jerk with the result that my bullet struck a tree a few yards from where I was standing. Losing one's temper anywhere does no good, least of all in a jungle. The forest guard, who did not know what the piled-up leaves implied and who had not seen the tiger, was under the impression that he had saved my life by drawing my attention to the dreaded bears, so there was nothing to be said. Alarmed by my shot the bears lumbered away while my companion urged me with a catch in his throat, 'Maro, maro!' ('Shoot, shoot!').

A very dejected forest guard walked back with me to Dabidhura, and to cheer him up I asked him if he knew of any place where I could shoot a ghooral, for my men were still without meat. Not only did the game little man know of such a place but he also volunteered, blisters and all, to take me to it. So after a cup of tea we set off accompanied by two of my men who, the forest guard said, would be needed to carry back the bag.

From the veranda of the Rest House the hill falls steeply away. Down this hill the forest guard led me for a few hundred yards until we came to a foot-wide ghooral track running across the face of the hill. I now took the lead and had proceeded for about halt a mile to the right when, on coming to a rocky ridge, I looked across a deep ravine and saw a ghooral on the far side standing on a projecting rock and looking into space, as all goats including tahr, ibex, and markor have a habit of doing. It was a male ghooral, as I could see from the white disk on its throat, and the distance between us was a shade over two hundred yards. Here now was an opportunity not only of procuring meat for my men but also of testing the accuracy of my new rifle. So, lying down, I put up the two hundred-yard leaf sight and, taking very careful aim, fired. At my shot the ghooral sank down on the rock on which he had been standing, which was very fortunate, for below him was a sheer drop of many hundred feet. A second ghooral, which I had not seen, now ran up the far side of the ravine followed by a small kid, and after standing still and looking back at us several times, carried on round the shoulder of the hill.

While the forest guard and I had a smoke, my two men set off to retrieve the bag. Deprived of his share of the bear's fat the forest guard was made happy by being promised a bit of the ghooral and its skin, which he said he would make into a seat for his father who, owing to age and rheumatism, spent all his days basking in the sun.

6

A visit to the valley early next morning confirmed my suspicion that the tiger would not return to his kill, and that the bears would. Little but the bones were left when the three bears had finished with the kill, and that little was being industriously sought by a solitary king vulture when I arrived on the scene.

The morning was still young so, climbing the hill in the direction in which the tiger had gone the previous day, I went over the ridge and down the far side to the Loharghat road to look for tracks of the man-eating leopard. On my return to the Rest House at midday I was informed of yet another tiger kill. My informant was an intelligent young man who was on his way to Almora to attend a court case and, being unable to spare the time to show me where he had seen the tiger killing a cow, drew a sketch for me on the floor of the veranda with a piece of charcoal. After a combined breakfast and lunch I set out to try to find the kill which—if the young man's sketch was correct—had taken place five miles from where I had fired at the tiger the previous day. The tiger, I found, had come on a small herd of cattle grazing on the banks of the stream flowing down the main valley and, judging from the condition of the soft ground, had experienced some difficulty in pulling down the victim he had selected. Killing a big and vigorous animal weighing six or seven hundred pounds is a strenuous job and a tiger after accomplishing this feat usually takes a breather. On this occasion, however, the tiger had picked up the cow as soon as he had killed it—as the absence of blood indicated—and crossing the stream entered the dense jungle at the foot of the hill.

Yesterday the tiger had covered up his kill at the spot where he had done his killing, but today it appeared to be his intention to remove his kill to as distant a place as possible from the scene of killing. For two miles or more I followed the drag up the steep face of the densely wooded hill to where the tiger, when he had conveyed his heavy burden to within a few hundred yards of the crest, had got one of the cow's hind legs fixed between two oak saplings. With a mighty jerk uphill, the tiger tore the leg off a little below the hock, and leaving that fixed between the saplings went on with his kill. The crest of the hill at the point where the tiger arrived with his kill was flat and overgrown with oak saplings a foot or two feet in girth. Under these trees, where there were no bushes or cover of any kind, the tiger left his kill without making any attempt to cover it up.

I had followed the drag slowly, carrying only my rifle and a few cartridges; even so, when I arrived at the crest my shirt was wet and my throat dry. I could imagine, therefore, the thirst that the tiger must have acquired and his desire to quench it. Being in need of a drink myself I set out to find the nearest water, where there was also a possibility of finding the tiger. The ravine in which I had shot the bear was half a mile to the right and had water in it, but there was another ravine closer to the left and I decided to try that first.

I had gone down this ravine for the best part of a mile and had come to a place where it narrowed with steep shaly banks on either side when, on going round a big rock, I saw the tiger lying in front of me at a range of twenty yards. There was a small pool of water at this spot, and lying on a narrow strip of sand between the pool and the right-hand bank was the tiger. Here the ravine took a sharp turn to the right, and part of the tiger was on my side of the turn and part round the bend. He was lying on his left side with his back to the pool and I could see his tail and part of his hind legs. Between me and the sleeping animal was a great mass of dry branches that had been lopped from overhanging trees some time previously to feed buffaloes. It was not possible to negotiate this obstacle without making a noise, nor was it possible to go along either of the steep banks without causing small landslides of shale. So the only thing to do was to sit down and wait for the tiger to give me a shot.

After his great exertion and a good drink, the tiger was sleeping soundly and for half an hour he made no movement. Then he turned on to his right side and a little more of his legs came into view. In this position he lay for a few minutes and then stood up, and withdrew round the bend. With finger on trigger I waited for him to reappear, for his kill was up the hill behind me. Minutes passed and then a kakar a hundred yards away went dashing down the hill barking hysterically, and a little later a sambar belled. The tiger had gone; why, I did not know, for he had already taken as much exercise as any tiger needed to take, and it was not a case of his having scented me, for tigers have no sense of smell. It did not matter, however, for presently he would return to the kill he had been at such pains to take to the top of the hill, and I would be there to receive him. The water in the pool where the tiger had drunk was ice-cold, and having slaked my thirst I was able to enjoy a long-deferred smoke.

The sun was near setting when I made myself comfortable on an oak tree ten yards to the east and a little to the right of the kill. The tiger would come up the hill from the west and it was not advisable to have the kill directly between us, for tigers have very good eyesight. From my seat on the tree I had a clear view of the valley and of the hills beyond; and when the setting sun, showing as a great ball of fire, was resting on the rim of the earth bathing the world in red, a sambar belled in the valley below me. The tiger was on the move and there was plenty of time for him to arrive at his kill while there was still sufficient daylight for accurate shooting.

The ball of fire dipped below the horizon; the red glow died of the earth; twilight gave place to darkness; and all was silent in the jungle. The moon was in its third quarter, but the stars— nowhere more brilliant than in the Himalayas— were giving enough light for me to see the kill, which was white. The head of the kill was towards me and if the tiger came now and started to eat at the hindquarters I would not be able to see him, but by aligning my sights on the white kill and then raising the rifle and pressing the trigger, as the kill disappeared from view, there was a fifty-fifty chance of hitting the tiger. But here was no man-eater to be fired at under any conditions. Here was a 'temple' tiger who had never molested human beings and who, though he had killed four head of cattle in four consecutive days, had committed no crime against the jungle code. To kill him outright would benefit those who were suffering from his depredations, but to take an uncertain shot at night with the possibility of only wounding him and leaving him to suffer for hours, or if unrecovered to become a man-eater, was not justifiable in any circumstances.

Light was coming in the east, for the boles of the trees were beginning to cast vague shadows, and then the moon rose, flooding the open patches of the jungle with light. It was then that the tiger came. I could not see him but I knew he had come, for I could feel and sense his presence. Was he crouching on the far side of the kill with just his eyes and the top of his head raised over the brow of the hill watching me? No, that was not possible, for from the time I had made myself comfortable on my seat I had become part of the tree and tigers do not go through a jungle scanning, without a reason, every tree they approach. And yet, the tiger was here, and he was looking at me.

There was sufficient light now for me to see clearly, and very carefully I scanned the ground in front of me. Then as I turned my head to the right, to look behind, I saw the tiger. He was sitting on his hunkers in a patch of moonlight, facing the kill, with his head turned looking up at me. When he saw me looking down on him he flattened his ears, and as I made no further movement, his ears regained their upright position. I could imagine him saying to himself, 'Well, you have now seen me, and what are you going to do about it?' There was little I could do about it, for in order to get a shot I would have to turn a half-circle and it would not be possible to do this without alarming the tiger, who was looking at me from a range of fifteen feet. There was, however, just a possibility of my getting a shot from my left shoulder, and this I decided to try to do. The rifle was resting on my knees with the muzzle pointing to the left, and as I lifted it and started turning it to the right the tiger lowered his head and again flattened his ears. In this position he remained as long as I was motionless, but the moment I started to move the rifle again, he was up and away into the shadows behind.

Well, that was that, and the tiger had very definitely won another round. As long as I sat on the tree he would not return, but if I went away he *might* come back and remove the kill; and as he could not eat a whole cow in a night I would have another chance next day.

The question that now faced me was where to spend the night. I had already walked some twenty miles that day and the prospect of doing another eight miles to the Rest House—through forest all the way—did not appeal to me. In any other locality I would have moved away from the kill for two or three hundred yards and slept peacefully on the ground, but in this locality there was a man-eating leopard, and man-eating leopards hunt at night. While sitting on the tree earlier in the evening, I had heard the distant pealing of cattle-bells, coming either from a village or from a cattle-station. I had pin-pointed the sound and I now set out to find where it had come from. Cattle-lifting is unknown in the Himalayas, and throughout Kumaon there are communal cattle-stations situated in the jungles close to the grazing grounds. I traced the bells I had heard to one of these stations, in which there were about a hundred head of cattle in a large open shed surrounded by a strong stockade. The fact that the station was in the depth of the jungle, and unguarded, was proof of the honesty of the hillfolk, and it was also proof that until my arrival cattle in the Dabidhura area had not been molested by tigers.

At night all animals in the jungle are suspicious, and if I was to spend the night under the protection of the inmates of the shed I would have to disarm their very natural suspicion. The tenants of our village at Kaladhungi keep about nine hundred head of cows and buffaloes, and having been associated with cattle from my earliest childhood I know the language they understand. Moving very slowly and speaking to the cattle I approached the shed, and on reaching the stockade sat down with my back to it to have a smoke. Several cows were standing near the spot where I sat and one of them now advanced and, putting its head through the bars of the stockade, started to lick the back of my head; a friendly gesture, but a wetting one, and here at an altitude of eight thousand feet the nights were cold. Having finished my cigarette, I unloaded my rifle and, covering it with straw, climbed the stockade.

Care was needed in selecting a place on which to sleep, for if there was an alarm during the night and the cattle started milling round it would be unsafe to be caught on the ground. Near the centre of the shed, and close to one of the roof-supports up which I could go if the need arose, there was an open space between two sleeping cows. Stepping over recumbent animals and moving the heads of standing ones to get past them, I lay down between the two that were lying back to back. There was no alarm during the night, so the necessity for me to shin up the roof-support did not arise, and with the warm bodies of the cows to keep off the night chills and with the honey-sweet smell of healthy cattle in my nostrils I slept as one at peace with all the world, tigers and man-eating leopards included. The sun was just rising next morning when, on hearing voices, I opened my eyes and saw three men, armed with milking pails, staring at me through the bars of the stockade. The water I had drunk at the tiger's pool was all that had passed my lips since breakfast the previous day, and the warm drink of milk the men gave me—after they had recovered from their amazement at finding me asleep with their cattle—was very welcome. Declining the men's invitation to accompany them back to their village for a meal, I thanked them for their board and lodging and, before returning to the Rest House for a bath and a square meal, set off to see where the tiger had taken his kill. To my surprise I found the kill lying just as I had left it, and after covering it over with branches to protect it from vultures and golden-headed eagles I went on to the Rest House.

In no other part of the world, I imagine, are servants as tolerant of the vagaries of their masters as in India. When I returned to the Rest House after an absence of twenty-four hours, no surprise was expressed, and no questions asked. A hot bath was ready, clean clothes laid out, and within a very short time I was sitting down to a breakfast of porridge, scrambled eggs, hot chapatis and honey—the last a present from the old priest—and a dish of tea. Breakfast over, I sat on the grass in front of the Rest House admiring the gorgeous view and making plans. I had set out from my home in Naini Tal with one object, and one object only, to try to shoot the Panar man-eating leopard; and from the night it had tried to drag the herdsman off the temple platform nothing had been heard of it. The priest, the bania, and all the people in near and distant villages that I questioned informed me that there were occasions when for long periods the man-eater seemed to disappear off the face of the earth and they were of the opinion that one of these periods had now started, but no one could say how long it would last. The area over which the man-eater was operating was vast, and in it there were possibly ten to twenty leopards. To find and shoot in that area one particular leopard—that had stopped killing human beings—without knowing where to look for it, was a hopeless job.

My mission as far as the man-eater was concerned had failed, and no useful purpose would be served by my prolonging my stay at Dabidhura. The question of the temple tiger remained. I did not feel that the killing of this tiger was any responsibility of mine; but I did feel, and felt very strongly, that my pursuit of him was inducing him to kill more cattle than he would otherwise have done. Why a male tiger started killing cattle on the day of my arrival at Dabidhura it was not possible to say, and whether he would stop when I went away remained to be seen. Anyway, I had tried my best to shoot him; had paid compensation for the damage he had done to the full extent of my purse; and he had provided me with one of the most interesting jungle experiences I had ever had. So I harboured no resentment against him for having beaten me at every point in the exciting game we had played during the past four days. These four days had been very strenuous for me, so I would rest today and make an early start next morning on the first stage of my journey back to Naini Tal. I had just come to this decision when a voice from behind me said, 'Salaam, Sahib. I have come to tell you that the tiger has killed one of my cows.' One more chance of shooting the tiger, and whether I succeeded or not I would stick to my plan of leaving next morning.

7

Annoyed at the interference of human beings and bears, the tiger had shifted his ground, and this last kill had taken place on the eastern face of the Dabidhura mountain several miles from where I had sat up for him the previous evening. The ground here was undulating, with patches of scrub and a few odd trees dotted here and there; ideal ground for chukor (hill partridge), but the last place in which I would have expected to find a tiger.

Running diagonally across the face of the mountain was a shallow depression. In this depression were patches of dense scrub, interspersed with open glades of short grass. At the edge of one of these glades the cow had been killed, dragged a few yards towards some bushes, and left in the open. On the opposite or downhill side of the glade to the kill, there was a big oak tree. On this tree, the only one for hundreds of yards around, I decided to sit.

While my men warmed a kettle of water for tea I scouted round to see if I could get a shot at the tiger on foot. The tiger I felt sure was lying up somewhere in the depression, but though I searched every foot of it for an hour I saw no sign of him.

The tree that was to provide me with a seat was leaning out towards the glade. Excessive lopping had induced a crop of small branches all along the trunk, which made the tree easy to climb but obscured a view of the trunk from above. Twenty feet up a single big branch jutted out over the glade, offering the only seat on the tree but not a comfortable one or one easy to reach. At 4 p.m. I sent my men away, instructing them to go to a village farther up the hill and wait for me, for I had no intention of sitting up after sundown.

The kill, as I have said, was lying in the open, ten yards from me and with its hindquarters a yard or so from a dense clump of bushes. I had been in position for an hour and was watching a number of red-whiskered bulbuls feeding on a raspberry bush to my right front, when on turning my eyes to look at the kill I saw the tiger's head projecting beyond the clump of bushes. He was evidently lying down, for his head was close to the ground, and his eyes were fixed on me. Presently a paw was advanced, then another, and then very slowly and with belly to ground the tiger drew himself up to his kill. Here he lay for several minutes without movement. Then, feeling with his mouth, and with his eyes still fixed on me, he bit off the cow's tail, laid it on one side and started to eat. Having eaten nothing since his fight with the bear three days before, he was hungry, and he ate just as man would eat an apple, ignoring the skin and taking great bite of flesh from the hindquarters.

The rifle was across my knees pointing in the direction the tiger, and all I had to do was to raise it to my shoulder.

I would get an opportunity of doing this when he turned his eyes away from me for a brief moment. But the tiger appeared to know his danger, for without taking his eyes off me he ate on steadily and unhurriedly. When he had consumed about fifteen or twenty pounds of flesh, and when the bulbuls had left the raspberry bush and, joined by two black-throated jays, were making a great chattering on the bushes behind him, I thought it was time for me to act. If I raised the rifle very slowly he would probably not notice the movement so, when the birds were chattering their loudest, I started to do this. I had raised the muzzle possibly six inches, when the tiger slid backwards as if drawn back by a powerful spring. With rifle to shoulder and elbows on knees I now waited for the tiger to project his head a second time, and this I felt sure he would presently do. Minutes passed, and then I heard the tiger. He had skirted round the bushes and, approaching from behind, started to claw my tree where the thick growth of small branches on the trunk made it impossible for me to see him. Purring with pleasure the tiger once and again clawed the tree with vigour, while I sat on my branch and rocked with silent laughter.

I know that crows and monkeys have a sense of humour, but until that day I did not know that tigers also possessed this sense. Nor did I know that an animal could have the luck, and the impudence, that particular tiger had. In five days he had killed five cows, four of them in broad daylight. In those five days I had seen him eight times and on four occasions I had pressed a trigger on him. And now, after staring at me for half an hour and eating while doing so, he was clawing the tree on which I was sitting and purring to show his contempt of me.

When telling me of the tiger the old priest said, 'I have one objection, Sahib, to your *trying* to shoot this tiger but neither you nor anyone else will ever succeed in *killing* it.' The tiger was now, in his own way, confirming what the priest had said. Well, the tiger had made the last move in the exciting game we had played without injury to either of us, but I was not going to give him the satisfaction of having the last laugh. Laying down the rifle and cupping my hands I waited until he stopped clawing, and then sent a full-throated shout echoing over the hills which sent him careering down the hill at full speed and brought my men down from the village at a run. 'We saw the tiger running away with his tail in the air,' the men said when they arrived, 'and just see what he has done to the tree.'

Next morning I bade farewell to all my friends at Dabidhura, and assured them I would return when the man-eater got active again.

I visited Dabidhura several times in subsequent years while hunting man-eaters, and I never heard of anyone having killed the temple tiger. So I hope that in the fullness of time this old warrior, like an old soldier, just faded away.

STORIES AND ENTERTAINMENTS

A FAMILY OF TIGERS

DHAN GOPAL MUKERJI

The first immigrant from South Asia to make a mark as a writer in America, and perhaps the first South Asian to write full-time in English, Dhan Gopal Mukerji (1890-1936) published several volumes of poetry, drama, memoirs and fiction for both adults and children. The following is a chapter from his novella Ghond, the Hunter. *Here, as in almost all his stories, especially for children, he wrote of life in the jungles and villages of eastern India in prose that has a fable-like quality.*

THE ceremony of my initiation [as a warrior-hunter] had a strange effect upon me. It burnt into my soul that no matter what vocation we choose, it should be considered as a responsibility and not as a holiday. I asked other boys who were initiated into other crafts, and they bore me out in my conclusion. A weaver lad who was initiated a month before me said: 'I know now that weaving is not only a vocation but also an adoration of God. I try to make beautiful fabrics to proclaim that I have not scamped my work, nor tried to hoodwink the Invisible.'

Later, when I became a hunter by profession, my observation of animal life revealed to me that animals [too] perform their own adoration of the sanctities, and also train and initiate their young.

Adoration of sunset and sunrise among birds and beasts is a common thing. In their eyes the light of the sun is the only God. So when he, the Lord of day, arises, eagles wheel at the gates of the east like the ritual dancers in the temple of Nataraja; monkeys sit in silence on tree-tops, even squirrels interrupt their eternal quest for nuts and sit still on their branches till the hour of Light has passed. Sunset too they observe in similar fashion[.]

Let me tell you now the tale of an animal's initiation. It was after I was thirty that one day I encountered a family of tigers. The parents were about six years old, and the younglings hardly four months. They were living in the Sunderbans, those beautiful woods of the deltas at the mouth of the Ganges. What a place, the Sunderbans! There the rivers are full of crocodiles and the ground savage with tigers, leopards, panthers and rhinoceros, not to mention wild buffaloes, vipers and tarantulas. The crocodiles were the most dangerous of these, I think, though troubles came from the large cats, and I was appointed by the State to find out why the tigers of the Sunderbans ate man.

I took up my abode in a village of about three score families on the bank of the Ganges. The river was tawny and so broad in those regions that you could hardly see the opposite shore. The village fronted the water as all Hindu settlements do, and behind us, beyond some cultivated land about two miles long and half a mile broad, lay the jungle. The jungle was about ten miles deep, separating us from the village on the other side of the delta. That human habitation was very large and had a weekly boat service to Calcutta about two hundred miles up the sacred river. This village was named Sundari, Beauty.

Our own village had the magnificent name of Tajjabpore, Seat of Wonder. It was my duty to accompany the postman of Tajjabpore once a week across the jungle, going on a Tuesday and returning on a Thursday. It was during one of these trips, about the middle of June, that we came across Bagh [the tiger], his wife Baghini [the tigress], and their son and daughter. It was a very hot summer and the rain had not yet fallen in large quantities.

During the season of drought, animals, especially deer, elephant and wild buffaloes, come near human habitation and assuage their hunger by eating up the growing grain fields. And since every animal follows its food, the big cats followed the vegetarians.

So one Tuesday morning as we crossed the grain fields and entered the woods, we came upon fourfold tiger pugs. Since it was nearly eight in the morning the postman and I concluded that all the tigers were 'fast asleep' by now and it would do us no harm to go on their track. In another twenty minutes we came across a very clear place where the postman said that he saw something moving. We went forward to investigate, and came upon an amazing sight. There lay father and mother tiger on the bank of a small pond not far away. Since the rivers are full of crocodiles, in order to avoid trouble, wild animals generally drink from inland pools that never dry up. The sunlight fell profusely on the waters, and patches of it played on the plants and thorn bushes that framed them.

In order to find out what had happened to the two youngsters, we climbed up a tree and looked down. We distinctly saw the raw skeleton of an animal lying between the parents, and before them, about ten feet away, the two cubs were slowly approaching the water's edge to take a drink. It looked as if this was the first time they had gone to the water unaccompanied by Bagh and Baghini, for they stepped gingerly: brother, who was the larger of the two, leading sister. They nosed about the shore until they came upon the tracks of the past, and no doubt inferred that since tigers had gone to the drinking place on that path before, the precedent must be adhered to.

First, brother stood over the water, looking about to make sure that no danger presented itself from any direction, then lowering his head—imitating the gestures of an old tiger—he took his drink. Next he turned round, making room for sister. She nosed his ear, as much as to say: 'Guard my rear while I drink.'

The boy did so with the gallantry of a young gentleman, then they slowly retraced their steps on their previous track to their parents. That display of caution—the sense that one should keep to the old and trusted paths—told me how sagacious young animals generally are.

Now that I had found them, I made up my mind to study as closely as possible the way tigers brought up their young, so I spent the following two months in tracking and watching them. It proved an easy task, for the little ones could not wander very far. The shortness of their legs permitted them no long hunting trips. Even though the monsoon had come and more rain had fallen, yet they stayed between the two villages that lay at either end of the jungle.

The way the parents taught the cubs to hunt was a superb lesson in education. Step by step they were taught.

The day they killed their first large calf, I was with them. This was what happened. Towards the end of June it had rained steadily for a whole week. At the end of it when the sun shone again, the cattle of the village went to graze in the forest, for there, like steady green sparks from an anvil, the grass had suddenly shot up. But monsoon weather is freakish. About mid-day a swift thunderstorm frightened the cows, and their herdsmen sped them home without waiting to count the heads of the cattle. That is why they did not round up a large calf who was left to find his way home all alone after the storm had passed.

I, who was on a tree during the rain, beheld him straggling along and eating all he could of the tender grass. Suddenly I saw two yellow and purple streaks run in the sunlight, and stop facing the poor calf. It was mother tiger and her son.

Soon the wind blew the odour of their presence towards the lost creature. He whinnied almost like a horse as he smelt tiger and, turning round, dashed for the jungle. There in the shadows he saw father tiger and daughter. I shouted from the treetop—but too late. A flash of purple, yellow and black—the calf's tail raised stiff in the air—and then…

That evening when I returned to Tajjabpore and told the villagers what had happened, they scolded me for not saving that poor calf. It never entered their heads that had I come between the four cats and their food, I would not be there to tell the tale! I never shoot an animal, as a rule, except from great necessity, and on this particular afternoon, I had not taken my rifle with me, though as a forest warden of the State I was allowed a gun. I explained to the villagers that tigers, even the born man-eaters, do not kill their first human victim until he comes between them and their prey at a critical moment. But once the tiger has tasted human blood, and learns the helplessness of his prey, he does not hesitate to kill whenever he corners man. Moreover, man is a biped: he cannot run away as fast as a deer or any other quadruped, and that makes any human being without a rifle helpless before the striped and spotted enemy.

After the killing of that large calf, the village was nervous, and set up special watches for its cattle. As for human beings, none ventured abroad after nightfall. I said, 'If a man carries a burning torch or a well-lit hurricane lantern, no beast of prey will go out of its way to meet him. The more you are seen at night, the wider berth they will give our village, but if you do not take the offensive, the animals will become aggressive. They smell fear more quickly than you know, and your fear will frighten them to attack you.' But only the postman agreed with me. It was the two of us out of that entire village who ever went abroad at any hour, day or night. Though I always carried a torch, I rarely lighted it. My eyes were extremely keen: in fact, the keenest of all the hunters of my time. I could see in the dark better than antelopes. Sometimes I was credited with the eye-power of the tiger, so at night, unless I wanted to keep the animals far away, I never carried a flaming torch.

So now my eyes had to serve me to the utmost, for I was studying the two cubs and their education at all hours, and they led me into all kinds of places. At first, the parents, I noticed, did all the hunting, though the children stalked the prey and frightened them, yet the cubs were not pushed to leap and kill. That final deed the parents shared between them. Watching the parents educated the children considerably, yet in spite of this, the parents took the children to places where it would be possible for them to leap and kill if they wished.

One day, I saw them do an interesting thing. It was around mid-day, near the drinking place. The parents and the children were lying wide-awake near the pond. The wind was blowing from the opposite direction. Soon at the other end of the pond came a wild buffalo family. Father and mother stood on either side while the young steer, about two months old, drank his fill. Then the father took his drink while the other two watched. Last drank the cow, whose rear the bull and the calf protected. Then the parents lay down, their backs to the water, and before them in the jungle their child grazed and frisked about. From my tree-top I could see mother tiger pushing away her babies from her as if they were too big to be cuddled. So they trotted out, and soon caught the scent of the buffaloes. For a while I lost sight of them, and then I saw them coming towards the guileless bull calf playing in the grass. Now quickly the cubs crouched and vanished again from sight, but they crawled nearer and nearer, as I could tell from the protruding of their snouts every few seconds from under leaves or saplings here and there. At last they attacked the young steer who mooed for help. Moo!...

Instantly, like two black rocks, the cow and the bull charged. Their bellowing filled the jungle with terror. The tiger cubs fled helter-skelter. Why the buffaloes waited so long before they ran to the protection of their calf I could not make out, but probably they too were educating him as the tigers were educating their young. When the cubs reached home, they looked crestfallen. The daughter went to her father and the boy put his head under his mother's chin.

Another time, the young male cub attacked a baby monkey. No sooner had he done so than the father and mother monkeys fell on him like two fiends. They slapped his face so hard that he let go of the baby monkey whose tail his paws had held like a vice. No sooner had he released it than all three of them scurried up a tree and jabbered in terror. That set flocks and flocks of monkeys talking and racing from tree to tree, frightening in their turn birds who were taking their afternoon rest. What a din of screeching birds and howling monkeys!

In the meantime the defeated cub came home to his mother, for that day father and sister had gone off by themselves, and there they lay together near the drinking pond, mother licking and patting him. But on these and several other occasions that followed, the parents never interfered nor helped the children. It is the first requisite of a tiger's life that he should tackle his job, whether hunting or wandering, singly. At a certain time, in order to train them in self-reliance, the parents put their cubs in the way of work, but nothing more.

At last it rained so hard that I lost sight of them for more than a fortnight. It was about the beginning of August while the postman and I had gone across to the village of Sundari for the mail, that we heard of four tigers there who had killed three head of cattle in a week. This whetted my curiosity, and as soon as the mail was received the postman and I set out for the jungle. It did not take us long to find and recognize the family. The cubs had grown by now, the boy was almost as high as the mother, though not as long, his footprints resembled hers so closely that you could not distinguish them. Only one thing betrayed the cub, his step was not so long as the mother's. She took much wider strides. So when we saw two sets of identical pugs, with four in each of greater compass, we concluded that mother and son walked beside each other, while the daughter invariably kept the company of her father.

Having sighted their lairs, I went back to Tajjabpore with the postman. Then I hastened back to my four striped beasts. They moved ever closer to our village. In a couple of days they had come perilously close to it. As they emerged from the thick jungle I perceived that all was not going well with the family. The father was becoming increasingly jealous of the son. Every time the mother's back was turned, the old fellow attacked the boy with the intent to kill. At one time he came so close to slashing the boy's throat with his paw that the latter yelled for help. Then from nowhere leaped mother between them, and attacked her husband. They fought and fought, but at last she won. After that severe tussle he ran away—never to be seen again. Her job was now doubly difficult; she had to kill both for her two children and herself. But you know a tigress! She took no half measures; she forced the boy to fill his father's place, and he had to go and stalk the prey while mother waited at a given point to leap and kill.

One afternoon close to nightfall they changed plan. She and daughter did the stalking. They brought a big buffalo up to him and lo, he leaped! But instead of falling on its neck, he fell on its rear, and with a terrific kick of his legs the black bull cleared himself and ran. Not one of the three could catch him, so that night they went without food. Next evening the same thing happened, but when on the fourth occasion the mother and daughter drove up to him half a dozen big buffaloes whom he could not attack, the mystery of the situation cleared. She was giving him his last lesson. After this the family would break up, so he must learn to stalk and kill all by himself. What was most surprising, she was giving him the hardest thing to do first, but by failure at the great one he was learning the easier tasks with infallible power and skill.

How different that is from our human way of training people, with the easiest always first. In nature animals cannot afford such long drawn-out step-by-step training. Animal children cannot be segregated in the school-room from the sharp experiences of life. They have to be educated in the heart of life itself. The easy and the difficult befall them without any sequence. It is a pity that in civilization man has made the business of education so sequestered and slow.

However, to return to our tiger reaching his final initiation. I have already intimated that all three of them had gone without food for four days. Hunger was tearing their vitals. They were so famished that they curtailed their daylight sleep. Sister and brother, the fifth day, killed a baby monkey at the water hole. But it could not assuage their hunger. Late that afternoon, when the sun was setting, they came out towards our village on the riverbank and sat there looking at the bars of light vibrate and die on the high waters of the night of the full moon. In the village men and women sang as they finished their day's work, and Papias (Indian thrushes) sang in the sky—pa…p…i…aa…! The green jungle throbbed like an emerald cast in a garnet crucible.

How swiftly the tropical twilight passes! In a half-hour the moon had risen, sending currents of cold white fire through the waters and every bough of the trees. The three beasts of prey prowled around the village. But no cattle had gone astray, and men carrying torches were the only living creatures who passed and repassed on the roads. One of these men was myself. Seeing us, the tigers retreated from the village into the woods. I too went thither after putting out my torch, but circuitously. Hardly had I reached the edge of the jungle than I heard something start. With the celerity of an ape I went up a tree, and looking down I saw a milk-white buck going to graze on the ripe crop of the fields. Save his horns, the most of him was lost in the tall rice plants whose tops shivered in silver dance rhythms as he pushed through them. The moonlight was so bright that most animals could not sleep. Talk, talk, talk of birds and beasts rang like an insistent hammering on every nerve centre of one's body.

Slowly appeared against the wind a pair of emeralds. It was a tiger's eyes. He came up rapidly towards the rice crop in which the buck had buried himself. But all the time he kept closely under the shadow of the jungle. His purpose was to approach gradually until he reached the spot exactly behind the stag which would cut off the latter's retreat. Those green eyes grew larger, then vanished.

In a short time an odour of tiger, carried up by the slow breeze, told me that he was crouching under my tree. I knew because of the jungle noises that the greedy buck, lost in rice-eating, had not heard his approach. Afar off on the other side were coming, downwind, four green eyes. In a short time the stag sensed the odour of tiger. He turned round and dashed for the jungle. Alas, poor brother—that moment from almost six feet away leaped a silvery flash, which coiled itself around and hung from his neck. In two more minutes his throat was torn, and life had oozed out of him. Just then mother and sister leaped forward and claimed their share of the booty. But they were greeted with a sky-rending roar from the boy, that said: 'It is *my* kill. I did it all alone. *I* am the Master! *I* am the King!' Mother had apparently had previous experience in initiating children. She thrust a paw at sister who still insisted on claiming her share, and stilled her whining; then the two of them slunk away out of sight.

After he had eaten his fill, the cub roared and yelled as he went in the direction of the water hole. His cry of triumph told all the world that he had graduated from school. The far-off panic-stricken echoes shouted, 'Here comes the King of the beasts.'

Now mother and daughter emerged from the shadows and fell upon the remains of the dead buck. They ate long and well. After all, they had to feed the hunger of nearly a week.

From that night on, we saw no more triple pug marks. For several days we noticed a solitary tiger's track in the deep jungles, and the other two, the mother and daughter, went in the opposite direction…

RITES OF PASSAGE

A.I.R. GLASFURD

A captain in the British Indian Army, Glasfurd was a hunter who wrote of the jungles of Central India in lyrical prose, with surprising empathy and a rare knowledge of their flora and fauna. This piece, which reads like a long short story, is a chapter, abridged and lightly edited for this collection, from his book Rifle and Romance in the Indian Jungle *(1905).*

AS the piercing rays of the blistering sun decline towards late afternoon, and are intercepted by the taller trees, the jungle begins to awake from the diurnal siesta to the anticipated delight of another tropical night. Cooler airs begin to move with light stirrings to and fro. The brief respite between the cruel, blazing day and soft, dangerous night is now taken advantage of by those creatures that have reason to avoid both. The painted sandgrouse come chuckling and whirling in twos and threes along the winding riverbed, drop suddenly on the damp sand, and run to become brown stones at the water's shining edge. The monkeys whoop and swing; the red spur-fowls cackle in the rustling leaves; the kakar barks hoarsely to his mate on the hillside.

'Whe-e-e-ew! Kuck-kaya-kya-kuck'm!' It is the golden-hackled jungle-cock's salute to the dying day.

Under the bamboo clumps, a frog croaks sleepily in the riverbed; from the forest beyond it a nightjar utters his first low 'Chuckoo-chuckoo'; something heavy is heard in the distance, stealthily crackling in the leaves uphill; a tiny fluffy owlet emerges, round and wonder-eyed, from a hole in a great dead tree, and chatters volubly of the coming night.

Then, somehow or other, it is full yellow moonlight; a light scarcely less bright than the evening glow so lately departed, but such a wondrous welcome change from its heat, turning greens to blue, blues to grey, casting a silvern fairy charm over the calm scene with its soothing, cool, deliciously peaceful effulgence.

The greater fauna of the jungle are now issuing forth to seek food and water; to roam, prowl, browse, slay, or be seized in turn, until the breaking of the distant dawn. Above them all, it is the tiger's hour.

Away in the distance, faint but clear, rises the unaccustomed sound of a cart bumping over the rough boulders of the dry Sipna river, and the staccato cry of a jungle-man, no doubt anxiously urging on his belated bullocks as they return to their forest village.

A couple of years or thereabouts had passed by, during which time the tigress and her cubs [daughter and son] had roamed the jungles together, the same inseparable trio; she teaching them their trade by practical demonstration, watching them as they practised on the smaller creatures on which they preyed, killing the larger animals for them when necessary, driving off any possible enemies by terrifying demonstrations, and generally bringing up her family in the way that every right-minded tiger should do. The cubs learned discretion when mother avoided the sneering patriarchal wild boar; or when the excitable sloth bear, short-sighted and hard of hearing, was left to grub in peace.

Of man also, that mysterious being, they had acquired the necessary knowledge, giving him as wide a berth as the jungle folk gave them; although they were aware of their own power under pressure of circumstances even in this direction, having joined in a horrible uproar one morning when a party of woodcutters happened suddenly and by chance on their retreat, and mother, springing forward to display all those intimidating qualities with which Nature had endowed her, chased them flying in panic before her terrible voice.

Thus, season had succeeded season, and the hot weather found the tigress, and her now nearly full-grown cubs, once more in the valley of the Sipna, on just such an evening as has been described.

Amid the darkly enfolding jungle, a little clearing of yellow grass, a moonlit cart-track smothered in silent dust; and the three tigers, grey shadows casting black shade as they stood listening under the moon. The waking consciousness of his growing power and strength possessed the young tiger. Mother uttered no sound, but all three understood their domain, with a grim joy of lordship over the jungle and its watchful, wandering inhabitants.

And so, gently on, strolling through the tropic night. It may have been towards the small hours of the night, nearer morning, that the striped night-walkers reached the head of the winding ravine of the Khari, at a point where the little river splits off in every direction, sending its now shrunken fingers into low, jungly hills; and it was after passing up one of these dry upper reaches that the sudden up-springing of a querulous screaming plover and the faint croaking of frogs betokened the proximity of water.

Round the next bend of the watercourse a few huge wild mango trees reared their dark trunks aloft, and drooped and stretched out thick, gnarled, leafy arms, casting a black and impenetrable shadow over the bed of the narrow glen. Under the trees the air was damp and chill. Some small animal ran, suddenly startled, away, passed into the moonlit grass and vanished.

A slender shaft of moonlight pierced the pitchy canopy of mango leaves and fell, drawing a silver line, at the margin of one little lonely pool.

A silent, lone, and secret spot.

Round this rare and precious remnant of the life-sustaining fluid, the soft black mud had been stirred and puddled, stamped and soiled by innumerable nightly hoofs of the wild pig and deer that inhabited the neighbouring solitudes, and were dependent on this one spot to slake their impatient thirst. Down the steep confining banks many well-worn and dusty little paths through the long grass showed where and how they made their breakneck descents to the water.

The tigress and her young had passed into the shadows beyond the pool. A slight, low purring breathing was heard for a moment, and a stone turned gently—once.

The disturbed plover wheeled a few times against the luminous starry sky; settled; rose again shrieking; then finally settled down in the riverbed, cried 'Did did did-he-do-it!' or 'Tit-tit-teri!' (as the native will translate this bird's cry) and relapsed into silence. The big black trees, the quiet, unruffled pool, the white moonlight here, the inky shadow there—save for the low chirpings of crickets, or a wakeful frog at intervals, and the quick 'Chuckoo-chuckoo-chuckoo!' of a far-away nightjar, all was as still and apparently as deserted as the grave.

Now and then a ripened jungle mango would slip from its stalk and drop with a little thud to the ground.

On an Indian night sounds fall from afar. For long had a most remotely faint rustling been heard beyond the precipitous grass-clothed bank above that pool of the deep-hidden Khari; but not until many more long minutes had passed did the crackle of undergrowth and brushing aside of the harsh grass grow slightly sharper and clearer. Then it stopped. And then some crumbling earth and loose stones slid rolling down the side of the little gorge.

Long after this, the grass rustled gently again. Something was apparently moving about stealthily, undecided whether to advance.

The moon had passed across the sky, until the slope of the bank itself lay in sable shadow, but the line of grass fringing its crest was silver, and clearly defined. Very slowly some large dark objects came up from behind it, loomed against the moonlit skyline, stood motionless for a long time; then descended, and approached in the dark. Extremely faint noises were heard, as if something was coming down the bank towards the waterhole; a leaf cracked once or twice. Whatever the creatures were, they were approaching with infinite caution and the wariest of steps.

They came on slowly. And in lapse of time a hesitating footfall sounded on the pebbly bed of the Khari.

Beyond the little pool the dry ravine swept round out of the shadow of the mango trees, and here its stony course shone white with saline incrustations in the bright rays of the moon. And it was against this luminous background that something showed black as it moved round the water's edge. There came slowly into view the lean muzzle and big alert ears of the sentinel hind!

There was a soft squelching in the dark, and a sucking noise, as the other deer stood about in the mire round the pool, and lowered their grateful noses to the cool liquid at their feet. Small sounds, as of drinking, of drippings from wet muzzles, came at intervals; but for the most part the small herd of sambar observed a profound quiet. The moon shone clear out in the open, the gentle night swung on her soft sweet course, the stars twinkled down on the silent scene. All was wrapped in a calm, kindly peace, a perfection of lulling repose that seemed to woo every sense into a feeling of quiet security; but it was the smooth treachery, the deadly dissimulation of the jungle by night.

Suddenly, noiseless as a shadow, another figure joined that of the sentry, and two hinds were now clearly outlined in silhouette. Their muzzles began to go out and down to be quickly raised again with a jerk! Their great ears hinged forward, then back, then forward again. They were gazing intently, fixedly, into the velvety shadows of the big trees.

All of a sudden one of them ran a few quick steps and halted, watchful, with outstretched neck. 'Ponk!' rang out her abrupt trumpet-note of warning, and echoed up the narrow glen.

'Whee-onk!' she belled again. 'Whee-onk!' And startled hoofs were heard stamping in the dark round the pool. Then they too ceased, and all was still as before.

The old hind remained listening, her long head poked anxiously forward, her cold wet muzzle glistening in the moonlight into which she had now emerged, her large widespread ears twitching slowly now and again. Often had she played this game before—better far to stand thus than run into some unknown danger. Perhaps, after all, it was some false alarm, and the peril was one of imagination alone.

So long did this phase continue that her stiffly posed shape might well have been taken for that of a spectral deer, or perhaps some fantastically twisted tree-stump. But there was a feeling of vague unrest, of danger in the air of the old Khari that night, a mysterious menacing fear, brooding and lurking under the heavy trees.

A sudden clattering of strong, widespread hoofs, and the big hind was galloping in terror up the bed of the ravine. Heavy feet scattered the loose stones and shingle, rushing madly away in other directions in the dark. Then into the moonlight, from the gloom of the big mangoes, shot a long, low, heavy something that rushed swiftly to cut off her course with a rattling throaty sound, and a striking right and left with keen hooking claws. One of those blows went home as the wretched hind reached some long grass in the stream-bed, and a hind leg went down. The momentary check sufficed to seal her fate. Something of enormous weight and strength clutched the nape of her neck, five more cruelly lacerating claws fixed immovably into her long, sensitive nose, and her throat under the ears was seized from below in a terrible grip.

For a moment or so the tigress and her prey remained motionless in this fearsome posture.

Then there was a sudden quick movement, a dull crack, and the poor old hind sank down under her murderess, sank stone-dead, her cervical vertebra neatly dislocated by a past mistress in the art of practical osteology.

Hardly had these kaleidoscopic occurrences flashed by in swift succession than the young tiger dashed up, tail on end, coughing, glaring, and rattling his throat most diabolically. Scarcely less swift than mother, he rushed in. With a horrible snarl he flung himself on the 'kill' just as mother relaxed that awful grip of her jaws on the hind's neck and raised her beautiful, victorious head in the moonlight; and in an instant the tiger's whiskers were buried and bedabbled in the hind's warm gory neck, which he twisted ferociously from side to side, his ears depressed, as he made most unfilial faces at his parent.

But the time was very unpropitious. Mother was not at that moment at all in a frame of mind to brook any sort of interference. She made a horrid, warning, vomiting kind of noise in her great throat. Then her ears went tightly back, her nose puckered up, a deep, brassy 'Wroof!' rent the still night air; she plunged forward, her huge paw went out correctively, tentatively, thoughtfully, more in sorrow than in anger, and the erring cub rolled over on to his back and into oblivion.

—

The moon had set. Above the dark outline of distant hills a faint and evanescent sheen lingered in the western sky, and a complete hush had descended. Even the insects had ceased to shrill and the gentle breathing of the sleeping forest become almost inaudible. The pool of the Khari ravine, where, so short a while before, such scenes of savagery had been enacted, lay as dark as its enfolding trees. Not a frog croaked.

It is at this hour, the dark before the dawn, that even the most persevering of hunters finds it almost impossible to fight against an insidious somnolence brought on by the slight lowering of the tropical temperature.

Slowly the atmosphere chills. A very slight dew is condensing.

High towards the zenith the faintest suggestion of luminosity seems to grow and spread. It is hardly to be distinguished from the star-dust already shining there; but, as we watch and conjecture, there is at last a distant twinkle through the spectral limbs of leafless trees, and a bright star slowly rises and glitters on the eastern horizon. We were right. It is the dawn. And that is Lucifer—morning star and light-bringer.

The slumbering forest stirs gently. Somewhere far away the crow of a jungle-cock rises clear. It is instantly answered by the loud mewing of peafowl from every point of the surrounding woods, where the great birds are perched roosting on the limbs of the largest trees they can find—

'Maa-oo! Aah-oon! Aaow! Aa-aa-o-o! Paa-aa-oo!'

A faint twittering of bulbuls commences in the undergrowth; and soon, in all directions, the jungle-cocks are busily crowing.

Now the faintest greenish suffusion is gradually mounting into the sky, pushing the morning star ever higher and paler, and before long that great materialistic sun, with his mighty glowing orb, reddens the distant horizon…

A flight of chattering parakeets goes whirling up the valley, and the tree-tops catch a golden glint as the level sunbeams run like long, bright fingers through the newly awakened jungle.

A distant 'Caw!' comes floating through the air, and a couple of the black scouts of the wilderness are seen winging high over the forest, till something suddenly arrests their keen eyesight. They wheel, cawing, in descending circles and swoops, and settle expectantly not far away.

There was a great screaming of small birds that morning among the bushes of the little riverbed; they congregated in ever-growing numbers, chattering, hovering, and scolding over some as yet unseen object at the edge of the grass. As the early sun appeared over the bank and shone hotly down into the ravine, a striped head slowly rose and gazed out with dazed and blinking eyes. Then it sank out of sight.

Next time, the body slowly followed the head, and the young tiger stood up unsteadily, the birds darting and diving round him in the air with harsh, angry cries. He sluggishly stretched himself, looked over his shoulder, and began to walk heavily down to the pool. He was still shaken from that correcting slap dealt him by mother the previous night, and he stood dejectedly awhile at the water's edge before lowering his head and lapping weakly. Then he turned away, and after looking about him for a time, extended himself flat on the warm, dry sand. As the sun climbed higher and hotter, he stirred uneasily once or twice. Finally he rose to his feet and paced slowly up the nullah. Where had the others gone?

As he wandered sulkily along and passed close to some tall rank grass, he suddenly stopped, sniffed slowly, gazed round suspiciously, then, still sniffing with outstretched head, cautiously followed a grass-crushed trail into some bamboo-shaded rocks.

Round the corner lay the few unconsumed remains of the hind sambar which had been the cause of his trouble. The cub lay down at a respectful distance, and waited patiently with his eyes on the carcass. But this time nothing happened. Half an hour later he had crept up in the shade, and was smelling the raw red flesh. Tigers seldom touch their food much after dawn or much before nightfall; but this cub was very hungry. So, with many suspicious halts to listen, he began to feed.

Lying on his side, rolling on his back, growling softly to himself, or patting the 'kill' with protruded claws, he fed and gnawed. Once he wandered off to the pool for another drink but that was very warm, and a puff of hot air, like that from a furnace-mouth, met him as he passed across the burning sand. When he returned there were some vultures seated inquiringly on a tree above; and a couple of crows who had been extremely busy during his absence flew silently up and perched close by, wiping their strong black beaks.

The tiger now dragged the carcass away under some thick bamboos, and 'lay up' not far off. Then he slept.

Slowly the intolerable hot-weather day wore away in silence—but for the creaking of the parched bamboos in the occasional breaths of burning air, an occasional 'caw' from the indefatigable crows, and the squeaking hiss of the quarrelsome vultures as they greeted the heavy flappings of some new-comer settling among them. The jungle—grass, sand, trees, bamboos, rocks—all were quivering yellow-white in the furious glare of the summer sun, and stood out blindingly against the relentless sky. Such birds as could be seen hiding in the shade held their beaks permanently agape, and all nature seemed to be fainting and gasping in the dreadful heat.

Towards dusk of that day the sense of loneliness overcame the young tiger afresh. Following them by some instinct, the young tiger prowled after his lost family all that night, but, as they were now some miles ahead of him, to little purpose.

Then it was dawn again, and day. Once more the hot-weather sun, although but a hand's breadth above the horizon, rose to a terrible heat, and again the creatures of the jungle retired before his blazing face to seek shade and repose.

In the neighbouring ravine were strips of bright green jamun bushes, overhanging nooks paved with damp sand and screened by tall grass, but it was hot and stuffy down there. The young tiger therefore paced slowly along the banks of the ravine, pausing at intervals in the slight shade of leafless trees.

The ravine was bordered by terrace-like hillsides clad with harsh dry grass and strewn with the brittle fallen leaves of the teak and other deciduous trees that, gaunt and bare, studded the surrounding slopes like an array of yellow skeletons. Through this parched-up wilderness a tiny path twisted its way uphill. On the edge of the terrace above, a spreading, many-rooted banyan tree cast the deep shade of its fresh and sappy blue-green foliage, and was stirred at intervals by a faint breeze. The cub took the upward path towards it, and, as he slowly climbed, his smaller footprints unconsciously overlaid the huge square pugs of one who had preceded him earlier that very morning.

At the edge of the little plateau he wound between big slabs of piled black basalt, and emerged into the dry breeze, gasping with the heat. He paced gratefully towards the shade of the mighty banyan. Stepping incautiously on a dry leaf, which broke with a heavy crunch under his forepad, he instantly sprang away from the tree with a short, startled roar…

Satisfied with the respect which he had so quickly inspired with merely the twitch of an ear, the big tiger again stretched out at his ease in the shade. The cub watchfully retired to a small tree higher up the hillside, and inhabited its somewhat scanty shadow. In this manner, with an eye ever half open for the striped majesty under the big banyan, he passed that day.

When evening at last left the valley in shadow and the cool zephyrs of dusk began to stir in the riverbed, the weaker denizens of the jungle might have been heard suddenly calling to each other with sharp, warning voices. 'Tiger!' they cried. 'Danger!' And the call was taken up and passed on rapidly. 'Danger!' cackled the brown spur-fowl. 'Tiger!' belled the sambar, coughed the monkeys, 'tok-tokked' the peafowl. Not long afterwards the moon's yellow rising disc revealed the big tiger perambulating riverbed or dusty game-path, and behind him followed ever respectfully, but perseveringly, the lonely, homesick cub. Towards midnight the big tiger found a sounder of wild hogs, and secured a juicy sow. Twice or thrice during the remainder of the night he had to leave his 'kill' and charge out woofing angrily into the moonlight. And so it was that again the cub went wandering on by himself.

From glen to glen he roamed of nights, past jungle hamlets, snuffing disconsolately in the direction of the cattle-pens along forest roads, over open glades, by the beds of ravines, and 'lying-up' in convenient spots when the dawn found him out. Up and down many a jungly khora he travelled, calling, as he went, in a moaning growl for his lost family circle, and pouncing on anything that might allay the increasing pangs of hunger—frogs in the nullahs, lizards among the rocks, or a writhing spitting ichneumon in the dry grass. A porcupine he tried one night, but it left a sharp black and white quill to remain embedded in the muscles of his cheek long after those in his paws had worked their painful way out.

More than ten days had passed in this manner since that eventful night at the pool of the Khari, and starvation now exercised its irresistible compulsion on his wanderings, while his voice changed from querulous moaning to a harsh and grating insistence.

In this condition of straitened circumstances he found himself, one hot evening, descending a steep, dry watercourse. All around were big dark hills, and the rocky way sank to a deep valley below. When he reached its stifling depths the sun had set. The air was still, a curl of thin smoke was rising beyond some distant trees, and a native drum was throbbing softly. There was a little Korku village down there; it was Sirisban, and around it the jungle grows almost up to the doors of the few tiny huts.

A soft clacking of rude cattle-bells could now be heard as the village kine approached their home, wending their way in slowly from the daily grazing-grounds.

The little mob of hill cattle came slowly into view, herded by a couple of children. They were pacing slowly and sleepily onwards in the yellow afterglow, past the steep bank of the nullah, past a depression filled with rank undergrowth and a tangle of dried creepers. All was peaceful, tranquil, and still. The herd passed on. Behind, one of them lingered in the rear. Then he too was passing the outskirts of the jungle and into the village commons.

Suddenly there was a silent rush, and immediately a furious clatter arose; every tail stuck up affrightedly in air; and in an instant the cattle were stampeding and galloping madly away, leaving the laggard struggling violently with a strange striped object. The herd-boys screamed out, pluckily beating their hollow bamboo cudgels on the ground. Next moment the released bullock, bleeding about the neck and shoulders from a number of deep scratches, went rushing frantically after his fellows towards the village, while something long and low glided away into the shadows whence it had come.

There was a confused uproar and shouting round the cattle-pens for some time after this; but the night soon fell swiftly dark, and the disturbance gradually came to an end.

The young tiger's timidity had been but temporary, and this repulse only left his appetite whetted to a yet keener edge. He crept out from his covert and furtively approached the village in the dark. Long he sat there, at a little distance, his chest a faint whitish patch in the shadows, and watched the twinkling village fires. Then the Korkus' evening meal was completed, the fires died down, silence reigned supreme; and as he began to prowl round close to the huts, his questing voice rose incontinently on the night air—

'Aaungh-ah! Aaungh-ah! Aaungh-ah!' repeated six or seven times consecutively, and followed by silence for some minutes before the deep call again grated forth.

In the village somebody yelled, and waved a firebrand; but the disappointed tiger continued his famished perambulations undeterred, and the watcher fell asleep.

In the jungle immediately west of Sirisban the stony ravine curves round under mossy old wide-branching mango trees, and here is the crude village well. As the young tiger approached this spot on his hungry prowl, he suddenly halted, and slowly sank down apparently into the very ground. In that dark glade the keenest human eye would have distinguished nothing save perhaps an indefinite suggestion of something vaguely white, but the tiger's acute senses had at once acquainted him with the surprising but delightful fact that a white heifer, no doubt overlooked in the confusion that evening and now playing truant, was standing there under the trees by the little pathway. Some rocks and a low bank separated the young tiger from the little cow; and, crouching very slowly, he now lay flattened out on his belly, intently contemplating his prospective meal. The heifer stood on, unconscious of any impending harm.

At last a paw of the stalker went out, with infinite caution; and remained there. Very slowly indeed another followed and passed it. And thus, inch by inch, paw by paw, each advanced in turn with almost inconceivable stealth, a grey shadow, a mere suggestion of shape, began to creep along under the tiny bank. So slowly did it travel, this phantom form only a few inches in height, that it was only after long intervals of time that it seemed to have moved a little nearer.

Under such conditions of extreme and breathless tension, time appears to stand still.

If the heifer had made the slightest movement, her creeping foe would have rushed on her instantly; but the foolish creature seemed to be wrapped in a silly, sleepy unconsciousness, perversely happy in her successful evasion of the cattle-pen's restraints.

Nearly half an hour must have passed thus, without a suspicion of the faintest sound or stir in the stillness of night, but now at last, within a few feet of the doomed cow, there might have been perceived a minute twitching movement, a movement barely discernible in the very faint light reflected from the starlit sky. This was the extreme tip of a round, thick tail curving from side to side in small spasmodic twists. And now, vaguely attracted by this strange motion, but without any change in her attitude of foolish rumination, the petrified heifer gradually realized that she was staring with distended eyeballs and wide-blown nostrils at something altogether frightful that lay at her very feet. Instantaneously deprived of all power of movement, of volition, the wretched little animal remained rooted to the spot. Her senses seemed to have been frozen by the mesmeric power that held her glued there—that extraordinary expression lent to the mask of a tiger engaged in stalking his prey, by virtue of the peculiar glaring white eye-spaces, with their frowning black angular markings, topped by a strange, intent black-barred forehead. Behind the paralyzing stare of this appalling headpiece the lithe and muscular frame was gathered up like the most powerfully compressed steel spring, ready and itching to 'take off' from the ground in its first sudden rush.

Thus did the two actors in this grim drama remain suspended, immobile, almost inanimate, in their respective poses—the smooth, white, shining skin of the little heifer faintly luminous in the dark of the trees, the horrible shadowy shape of her destroyer pressed close against the stones of the dim watercourse.

Every influence of the hour and place lent an increased paralysis to the sensation of terrible danger. An owl had now begun hooting mournfully in the forest beyond and the feeble chirping of crickets and tree-frogs made the silence yet more horribly expectant.

After a very long time there was another movement in that dark place—it was the heifer protruding her damp and helplessly fascinated nose, as she stretched it slowly downwards and outwards in the direction of that awful 'something' at her feet.

In that one instant the tension snapped.

A shadowy mass rose at once, seizing her by the throat and over the nape of the neck, and forthwith a fearful struggle set in amid the furious rattlings and rollings of stones.

The tiger, it must be remembered, was young and inexperienced; this was his first independent attempt at procuring his own food; and the cow, though little more than half-grown, was possessed of frantic strength born of the active terror which had succeeded her paralysis of fear. So both seizer and seized continued to battle violently together.

In the course of the struggle the tiger's jaws had been suddenly and dexterously shifted from under the throat to the nape of the heifer's slim neck, his rigidly protruded claws were deeply fixed—one forepaw over her shoulder, the other on her face—and his efforts seemed to be directed towards suddenly bending her head inwards and upwards. In this ghastly embrace the pair heaved and swung, now here, now there, with short, rapid, panting rushes. Then, as the cow, frantically struggling, succeeded in rearing her head and neck momentarily upwards, her murderer, with bent back and swiftly clambering hind feet, ripped and scored long, deep gashes down her stiffly protruded forelegs. Down she came again; and a tremulous moan of despair began to well from her straining throat.

At last there was a heavy squelch, as the miserable creature gave way and fell on her side. As she rolled over, the tiger slightly relaxed his hold. Up she sprang again, and went staggering off, tail in air. But, poor beast, she had not gone far before her hind legs were struck violently from under her, and she was once more in that merciless grip. This time the maddened tiger exerted all his strength. Almost at once there came a dull, thick, creaking snap and a stifled groan! There followed another heavy fall in the darkness; the sound of feeble kicking; a few deep, convulsive breaths, and a slow expiring sigh. Then absolute silence.

Long after this was heard a queer low sound as of bubbling, frothy breathing, and a ripping tearing noise. Then it ceased, and a deep throaty purr vibrated. The tiger was now wandering round and smelling his 'kill' in the dark. In course of time a dragging sound ensued, and stones rattled. He was endeavouring to convey his prey to a distance, after the instincts of his race.

All night long the young tiger fed voraciously. Beginning at the soft portions between the hinder limbs, he ate steadily forwards, gradually demolishing almost all of both hind quarters. But not yet had he attained to the scientific butchery of his kind; and the carcass remained uncleaned.

A thin sickle moon appeared over the eastward mountains towards morning, and the tiger began to drag the remains of his 'kill' yet further into the jungle, with a view to concealing it against his return next night. As he was transporting it along a steep incline it escaped from his hold and rolled down to the bottom of a ravine. He followed, and ate a little more; then, as day began to break, instinctively covered up the gory carcass with leaves and grass, scratching them together like a great cat. Water was his next consideration; and, after that, a siesta in some cool nook. As the sun rose he might have been seen near a pool farther down the nullah, reaching up and deeply scoring down the soft white bark of a taklai tree with lazy, luxurious claws; then he climbed the hillside slowly, contentedly. He had fed and drunk his fill, and up went his round tail after the pleasurable fashion of all cats. He passed on upwards, a handsome, sleek young murderer, seeking a shady spot for the day, and wearing an appearance of mild benignity very much at variance with his horrible work of the night. But all Nature is cruel, and tigers too must live; poor brute! He had only fulfilled his mission after all…

The young tiger now rapidly left his cubdom behind. He could kill for himself, provided that the beast he found was not too big and strong for him; and the longings for mother and the old life soon passed away. He struck out an independent career, and each day brought some fresh and useful experience.

It would not be difficult to paint in the life story of our tiger, becoming an adult, in ultra-lurid tints and make him into a dreaded man-eater, a monster, the terror of a countryside—for such things are too literally true. But they are the exception; based on the writer's own personal experience, in the ordinary everyday habits and incidental life of the jungle-king, usually one of retirement and inoffensive monotony, such things have no place.

The life of the jungle and its denizens runs its course full of incident and colour, tragedy and romance, with the ever-recurring refrain of unalterable savage Nature. And that of the tiger is no exception. He follows the seasons—hot, cold and wet—wandering on lengthy rounds or tied to a locality. He goes hungry or luxuriates in easy circumstances at the nod of Fate.

Thus some five years rolled by, and our tiger attained to the full size and strength of his magnificent prime. His headquarters were situated on the line of the same old jungly Sipna, but his regular beat extended over many long miles of the neighbouring hills and glens; and in days of parching hot weather he would temporarily shift his quarters to the higher ranges. A tiger of the heavy, continuous, well-watered forests of Melghat, his was the life of a great wanderer, a beast now here, now there…

MRS PACKLETIDE'S TIGER

SAKI

A delightful story about the absurd obsession with shikar, and the comedy of it, by the great satirist Saki (born H.H. Munro in 1870) who may well have met a lady like Mrs Packletide during his short stint as a young police officer in Burma in 1893-94. Burma was then part of the British Indian Empire.

IT was Mrs Packletide's pleasure and intention that she should shoot a tiger. Not that the lust to kill had suddenly descended on her, or that she felt that she would leave India safer and more wholesome than she had found it, with one fraction less of wild beast per million of inhabitants. The compelling motive for her sudden deviation towards the footsteps of Nimrod was the fact that Loona Bimberton had recently been carried eleven miles in an aeroplane by an Algerian aviator, and talked of nothing else; only a personally procured tiger-skin and a heavy harvest of Press photographs could successfully counter that sort of thing. Mrs Packletide had already arranged in her mind the lunch she would give at her house in Curzon Street, ostensibly in Loona Bimberton's honour, with a tiger-skin rug occupying most of the foreground and all of the conversation. She had also already designed in her mind the tiger-claw broach that she was going to give Loona Bimberton on her next birthday. In a world that is supposed to be chiefly swayed by hunger and by love Mrs Packletide was an exception; her movements and motives were largely governed by dislike of Loona Bimberton.

Circumstances proved propitious. Mrs Packletide had offered a thousand rupees for the opportunity of shooting a tiger without over-much risk or exertion, and it so happened that a neighbouring village could boast of being the favoured rendezvous of an animal of respectable antecedents, which had been driven by the increasing infirmities of age to abandon game-killing and confine its appetite to the smaller domestic animals. The prospect of earning the thousand rupees had stimulated the sporting and commercial instinct of the villagers; children were posted night and day on the outskirts of the local jungle to head the tiger back in the unlikely event of his attempting to roam away to fresh hunting-grounds, and the cheaper kinds of goats were left about with elaborate carelessness to keep him satisfied with his present quarters. The one great anxiety was lest he should die of old age before the date appointed for the memsahib's shoot. Mothers carrying their babies home through the jungle after the day's work in the fields hushed their singing lest they might curtail the restful sleep of the venerable herd-robber.

2

The great night duly arrived, moonlit and cloudless. A platform had been constructed in a comfortable and conveniently placed tree, and thereon crouched Mrs Packletide and her paid companion, Miss Mebbin. A goat, gifted with a particularly persistent bleat, such as even a partially deaf tiger might be reasonably expected to hear on a still night, was tethered at the correct distance. With an accurately sighted rifle and a thumb-nail pack of patience cards the sportswoman awaited the coming of the quarry.

'I suppose we are in some danger?' said Miss Mebbin.

She was not actually nervous about the wild beast, but she had a morbid dread of performing an atom more service than she had been paid for.

'Nonsense,' said Mrs Packletide, 'it's a very old tiger. It couldn't spring up here even if it wanted to.'

'If it's an old tiger I think you ought to get it cheaper. A thousand rupees is a lot of money.'

Louisa Mebbin adopted a protective elder-sister attitude towards money in general, irrespective of nationality or denomination. Her energetic intervention had saved many a rouble from dissipating itself in tips in some Moscow hotel, and francs and centimes clung to her instinctively under circumstances which would have driven them headlong from less sympathetic hands. Her speculations as to the market depreciation of tiger remnants were cut short by the appearance on the scene of the animal itself. As soon as it caught sight of the tethered goat it lay flat on the earth, seemingly less from a desire to take advantage of all available cover than for the purpose of snatching a short rest before commencing the grand attack.

'I believe it's ill,' said Louisa Mebbin, loudly in Hindustani, for the benefit of the village headman, who was in ambush in a neighbouring tree.

'Hush!' said Mrs Packletide, and at that moment the tiger commenced ambling towards his victim.

'Now, now!' urged Miss Mebbin with some excitement, 'if he doesn't touch the goat we needn't pay for it.' (The bait was an extra.)

3

The rifle flashed out with a loud report, and the great tawny beast sprang to one side and then rolled over in the stillness of death. In a moment a crowd of excited natives had swarmed on to the scene, and their shouting speedily carried the glad news to the village, where a thumping of tom-toms took up the chorus of triumph. And their triumph and rejoicing found a ready echo in the heart of Mrs Packletide; already that luncheon-party in Curzon Street seemed immeasurably nearer.

It was Louisa Mebbin who drew attention to the fact that the goat was in death-throes from a mortal bullet-wound, while no trace of the rifle's deadly work could be found on the tiger. Evidently the wrong animal had been hit, and the beast of prey had succumbed to heart-failure, caused by the sudden report of the rifle, accelerated by senile decay. Mrs Packletide was pardonably annoyed at the discovery; but, at any rate, she was the possessor of a dead tiger, and the villagers, anxious for their thousand rupees, gladly connived at the fiction that she had shot the beast. And Miss Mebbin was a paid companion. Therefore did Mrs Packletide face the cameras with a light heart, and her pictured fame reached from the pages of the *Texas Weekly Snapshot* to the illustrated Monday supplement of the *Novoe Vremya*. As for

Loona Bimberton, she refused to look at an illustrated paper for weeks, and her letter of thanks for the gift of a tiger-claw brooch was a model of repressed emotions. The luncheon-party she declined; there are limits beyond which repressed emotions become dangerous.

From Curzon Street the tiger-skin rug travelled down to the Manor House, and was duly inspected and admired by the county, and it seemed a fitting and appropriate thing when Mrs Packletide went to the County Costume Ball in the character of Diana. She refused to fall in, however, with Clovis's tempting suggestion of a primeval dance party, at which every one should wear the skins of beasts they had recently slain. 'I should be in rather a Baby Bunting condition,' confessed Clovis, 'with a miserable rabbit-skin or two to wrap up in, but then,' he added, with a rather malicious glance at Diana's proportions, 'my figure is quite as good as that Russian dancing boy's.'

4

'How amused everyone would be if they knew what really happened,' said Louisa Mebbin a few days after the ball.

'What do you mean?' asked Mrs Packletide quickly.

'How you shot the goat and frightened the tiger to death,' said Miss Mebbin, with her disagreeably pleasant laugh.

'No one would believe it,' said Mrs Packletide, her face changing colour as rapidly as though it were going through a book of patterns before post-time.

'Loona Bimberton would,' said Miss Mebbin. Mrs Packletide's face settled on an unbecoming shade of greenish white.

'You surely wouldn't give me away?' she asked.

'I've seen a week-end cottage near Darking that I should rather like to buy,' said Miss Mebbin with seeming irrelevance. 'Six hundred and eighty, freehold. Quite a bargain, only I don't happen to have the money.'

Louisa Mebbin's pretty week-end cottage, christened by her 'Les Fauves', and gay in summer-time with its garden borders of tiger-lilies, is the wonder and admiration of her friends.

'It is a marvel how Louisa manages to do it,' is the general verdict.

Mrs Packletide indulges in no more big-game shooting.

'The incidental expenses are so heavy,' she confides to inquiring friends.

THE TIGER-CHARM

ALICE PERRIN

Born in Mussoorie in 1867, Alice Perrin was sent to school in England and returned to India in 1886, where she lived with her husband for the next two decades. Most of Perrin's stories and novels are based on her experiences in India, and some critics have rated her higher than Kipling, especially as a short-story writer. 'The Tiger Charm' is a lightly edited version of a story that first appeared in East of Suez, *a collection of supernatural stories published in 1901.*

THE sun, the sky, the burning dusty atmosphere, and the waving sea of tall yellow grass seemed molten into one blinding blaze of pitiless heat to the aching vision of little Mrs Wingate. In spite of blue goggles, pith sun hat and enormous umbrella, she felt as though she were being slowly roasted alive, for the month was May, and she and her husband were perched on the back of an elephant, traversing a large tract of jungle at the foot of the Himalayas.

Colonel Wingate was one of the keenest sportsmen in India, and every day for the past week had he and his wife, and their friend, Captain Bastable, sallied forth from the camp with a line of elephants to beat through the forests of grass that reached to the animal's ears; to squelch over swamps, disturbing herds of antelope and wild pig; to pierce thick tangles of jungle, from which rose pea-fowl, black partridge, and birds of gorgeous plumage; to cross stony beds of dry rivers—ever on the watch for the tigers that had hitherto baffled all their efforts. 'That howdah is not big enough for two people,' shouted Captain Bastable, coming to the rescue. 'Let Mrs Wingate change to mine. It's bigger, and my elephant has easier paces.'

Hot, irritated, angry, Colonel Wingate commanded his wife to betake herself to Bastable's elephant, and to keep her infernal umbrella closed for the rest of the day, adding that women had no business out tiger-shooting; and why the devil had she come at all?—oblivious of the fact that Mrs Wingate had begged to be allowed to stay in the station, and that he himself had insisted on her coming.

She well knew that argument or contradiction would only make matters worse, for he had swallowed three stiff whiskies and sodas at luncheon in the broiling sun, and since the severe sunstroke that had so nearly killed him two years ago, the smallest quantity of spirits was enough to change him from an exceedingly bad-tempered man into something little short of a maniac.

She had heedlessly married him when she was barely nineteen, turning a deaf ear to warnings of his violence, and now, at twenty-three, her existence was one long fear. He never allowed her out of his sight, he never believed a word she said; he watched her, suspected her, bullied her unmercifully, and was insanely jealous. Unfortunately, she was one of those nervous, timid women, who often rather provoke ill-treatment than otherwise.

This afternoon she marvelled at being permitted to change to Captain Bastable's howdah, and with a feeling of relief scrambled off the elephant, though trembling, as she always did, lest the great beast should seize her with his trunk or lash her with his tail that was like a jointed iron rod. Then, once safely perched up behind Captain Bastable, she settled herself with a delightful sense of security. He understood her nervousness, he did not laugh or grumble at her little involuntary cries of fear; he was not impatient when she was convinced the elephant was running away or sinking in a quicksand, or that the howdah was slipping off. He also understood the Colonel, and had several times helped her through a trying situation; and now the sympathy in his kind eyes made her tender heart throb with gratitude.

'All right?' he asked.

She nodded, smiling, and they started again ploughing and lurching through the coarse grass, great wisps of which the elephant uprooted with his trunk, and beat against his chest to get rid of the soil before putting them in his mouth. Half an hour later, as they drew near the edge of the forest, one of the elephants suddenly stopped short, with a jerky, backward movement, and trumpeted shrilly. There was an expectant halt all along the line, and a cry from a native of 'Tiger! Tiger!' Then an enormous striped beast bounded out of the grass and stood for a moment in a small, open space, lashing its tail and snarling in defiance. Colonel Wingate fired.

The tiger, badly wounded, charged, and sprang at the head of Captain Bastable's elephant. There was a confusion of noise; savage roars from the tiger; shrieks from the excited elephants; shouts from the natives; banging of rifles. Mrs

Wingate covered her face with her hands. She heard a thud, as of a heavy body falling to the ground, and then she found herself being flung from side to side of the howdah, as the elephant bolted madly towards the forest, one huge ear torn to ribbons by the tiger's claws.

She heard Captain Bastable telling her to hold on tight, and shouting desperate warnings to the mahout to keep the elephant as clear of the forest as possible.

Like many nervous people in the face of real danger, she suddenly became absolutely calm, and uttered no sound as the pace increased and they tore along the forest edge, escaping overhanging boughs by a miracle. To her it seemed that the ponderous flight lasted for hours. She was bruised, shaken, giddy, and the crash that came at last was a relief rather than otherwise. A huge branch combed the howdah off the elephant's back, sweeping the mahout with it, while the still terrified animal sped on trumpeting and crashing through the forest. Mrs Wingate was thrown clear of the howdah.

Captain Bastable had saved himself by jumping, and only the old mahout lay doubled up and unconscious amongst the debris of shattered wood, torn leather and broken ropes. Netta Wingate could hardly believe she was not hurt, and she and Captain Bastable stared at one another with dazed faces for some moments before they could collect their senses. Far away in the distance they could hear the elephant still running. Between them they extricated the mahout, and, seating herself on the ground, Netta took the old man's unconscious head on to her lap, while Captain Bastable anxiously examined the wizened, shrunken body.

'Is he dead?' she asked.

'I can't be sure. I'm afraid he is. I wonder if I could find some water. I haven't an idea where we are, for I lost all count of time and distance. I hope Wingate is following us. Should you be afraid to stay here while I have a look round and see if we are anywhere near a village?'

'Oh, no, I sha'n't be frightened,' she said steadily.

Her delicate, clear-cut face looked up at him fearlessly from the tangled background of mighty trees and dense creepers; and her companion could scarcely believe she was the same trembling, nervous little coward of an hour ago.

He left her, and the stillness of the jungle was very oppressive when the sound of his footsteps died away. She was alone with a dead, or dying man, on the threshold of the vast, mysterious forest, with its possible horrors of wild elephants, tigers, leopards, snakes! She tried to turn her thoughts from such things, but the scream of a peacock made her start as it rent the silence, and then the undergrowth began to rustle ominously.

It was only a porcupine that came out, rattling his quills, and, on seeing her, ran into further shelter out of sight. It seemed to be growing darker, and she fancied the evening must be drawing in. She wondered if her husband would overtake them. If not, how were she and Jim Bastable to get back to the camp? Then she heard voices and footsteps, and presently a little party of natives came in sight, led by Jim and bearing a string bedstead.

'I found a village not far off,' he explained, 'and thought we'd better take the poor old chap there. Then, if the Colonel doesn't turn up by the time we've seen him comfortably settled, we must find our way back to the camp as best we can.'

The natives chattered and exclaimed as they lifted the unconscious body on to the bedstead, and then the little procession started. Netta was so bruised and stiff she could hardly walk; but, with the help of Bastable's arm, she hobbled along till the village was gained. The headman conducted them to his house, which consisted of a mud hovel shared by himself and his family with several relations, besides a cow and a goat with two kids. He gave Netta a wicker stool to sit on and some smoky buffalo's milk to drink, while the village physician was summoned, who at last succeeded in restoring the mahout to consciousness and pouring a potion down his throat.

'I die,' whispered the patient, feebly. Netta went to his side, and he recognised her.

'A—ree! Memsahib!' he quavered. 'So Allah has guarded thee. But the anger of the Colonel sahib will be great against me for permitting the elephant to run away, and it is better that I die. Where is that daughter of a pig? She was a rascal from her youth up; but today was the first time she ever really disobeyed my voice.'

He tried to raise himself, but fell back groaning, for his injuries were internal and past hope.

'It is growing dark.' He put forth his trembling hand blindly. 'Where is the little white lady who so feared the sahib, and the elephants, and the jungle? Do not be afraid, memsahib. Those who fear should never go into the jungle. So if [you see] a tiger, be bold, be bold; call him "uncle" and show him the tiger-charm. Then will he turn away and harm [you] not—' He wandered on incoherently, his fingers fumbling with something at his throat, and presently he drew out a small silver amulet attached to a piece of cord. As he held it towards Netta, it flashed in the light of the miserable native oil lamp that someone had just brought in and placed on the floor.

'Take it, memsahib, and feel no fear while [you have] st it, for no tiger would touch thee. It was my father's, and his father's before him, and there is that written on it which has ever protected us from the tiger's tooth. I myself shall need it no longer, for I am going, whereat my nephew will rejoice; for he has long coveted my seat. Thou shalt have the charm, memsahib, for thou hast stayed by an old man, and not left him to die alone in a Hindu village and a strange place. Some day, in the hour of danger, thy little fingers may touch the charm, and then thou wilt recall old Mahomed Bux, mahout, with gratitude.'

He groped for Netta's hand, and pushed the amulet into her palm. She took it, and laid her cool fingers on the old man's burning forehead.

'Salaam, Mahomed Bux,' she said softly. 'Bahut, bahut, salaam.' Which is the nearest Hindustani equivalent for 'Thank you'.

But he did not hear her. He was wandering again, and for half an hour he babbled of elephants, of tigers, of camps and jungles, until his voice became faint and died away in hoarse gasps.

Then he sighed heavily and lay still, and Jim Bastable took Mrs Wingate out into the air, and told her that the old mahout was dead. She gave way and sobbed, for she was aching all over and tired to death, and she dreaded the return to the camp.

'Oh, my dear girl, please don't cry!' said Jim distressfully. 'Though really I can't wonder at it, after all you've gone through today; and you've been so awfully plucky, too.'

Netta gulped down her tears. It was delicious to be praised for courage, when she was only accustomed to abuse for cowardice.

'How are we to get back to the camp?' she asked dolefully. 'It's so late.'

And, indeed, darkness had come swiftly on, and the light of the village fires was all that enabled them to see each other.

'The moon will be up presently; we must wait for that. They say the village near our camp lies about six miles off, and that there is a cart-track of sorts towards it. I told them they must let us have a bullock-cart, and we shall have to make the best of that.'

They sat down side by side on a couple of large stones, and listened in silence to the lowing of the tethered cattle, the ceaseless, irritating cry of the brain fever bird, and the subdued conversation of a group of children and village idlers, who had assembled at a respectful distance to watch them with inquisitive interest. Once a shrill trumpeting in the distance told of a herd of wild elephants out on a night's raid on the crops, and at intervals packs of jackals swept howling across the fields, while the moon rose gradually over the collection of squalid huts and flooded the vast country with a light that made the forest black and fearful.

Then a clumsy little cart, drawn by two small, frightened white bullocks, rattled into view. Jim and Netta climbed into the vehicle, and were politely escorted off the premises by the headman and the concourse of interested villagers and excited women and children.

They bumped and shook over the rough, uneven track. The bullocks raced or crawled alternately, while the driver twisted their tails and abused them hoarsely. The moonlight grew brighter and more glorious. The air, now soft and cool, was filled with strong scents and the hum of insects released from the heat of the day. At last they caught the gleam of white tents against the dark background of a mango-grove.

'The camp,' said Captain Bastable, shortly. Netta made a nervous exclamation.

'Do you think there will be a row?' he asked with some hesitation. They had never discussed Mrs Wingate's domestic troubles together.

'Perhaps he is still looking out for us,' she said evasively.

'If he had followed us at all, he must have found us. I believe he went on shooting, or back to the camp.'

There was an angry impatience in his voice. 'Don't be nervous,' he added hastily. 'Try not to mind anything he may say. Don't listen. He can't always help it, you know. I wish you could persuade him to retire; the sun out here makes him half off his head.'

'I wish I could,' she sighed. 'But he will never do anything I ask him, and the big-game shooting keeps him in India.'

Jim nodded, and there was a comprehending silence between them till they reached the edge of the camp, got out of the cart, and made their way to the principal tent. There they discovered Colonel Wingate, still in his shooting clothes, sitting by the table, on which stood an almost empty bottle of whisky. He rose as they entered, and delivered himself of a torrent of bad language.

He accused the pair of going off together on purpose, declaring he would divorce his wife and kill Bastable. He stormed, raved and threatened, giving them no opportunity of speaking, until at last Jim broke in and insisted on being heard.

'For Heaven's sake, be quiet,' he said firmly, 'or you'll have a fit. You saw the elephant run away, and apparently you made no effort to follow us and come to our help. We were swept off by a tree, and the mahout was mortally hurt. It was a perfect miracle that neither your wife nor I was killed. The mahout died in a village, and we had to get here in a bullock-cart.' Then, seeing Wingate preparing for another onslaught, Bastable took him by the shoulders. 'My dear chap, you're not yourself. Go to bed, and we'll talk it over tomorrow if you still wish to.'

Colonel Wingate laughed harshly. His mood had changed suddenly.

'Go to bed?' he shouted boisterously. 'Why, I was just going out when you arrived. There was a kill last night, only a mile off, and I'm going to get the tiger.' He stared wildly at Jim, who saw that he was not responsible for his words and actions. The brain, already touched by sunstroke, had given way at last under the power of whisky. Jim's first impulse was to prevent his carrying out his intention of going after the tiger. Then he reflected that it was not safe for Netta to be alone with the man, and that, if Wingate were allowed his own way, it would at least take him out of the camp.

'Very well,' said Jim quietly, 'and I will come with you.'

'Do,' answered the Colonel pleasantly, and then, as Bastable turned for a moment, Mrs Wingate saw her husband make a diabolical grimace at the other's unconscious back. Her heart beat rapidly with fear.

Did he mean to murder Jim? She felt convinced he contemplated mischief; but the question was how to warn Captain Bastable without her husband's knowledge. The opportunity came more easily than she had expected, for presently the Colonel went outside to call for his rifle and give some orders. She flew to Bastable's side.

'Be careful,' she panted; 'he wants to kill you, I know he does. He's mad! Oh, don't go with him—don't go—'

'It will be all right,' he said reassuringly. 'I'll look out for myself, but I can't let him go alone in this state. We shall only sit up in a tree for an hour or two, for the tiger must have come and gone long ago. Don't be frightened. Go to bed and rest.'

She drew from her pocket the little polished amulet the mahout had given her.

'At any rate, take this,' she said hysterically. 'It may save you from a tiger, if it doesn't from my husband. I know I am silly, but do take it. There may be luck in it, you can never tell; and old Mahomed Bux said it had saved him and his father and his grandfather—and that you ought to call a tiger "uncle" '—she broke off, half laughing, half crying, utterly unstrung.

To please her he put the little charm into his pocket, and after a hasty drink went out and joined Wingate, who insisted that they should proceed on foot and by themselves. Bastable knew it would be useless to make any opposition, and they started, their rifles in their hands; but, when they had gone some distance and the tainted air told them they were nearing their destination, Jim discovered he had no cartridges.

'Never mind,' whispered the Colonel, 'I have plenty, and our rifles have the same bore. We can't go back now; we've no time to lose.'

Jim submitted, and he and Wingate tiptoed to the foot of a tree, the low branches and thick leaves of which afforded an excellent hiding place, down-wind from the half-eaten carcass of the cow. They climbed carefully up, making scarcely any noise, and then Jim held out his hand to the other for some cartridges. The Colonel nodded.

'Presently,' he whispered, and Jim waited, thinking it extremely unlikely that cartridges would be wanted at all.

The moonlight came feebly through the foliage of the surrounding trees on to the little glade before them, in which lay the remains of the carcass pulled under a bush to shield it from the carrion birds. A deer pattered by towards the river, casting startled glances on every side; insects beat against the faces of the two men; and a jackal ran out with his brush hanging down, looked round, and retired again, with a melancholy howl.

Then there arose a commotion in the branches of the neighbouring trees, and a troop of monkeys fought and crashed and chattered, as they leapt from bough to bough. Jim knew that this often portended the approach of a tiger, and the moment afterwards a long, hoarse call from the river told him that the warning was correct. He made a silent sign for the cartridges; but Wingate took no notice: his face was hard and set, and the whites of his eyes gleamed.

A few seconds later a large tiger crept slowly out of the grass, his stomach on the ground, his huge head held low. Jim remembered the native superstition that the head of a man-eating tiger is weighed down by the souls of its victims.

With a run and a spring the creature attacked its meal, and began growling and munching contentedly, purring like a cat, and stopping every now and then to tear up the earth with its claws.

A report rang out. Wingate had fired at and hit the tiger. The great beast gave a terrific roar and sprang at the tree. Jim lifted his rifle, only to remember that it was unloaded.

'Shoot again!' he cried excitedly, as the tiger fell back and prepared for another spring. To his horror, Wingate deliberately fired the second barrel into the air, and, throwing away the rifle, grasped him by the arms.

The man's teeth were bared, his face distorted and hideous, his purpose unmistakable—he was trying to throw Bastable to the tiger. Wingate was strong with the diabolical strength of madness, and they swayed till the branches of the tree crackled ominously. Again the tiger roared and sprang, and again fell back, only to gather itself together for another effort. The two men rocked and panted, the branches cracked louder with a dry, splitting sound, then broke off altogether, and, locked in each other's arms, they fell heavily to the ground.

Jim Bastable went undermost, and was half stunned by the shock. He heard a snarl in his ear, followed by a dreadful cry. He felt the weight of Wingate's body lifted from him with a jerk, and he scrambled blindly to his feet. As in a nightmare, he saw the tiger bounding away, carrying something that hung limply from the great jaws, just as a cat carries a dead mouse.

He seized the Colonel's rifle that lay near him; but he knew it was empty, and that the cartridges were in the Colonel's pocket. He ran after the tiger, shouting, yelling, brandishing the rifle, in hopes of frightening the brute into dropping its prey; but, after one swift glance back, it bounded into the thick jungle with the speed of a deer, and Bastable was left standing alone.

Faint and sick, he began running madly towards the camp for help, though he knew well that nothing in this world could ever help Wingate again. His forehead was bleeding profusely, either hurt in the fall or touched by the tiger's claw, and the blood trickling into his eyes nearly blinded him. He pulled his handkerchief from his pocket as he ran, and something came with it that glittered in the moonlight and fell to the ground with a metallic ring.

It was the little silver amulet. The tiger-charm.

THE WHITE TIGER

A. MERVYN SMITH

This story first appeared in Sport and Adventure in India *(see 'The One-Eyed Man-Eater').*

'THE Sahib wishes to know which is the most dangerous animal I have ever killed? What do we baghmarees (tiger-slayers) know of danger, Huzoor? We set our traps, and it is naseeb ka baat (a question of luck) whether we kill or not. There is no danger. The bow is fixed in the evening, and we go to see next morning whether the arrow is shot. We follow the trail and generally get the animal that day or the next. Bears are the most difficult to kill; not only do they take longer to die, but they generally make off to their caves when wounded and die there. No, we never go near the wounded animal. We follow it up, and if it shows signs of life we go away and come later on, when it is dead. When we use cobra poison the wounded animal goes to sleep and dies in its sleep. Dakara (aconite) is also good. Krait (snake) poison is not so good. When the arrow has been poisoned with krait venom the animal may recover if there be much bleeding from the wound. Yes, we have antidotes for all the poisons. Sometimes a man is wounded by our poisoned arrows. If we know it in time, we apply certain jungle leaves as a poultice and the man recovers. If large water blisters form round the wound within half-an-hour, the man will recover. If no blisters come, he will die…'

What has all this to do with dangerous animals? the Sahib asks.

'Well, hear me, Huzoor. I was once in great danger. Twenty men were in fear of their lives for a week because of one animal. It was in Gangpore, seven years ago. The Sahib knows the motee-joad (twin pearls)? Yes of course, the Sahib has seen it; he shot one on the river a fortnight ago—the large brown-breasted wild duck that is called by us the motee-joad because when once these birds pair, their affection for one another is so strong that it has passed into a proverb with us—"As faithful as the motee-joad". Remember, when the Huzoor shot the wild duck, its mate would not leave the spot for hours although all its companions had taken to flight? The Huzoor could have shot it also but his heart is soft… At night these birds do not roost together, Huzoor, but rest on opposite sides of the river, and all night long you will hear their "qua! qua!" as they call to each other… Ah, the Sahib is impatient, but I am coming to my story of the white tiger. Yes, white tiger. Your servant does not lie. Why should I lie to the Sahib Huzoor? These eyes have seen it, and others have seen it but they are not here now. White tiger, not panther; does not your servant know the difference between a tiger and a leopard when he has lived all his life in the forest? Yes, there are white tigers in Gangpore, and I have killed one.

'It was at the ghur (Gainghur, the Raja's residence). A tiger had killed several cattle. The pugs were small and some said it was a panther; but I knew it was a tiger because the pugs of a tiger show the toe marks distinctly, whereas in a panther's pugs the toe marks are very faint, because it treads more on the ball of the foot, to preserve its claws for tree climbing. The tiger cannot climb trees but the panther can. I have seen it run up a tree like a squirrel and bite a man's leg on the topmost bough. On a tree you are safe from a tiger… So I said it was a tiger, and the Raja asked me to kill it. I set my bow and poisoned arrows near the next kill but the tiger did not come near it. I set it at several different kills but the thief of a tiger was too cunning. He would not come near it. The people laughed and said I was a tantee (weaver), and not a baghmaree (tiger-killer), and that I had better go back to my trade. But the Huzoor can see I am a man—' (stroking his moustache)—'and am not to be beaten by a janwar (wild animal). I took counsel with no one but walked the jungle every day to see if I could not circumvent this dog that had thrown dirt in my face and caused the villagers to laugh at me. I soon noticed that there were two sets of pugs, which went together. This led me to believe there were a tiger and a tigress. I went to every kill before the Khols got scent of it and carried away the flesh—as these people eat every kind of flesh, even rats and snakes and carrion—and I carefully noted that the trails all led in one direction—to a rocky hill covered with dense jungle. This was where the tigers had taken up their abode.

'I soon found that the tigers took a particular path to the river to drink. That was the clue I wanted, Huzoor. I would now have my revenge, and the villagers would see I was a real baghmaree, although only a weaver by caste. Shabash! I set my bow to command the path the tiger took when going to the river, and went home quite pleased with myself; but I did not tell anybody that I had set my trap, as I waited for my triumph to be complete. I hardly slept that night, and was away at grey dawn to see the trap. The bow was sprung and both arrows had taken effect as they were not to be found anywhere, while pug-marks, blood and signs of struggling were to be seen on the path. I knew the arrows would do their work, for I had put on some fresh cobra poison the previous day. Imagine my feelings, Sahib, when I saw I had triumphed! The bridegroom on his wedding-day, when the village girls anoint him with turmeric and oil; or when you have just secured a pair of strong buffaloes for your plough at half price; or when your field has yielded forty-fold; or when your enemy is dead—mine were all these feelings in one! I felt a hero.

'I gathered up my bow and ropes and walked to the village a new man. I went straight to the gathering-tree in the centre of the village and sat down. First came one and jibed, "Well, tantee, is that your loom you have rolled up?" pointing to my bow. "Make me a saree for my wife, and I will give you half a candy of grain when the crop comes," said another. Many joined in the laugh, but I waited quietly till the principal men of the village had assembled to talk, when I said, "Brothers, don't laugh any more, but come with the poor weaver. I have something to show"; and I strode on with the gait of an elephant with the great Maharaj on his back. All the village followed, and I led straight to the place where I had set my trap, and the trail from there was clear. Not two hundred yards off we found the body of the tiger. It was a white tiger. Pure white: no spot or stripe of any kind. Believe me, Sahib, when I tell you it was white.

A great shout went up from the villagers and I was happy. Such moments come seldom.

'After a time the villagers left and only the shikarees (hunters) of the village remained with me to do pooja. The oldest of the shikarees made a slight wound in my head and took some of the blood and rubbed it in on the head of the tiger. I walked three times round the body of the tiger, and then touched its body with my forehead while the others looked aside. We now slung the tiger to a pole and took it to the village in triumph. When we got there, the shikarees' wives came out and washed my feet with water and salaamed to me. You don't want to hear all that; you want to know where the danger came in. I will pass over the triumphs of the day; how the Raja gave me two rupees and a dhotee; how the villagers also rewarded me, each according to his means. I was a great man that day… Don't be impatient, Sahib; one likes to talk of one's victories, we are all alike.

'We skinned the tiger, and found it was very old—fifteen years old. How do we know a tiger's age? By the number of lobes in the liver. This one had fifteen distinct marks, one for each year. Panthers have these marks also, but not other animals. All shikarees know this, as we always take out the liver for medicine. This is how we judge of a tiger's age, and it is true. We pegged out the skin in the sun to dry, the head being boned and stuffed with straw and the mouth agape. At night we rolled up the skin and placed it on some sticks in an empty cow-shed. Our huts were about thirty yards away; but beside the empty shed was another in which several bullocks were stalled. It was barely dark when we heard the "oungh! oungh!" of the other tiger in the distance. This we knew was the tiger calling for his mate. The tiger seldom cries, only when calling its mate; it never speaks at other times. The "oungh oungh!" came nearer, and we knew the tiger had scented out his dead mate. Soon it was near the cattle-shed, and we could hear the cattle struggling in alarm. We all shouted together, but the tiger still kept prowling round and round the empty shed. He then sprang on to the roof and tore away the thatch. We now kept very quiet as we began to be afraid. We heard a purring sound and then a roar, and the tiger was inside the empty shed.

'Soon we heard a great crashing and breaking of wood, and the whole roof of the shed was torn down. He then passed into the next shed, where the bullocks were stalled. The bullocks were so terrified that they broke the barred gate and ran out; but the tiger was down among them and killed four, as we found next morning. He went back to the empty shed and kept alternately roaring and purring. He would go off a couple of hundred yards and roar, and finding no answering roar he would come back. He kept this up the whole night. The whole village was in a fright; not a soul slept. At dawn the tiger went off to the hills, still roaring occasionally. Next morning what a scene met our eyes! Thick bamboos had been bitten in two by the tiger in his rage. The shed was completely wrecked, but the skin was intact.

'We took the skin to the ghur, two miles away, where the Raja lived, and told our tale. An old Khol, who knew the habits of all wild beasts, said it was a motee-joad bagh (twin-pearl tiger), and that it would never leave its mate, but would kill all in the village unless we killed it. The Raja ordered the skin to be put into a strong shed where the grain was stored, and commanded twenty of the best shooters in the village to get up into machans near the shed and shoot the tiger when it came at night. Everybody strongly barricaded their doors that night. I was on a machan near the shed. Night came on, but no tiger roared. It grew late; half the night went by; and from fear and trembling we grew light-hearted, and began to twit the Khol about his knowledge of tigers, when suddenly we heard a roar at our very feet that made us lie down and cover our heads in fear. Then we heard a great scratching at the door of the shed where the skin was, and we knew the tiger was trying to break in. We could not see the tiger, so some of us shouted and others fired their guns, but he continued scratching and roaring. We then arranged to fire together at the door in the hopes of hitting him. We fired and heard a scream of rage and then a great scuffling, as if something was trying to climb the tree on which our machan was built. Of the eight men on my machan, six had fired off their matchlocks, and only two shots were left. If the tiger succeeded in climbing the tree we were dead men…

'I can assure you, Huzoor, I was like a twisted rag; there was no sap in me. The tiger would rush up the trunk of the tree, and then fall back. This he did several times, and then went back to the door and began his scratching. When the other men had reloaded, we arranged to fire four at a time. This we did several times, and at last it appeared as if we had struck him, for the scratching ceased, but he continued to roar. We kept on firing till all sounds from him ceased, and then we knew we had killed him, or he had gone off. In the morning we saw he was dead near the door and near to his mate. He had twenty shots in his body. He was, in truth, a motee-joad, Huzoor. He gave up his life rather than leave his mate!'

THE PETS

Two stories, probably true—one by David Wilson (see 'Tiger Tales from Burma'), the other by Stanley Jepson (editor of The Illustrated Weekly of India *in the 1930s)—about leopard cubs and their loving captors.*

The Object of His Affection

(Excerpted from 'The Big Pet Cat' by David Wilson)

ONE evening in the [1890s] I went to dine at the house of a friend in Burma, and was unexpectedly greeted at the entrance by a leopard almost fully grown. He received me with the same restful manner of dignified neutrality that may be seen on the features of a domestic cat, or of an old family servant, observing a strange visitor.

'Do the others know?' I asked the host, meaning the other dinner guests, not yet arrived.

'Yes, they all know him, but none of them like him, or maybe it is that *he* does not like *them*. I don't exactly know what is the matter…But he seems to feel by instinct that you're a friend. Dear old fellow!'

And the big cat laid his head confidentially on my host's thigh, and rolled his eyes dubiously in the way cats do, while a fat hand caressed his fine fur tenderly, lovingly.

'It'll be rare fun to see the rest arrive,' said the host.

It was indeed a pleasant entertainment to see that bachelor's house being entered as if a very distinguished hostess were receiving the visitors. The sight of 'Mr Spots' made the most free-and-easy a little constrained in manner. They kept their eyes upon him; and as he moved about at his ease, they made way for him with an agility of quick politeness more common in Frenchmen than in Englishmen. But though he engrossed their conversation as much as their thoughts, there was a lack of heartiness in their appreciation, which seemed to sadden their host. He tried to keep the fine animal beside himself.

'Pets should always be young and growing creatures,' he said, as he scratched its head, and with many mingled puffs and sighs went on to say, 'They are a nuisance when they grow up. You lose their affection, you see... Women are just the same. This beautiful beast does not heed me now, though at one time no puppy could be fonder. He would lie on his back to be tickled by a straw and play with me by the hour. He hardly ever snarled, even at the servants... Look at him!'

The gentle beast was made to show his teeth and opened a capacious mouth.

'Yes, indeed,' said one. 'I've done nothing but look at him since I came in, and have had my hand on my pistol already once.'

'He won't hurt you. He's had his dinner.'

Another visitor sent his dog home, and opportunely remarked that as leopards were fond of eating dogs, they felt at home with humanity as lions or tigers never could. It was hunger only that made these bigger beasts eat men. The normal tiger or lion would run away from a child, or at any rate pass it by. But even a well-fed leopard might take to 'long pig', meaning humanity, in simple wantonness, just for a change.

'I hope he always has plenty of salt with his food,' said one. 'Might I tell the boy to fetch some for him now?'

'Why in all the world?' asked our host.

'Because it is the salt in human flesh that is said to be the great attraction.'

'You don't suppose my leopard spends his time in studying chemistry, do you? I tell you, he would not eat you if you offered yourself. His belly's full.'

'Mr Spots' yawned and looked round the company with an air of royal indifference. His master continued to scratch his head. Then, in obedience to a gesture, he submitted quietly when a servant fastened a chain on his neck, and reluctantly but unresistingly he let himself be led away.

'I'm very sorry,' said his master, looking after him affectionately, almost as if apologising to the pet. 'That's what has been hurting his feelings,' he explained to us.

'What?'

'The chain—the restriction, the want of confidence, is spoiling his fine temper.'

After a pause he added, 'As I was saying, it's the lapse of time. Pets should always be adolescent, and women too.'

'Not women,' protested one, who quoted: 'Age cannot whither her nor custom stale her infinite variety.'

'It's not variety that I want,' cried the host. 'I *hate* change. I would like my pets never to grow up. It's the change I object to. It's horrid, these transfers…'

'Hillo! Are you transferred?' we cried, more interested than surprised; for, as readers are probably aware, the Europeans of every kind in the east are at the best respectable vagabonds, globe-trotters by trade, and only a few derelicts, who are settling down to die, can have a fixed abode.

'Transferred? No, no I don't mean that. I was thinking of transfers of affection,' our host explained, and he proceeded to discuss the claims of various zoos—and the chance of poor 'Mr Spots' being more happy in one than another—like a mother discussing her daughter's suitors.

Amidst the merriment that arose when all constraint was ended, our host was advised to wed, and seemed to take the advice most seriously.

He did send away the leopard, and did take a wife, not long afterwards; and as he was a good-hearted man, I believe she is a happy woman; but she little suspects who was her predecessor in her husband's affections.

Miss Bimbo

(Excerpted from 'The Mind of the Wild' by Stanley Jepson)

The first general impression which is gained by people who come into close contact with wild animals is that their actions are, more often than not, the outcome of instinct rather than of reason or even of personal experience. The seven-eighths of the brain in which rests the subconscious mind would seem to be dominant in the case of wild animals. Inherited instinct is their sure and safe guide. A little example may be given in the case of a baby panther, Miss Bimbo, which was kept for some months [in the 1930s] by my wife.

Bimbo was found deserted with another cub when they could not have been more than two or three days old. The big cats will sometimes desert one or two out of a litter of three or four, because they realise they cannot suckle so many young. There are incidents in zoos, etc., of pantheresses and tigresses which will kill and eat one or two of their cubs. The forest officer, whose guard found the cubs, did his best to return Bimbo and her brother to their mother, and a guard was put on duty up a tree with the two cubs in a box to which was attached a string. When the mother appeared, the string would be pulled and the cubs released. But in spite of long vigil the mother did not appear, so Miss Bimbo forsook the wild for the civilised (?) world. Her brother died, and an attempt was made to fly Bimbo to Whipsnade Zoo, but though Tata Sons' Aviation Department was willing to do this from Bombay to Karachi, Imperial Airways found they could not break their own regulations [and take her onwards to Britain]. It was feared ladies in the plane might be nervous with a panther aboard, though Miss Bimbo was hardly as big as a cat!

This preamble is by way of emphasising that the panther cub's mother could have taught her nothing. Yet Bimbo had all sorts of jungle habits which were firmly fixed in her mind through inherited instincts.

For instance, one favourite amusement was to drag her mistress's silk stockings (she had a liking for the best ones!) under a divan; she could easily have carried the stocking in her mouth, but she dragged it and everything else backwards after the manner of an adult tiger or panther dragging a kill. In spite of the fact that she had a dog to play with when very young, she developed the habit of moving about in exactly the same way as a tiger or panther in the jungle. For instance, she would never walk along the middle of a room but would take cover behind chairs, crouch down and slink along the side of the wall, make short and fast rushes from one piece of cover to another. On seeing a dog or any other animals when out for a walk, she would even as a small cub flatten herself immediately into the grass and watch. Afterwards she would stalk slowly forward in short, quick rushes, body low down on the ground. Her favourite toy was a small dog purse, and she would stalk this and pounce on it, gripping the neck in the approved panther style when killing a goat. She knew quite easily which were dangerous places when walking about the house, i.e., which places would have been dangerous if the house had been part of the jungle, so to speak. She would peer round doors always before going through them, and would rush over open spaces and crawl quietly where there was 'cover', i.e., furniture, etc. It was most amusing and enlightening to watch these jungle tactics applied to domestic environment.

Bimbo was an affectionate pet and most intelligent. She would come when called, would play with her claws held in, would stop biting on the command 'No bite!' and was taught to be clean much more easily and quickly than in the case of a puppy. When taken for a visit to the zoo, she stood, almost with hair on end, and replied to a big tiger's roars and bounces with snarls and equally fierce gestures.

After three months she could not exactly be described as a safe pet because her claws were so long. Although she was in no way vicious, she might have done damage unwittingly. She was accordingly presented to the Victoria Gardens' Zoo in Bombay, where she still recognises her former mistress and lies on her back asking to be tickled.